Praise for *Trends in Assessment*

"Whether you're a longtime assessment leader or a newcomer, this volume is a terrific tour of the movement's most important trends and developments: a more integrative vision of learning; more varied and authentic methods; new partners; and, most of all, a growing community of educators working together to improve student learning and success. While not glossing over challenges, *Trends in Assessment* is a heartening account of what is possible and where assessment can make a difference in the future." —*Pat Hutchings, Senior Scholar, National Institute for Learning Outcomes Assessment*

"Everyone engaged with assessment should read this important book. This well-conceived and incredibly useful volume presents a summary of trends and themes in the field. The writers concentrate on practical issues and on the big ideas and paradigm-shifting developments that can make assessment more powerful for student learning in the future. The volume is at once a primer and also a challenge, not afraid to ask the tough questions that assessment leaders struggle with every day."—*Barbara Walvoord, Professor Emerita, University of Notre Dame*

"The contributors to this *Festschrift*-like compilation summarize the major advances in student learning outcomes assessment, most of which have been featured at the annual Assessment Institute, the premier gathering of scholars and practitioners committed to documenting and improving student learning. Timely and authoritative, *Trends in Assessment* stands as the contemporary 'go-to' resource about promising assessment approaches for faculty and staff new to assessment work as well as seasoned practitioners."—*George D. Kuh, Chancellor's Professor Emeritus of Higher Education, Indiana University*

"I have been a participant and presenter at virtually every Assessment Institute since its founding. But I have always been frustrated by the impossibility of attending all the sessions I want to—a condition that has only worsened as the Institute has grown so dramatically and successfully. In *Trends in Assessment*, we finally have a volume that addresses this dilemma. The nine topical chapters focused on the Assessment Institute's recent tracks summarize the major features of the current assessment landscape in a common format that covers main points, methodological challenges, and future directions. Both veterans and newcomers will find it invaluable, and I will keep it close during the many future Assessment Institutes I plan to attend."—*Peter Ewell, President Emeritus, National Center for Higher Education Management Systems; NILOA Senior Scholar*

"Kudos! A must-read volume for new and experienced assessment practitioners, institutional researchers, and academic leaders. Hundley and Kahn have compiled an impressive collection of essays that speaks to not only the current state of assessment but also the many ways the field is moving forward, encouraging us to think about how to better integrate assessment into institutional practice. Most importantly, *Trends in Assessment* highlights the ways assessment permeates all areas of campus life—from student learning to faculty development to high-impact practices—and is essential for developing and sustaining a learning culture."—***Laura M. Gambino***, *Vice President, New England Commission of Higher Education*

"Stephen P. Hundley and Susan Kahn have provided a 'must-read' primer for anyone interested in assessment in higher education. This book offers much more than a collection of chapters on the trends in higher education assessment written by outstanding and knowledgeable authors (although it certainly does do that). *Trends in Assessment* gives us a timely, thoughtful, and integrated look at how the role of assessment has morphed and grown over the past four decades and how it might continue to evolve in the future. Assessment has come a long way, and this resource is a powerful reminder of the necessity and importance of the ongoing discussion about learning in higher education."—***Catherine M. Wehlburg***; *Dean of Sciences, Mathematics, and Education; Marymount University*

"A fitting tribute to the deliberations emerging from IUPUI's Assessment Institute, this book is a must-read for anyone who wants to understand how decades of practice have informed perspectives on where we are headed with the assessment conversation in higher education. Each chapter addresses its own pertinent topic and closes with a summary of historical trends in that area and questions to further the conversation."—***Marilee Bresciani Ludvik***, *Professor of Postsecondary Educational Leadership, San Diego State University*

"A thought-provoking and broad-ranging volume; *Trends in Assessment: Ideas, Opportunities, and Issues for Higher Education* offers critical insights into the world of assessment in higher education. This book uses the frame of current and future trends to provide stimulating discussions on a variety of important topics, beginning with a concise and accurate history of assessment work and ending with broad predictions for the future. Even those with a niche area of interest will find something intriguing here, with time dedicated to ePortfolios, learning improvement, assessment in student affairs, and the scholarship of assessment, among many others."—***Nicholas Curtis***, *Director of Assessment, Marquette University*

"*Trends in Assessment* offers an insightful historical perspective on the development of assessment from a state-based movement to a discipline aimed at transforming higher education. The editors and contributors offer the reader a glimpse of the critical moments that have built a more meaningful and authentic system of instruments, exercises, and methods guiding institutional quality assurance today. The book offers a continual reminder of the importance of looking toward a future of assessment—a future that encourages constant self-reflection, criticism, inclusion, and continuous development and growth of the field."—*Mac Powell, Senior Fellow, Northwest Commission on Colleges and Universities*

"Hundley and Kahn have brought together a distinguished group of authors who have synthesized multiple decades of work in higher education assessment to bring the profession a well-researched, historically grounded, and honest examination of the field. Written in clear, unambiguous language, every chapter unveils new insights into the evolution of assessment in higher education and presents trends that provide the profession a much-needed way forward for the advancement of student learning in higher education."—*Timothy S. Brophy; Director, Institutional Assessment; Professor, Music Education; and Chair, Academic Assessment Committee; University of Florida Office of the Provost*

"Imagine a resource that distills more than 30 years of learning about an endeavor as complex as postsecondary education itself: student learning outcomes assessment. What you imagine might include disruptive accountability demands that compel educators to accept responsibility for quality assurance, but not necessarily in ways that truly improve teaching and learning. This volume captures, with warts and all, the progression of this work according to the people who plan and deliver the annual Assessment Institute in Indianapolis. The chapters provide provocative and practical syntheses, frameworks, guidelines, and conclusions that should help shift our collective focus from assessment *per se* to its objective—improved student learning."—*Victor M.H. Borden, Senior Advisor to the Executive Vice President for University Academic Affairs, Indiana University Bloomington*

"*Trends in Assessment* is vital to the higher education field as accountability and pedagogy become more complex. It was developed with both practitioners and other stakeholders in mind, keeping the student learning experience at its core. Written by well-known experts in their respective areas, the book discusses past, present, and future assessment trends to keep in mind as we navigate a period of transformation in higher education. Each chapter provides a brief history of its topic, presents relevant educational issues or tensions among important concepts, and then offers thought-provoking projections for the future of assessment. This book is a must-have resource for understanding and digging into the future of higher education assessment."—**Robert W. Aaron**, *Executive Director of Student Affairs Assessment and Planning, Northwestern University*

TRENDS IN ASSESSMENT

TRENDS IN ASSESSMENT

Ideas, Opportunities, and Issues for Higher Education

Edited by Stephen P. Hundley and Susan Kahn

Foreword by Trudy W. Banta

STERLING, VIRGINIA

Published by Stylus Publishing, LLC.
22883 Quicksilver Drive
Sterling, Virginia 20166-2019

Library of Congress Cataloging-in-Publication Data

Names: Hundley, Stephen P., editor. | Kahn, Susan, 1952- editor.

Title: Trends in assessment : ideas, opportunities, and issues
for higher education / edited by Stephen P. Hundley and Susan
Kahn; foreword by Trudy W. Banta.

Description: First edition. | Sterling, Virginia : Stylus Publishing,
2019. Includes bibliographical references.

Identifiers: LCCN 2019017721 | ISBN 9781642670929
(cloth : acid free paper) | ISBN 9781642670936
(paperback : acid free paper) | ISBN 9781642670943
(library networkable e-edition) | ISBN 9781642670950
(consumer e-edition)

Subjects: LCSH: Education, Higher--United States--Evaluation. |
Education, Higher--Aims and objectives--United States. |
Universities and colleges--United States--Planning.

Classification: LCC LA227.4 .T744 2019 | DDC 378.73--dc23

LC record available at https://lccn.loc.gov/2019017721

13-digit ISBN: 978-1-64267-092-9 (cloth)
13-digit ISBN: 978-1-64267-093-6 (paperback)
13-digit ISBN: 978-1-64267-094-3 (library networkable e-edition)
13-digit ISBN: 978-1-64267-095-0 (consumer e-edition)

Printed in the United States of America

All first editions printed on acid-free paper
that meets the American National Standards Institute
Z39-48 Standard.

Bulk Purchases

Quantity discounts are available for use in workshops and
for staff development.

Call 1-800-232-0223

First Edition, 2019

To all past, present, and future participants of the
Assessment Institute in Indianapolis

CONTENTS

FOREWORD   ix
  Trudy W. Banta

PREFACE   xv
  Stephen P. Hundley and Susan Kahn

INTRODUCTION   1
An Overview of Trends in Assessment
  Stephen P. Hundley, Susan Kahn, and Karen E. Black

PART ONE: TRENDS IN ASSESSMENT

1 MOVEMENT AFOOT
  Fostering Discourse on Assessment Scholarship   19
    Natasha A. Jankowski and Gianina R. Baker

2 BECOMING MORE HIP
  Assessment Trends in High-Impact Learning Practices and Student Success   33
    Jennifer Thorington Springer, Amy A. Powell, Steven Graunke,
    Thomas W. Hahn, and Julie A. Hatcher

3 EVOLVING PRACTICES IN THE DEVELOPMENT AND ASSESSMENT
  OF GLOBAL LEARNING   45
    Leslie A. Bozeman, Dawn M. Whitehead, Darla K. Deardorff,
    and Gil Latz

4 ASSESSING COMMUNITY ENGAGEMENT   60
    Kristin Norris and H. Anne Weiss

5 UNDERSTANDING STUDENTS YESTERDAY, TODAY, AND
  TOMORROW
  Trends in Student Affairs Assessment   76
    A. Katherine Busby and A. Sonia Ninon

6 STEM EDUCATION AND ASSESSMENT
Evolving Through Evidence   91
Anthony Chase, Gabrielle Kline, and Stephen P. Hundley

7 ASSESSMENT AT THE HIGHEST DEGREE(S)
Trends in Graduate and Professional Education   107
Sarah B. Zahl, Sherry Jimenez, and Max Huffman

8 MEASURING FACULTY LEARNING
Trends in the Assessment of Faculty Development   124
Krista Hoffmann-Longtin, Kyle Fassett, John Zilvinskis, and
Megan M. Palmer

9 TRANSFORMING ASSESSMENT, ASSESSING TRANSFORMATION
ePortfolio Assessment Trends   137
Susan Kahn

PART TWO: LOOKING TO THE FUTURE

10 LOTS OF ASSESSMENT, LITTLE IMPROVEMENT?
How to Fix the Broken System   157
Keston H. Fulcher and Caroline O. Prendergast

11 USING ASSESSMENT TRENDS IN PLANNING, DECISION-MAKING,
AND IMPROVEMENT   175
Michele J. Hansen

12 META-TRENDS IN ASSESSMENT
Perspectives, Analyses, and Future Directions   194
Stephen P. Hundley, Susan Kahn, Jeffery Barbee, and
Partners of the Assessment Institute

EDITORS AND CONTRIBUTORS   215

INDEX   229

I am very pleased to introduce this new volume, *Trends in Assessment: Ideas, Opportunities, and Issues for Higher Education*, edited by my colleagues Stephen P. Hundley and Susan Kahn, with contributions from many other colleagues at Indiana University–Purdue University Indianapolis (IUPUI) and across the United States. *Trends in Assessment* is the first book to emerge from the Assessment Institute in Indianapolis, which has played such an important role throughout my career. This book's chapters draw, in particular, on the Institute tracks we began to offer in the early 2000s, as the American Institute program grew and as the practice of assessment found its way into new areas of the academy. I shall say more about this history in what follows.

Assessment Conference Beginnings in Tennessee

The forerunner of the Assessment Institute in Indianapolis began in Tennessee, just six years after I became involved in the new field of assessing the outcomes of higher education. In the late 1970s, the principals at the Tennessee Higher Education Commission, Grady Bogue and Wayne Brown, began pilot projects aimed at developing policy that would encourage all of Tennessee's state-supported higher education institutions, both two-year and four-year institutions, to assess outcomes and take actions to improve based on the findings.

As luck would have it, I happened to be a professor in an administrative internship in the office of the chancellor of the University of Tennessee, Knoxville (UTK) in 1979, when the pilot projects gave rise to the nation's first performance funding policy for public higher education. I had experience in applying my educational psychology background to evaluating local and state education projects, and Chancellor Jack Reese asked me in 1980 to coordinate the university's response to performance funding. This involved testing seniors in general education and their major field, surveying alumni, accrediting all accreditable programs, and showing how we were using findings from these efforts to improve academic programs and student services.

By 1985, Virginia, Colorado, and New Jersey had joined Tennessee in implementing performance funding initiatives intended to improve student outcomes. Then the U.S. Department of Education's Fund for the Improvement of Postsecondary Education (FIPSE) developed an interest in outcomes assessment. In 1986, my first proposal to FIPSE was funded, and I established the Center for Assessment Research and Development (CARD) at UTK. With my new associate Gary Pike, who would subsequently become a widely respected higher education methodologist, I set out initially to collect and disseminate information about good practice in outcomes assessment, wherever in the world it might be found. Three successive three-year FIPSE grants enabled the small staff at CARD to carry out research on the tests and surveys we were required to administer to address performance funding requirements.

The principal dissemination strategy for which we sought FIPSE support in 1986 was a national conference. We conducted our first assessment conference in Memphis, Tennessee, in early 1987. UTK was not the only recipient of a FIPSE grant that included a plan for a national conference series. The American Association for Higher Education (AAHE) also received such support in 1986. At the time, I thought it strange that FIPSE saw fit to support two national assessment conferences. But when the AAHE Assessment Conference series ended in 2005, the FIPSE decision seemed wise.

After the conference in Memphis, CARD staff decided we could develop the program more efficiently closer to home, and our next national conferences were in Knoxville. Holding the conference on campus also allowed UTK colleagues to share their own work in assessment and to learn from presenters from other institutions—a very important concept for me.

The Assessment Institute in Indianapolis

In 1992, I reluctantly (at first) agreed to leave my academic home of so many years in Tennessee to accept the position of vice chancellor for planning and institutional improvement and professor of higher education at IUPUI. Before I even moved to Indianapolis, I was conferring with colleagues at the IUPUI Conference Center and Hotel about moving the national assessment conference to my new campus. For the 1991 event in Knoxville, we attracted 160 people. In November 1992, 350 people joined us in Indianapolis, a city near the geographic center of population in the United States and nicknamed the Crossroads of America because 4 interstate highways intersect here. Location, location, location.

When the registration for what we soon began to call the Assessment Institute in Indianapolis topped 800 in 2005, we decided we had outgrown the on-campus facility, and we moved the event to a downtown hotel connected to the huge Indianapolis Convention Center. I had so appreciated the conference center on campus because it was easy for IUPUI faculty and staff to walk across the street and present, or sit in on, conference sessions. But I found that by the time we moved the event downtown, we had cultivated a substantial audience among our colleagues, and they continued to offer their sessions and attend others. In the larger venue, we quickly moved to more than 1,000 participants from almost every state and several other countries, an attendance mark that is still enjoyed by the Assessment Institute.

In keeping with my intention to make the Assessment Institute a means of strengthening outcomes assessment at my home institution, I invited IUPUI colleagues in various disciplines to become partners in sponsoring the Institute. Thus, we asked faculty in the Indiana University (IU) School of Nursing—our first partner—to plan their own conference track, offering presentations themselves and inviting proposals from nursing faculty colleagues at other universities. Soon, the IU School of Nursing was sponsoring its own national assessment conference! Then a colleague in the College of Pharmacy at Butler University, also located in Indianapolis, asked to create an Institute track for pharmacy faculty from across the country. We included that track, and after a few years the IU School of Medicine faculty expressed a similar interest, so we broadened the track to encompass health professions. Interest in these specialized tracks waxed and waned over the years, but we gradually expanded the concept to include more and more IUPUI colleagues in offering the AI program—more about this in a subsequent section.

The Assessment Conference Program

At the time of the first assessment conference in Memphis in 1987, few people were prepared to discuss publicly their experiences with outcomes assessment in higher education. So for a day we sat in one room and heard a series of plenary speakers and panels. When we moved to Knoxville, we were able to involve UTK colleagues who had done survey work or conducted research on various assessment instruments. In addition, assessment expertise was developing throughout Tennessee and in Virginia and other southeastern states, where in 1986 the Southern Association of Colleges and Schools had become the first of the regional accrediting associations to issue formal guidelines for assessment in the institutional accreditation process. So we were able to add some concurrent sessions to our program and extend it by a half day.

I always wanted to begin the conference with a plenary session that would provide a showcase for current developments and set the tone for learning new concepts throughout the program. I invited Peter Ewell, Tom Angelo, and Jeff Seybert, all well-known assessment scholars, to join me in talking about our recent experiences visiting college campuses and consulting with state and national organizations about outcomes assessment. Soon after I arrived in Indianapolis, I invited my IU higher education faculty colleague George Kuh to take on that responsibility with us. And soon we began to invite an additional national figure to speak for 20 minutes, then respond to questions we would pose in advance.

During the late 1990s and early 2000s, a very heartwarming thing for me happened: Leaders of academic support units at IUPUI became pioneers in using assessment evidence to assess and improve in their own areas. Scott Evenbeck, founding dean of IUPUI's University College and now the president of Guttman Community College in New York City, hired both quantitative and qualitative assessment specialists to gather and present evidence of the effectiveness of supplemental instruction, intrusive advising, summer bridge programs, and other initiatives designed to improve outcomes for IUPUI's beginning students—resulting in a number of national awards for University College. I invited Scott and his colleagues to develop a first-year experience track within the Assessment Institute.

Bob Bringle, Purdue University professor of psychology, was an early service-learning thought leader who created instruments to assess the effectiveness of coursework and other initiatives designed to promote community engagement among IUPUI students. Bob was invited to develop a service-learning track within the Assessment Institute.

Nancy Chism, professor of education and director of the IUPUI Center for Teaching and Learning, was a national leader in the field of professional development for faculty and staff. I saw faculty development as an essential resource in encouraging and preparing faculty to engage in outcomes assessment. Nancy was an early sponsor of a track within the Assessment Institute.

In the early 2000s, led by Susan Kahn, director of institutional effectiveness, IUPUI became a pioneer in the use of ePortfolios to demonstrate institution-wide effectiveness—from campus-wide programming to individual programs and courses. We incorporated ePortfolios as an Assessment Institute track.

Assessment in student affairs, in global learning, and in graduate education was championed by IUPUI leaders over the next 15 years, and each of these fields became the topic of an AI track. Other tracks added in more recent years are described in the preface of this book. And as track chairs developed their own careers, sometimes departing IUPUI for other institutions, many continued their involvement with the Institute. The Assessment Institute track leaders of today are thus a truly nationwide group.

The chapters that follow benefit from these national—and international—perspectives, as well as from the wealth of experience the track leaders bring to their topics. And as the chapters examine the history and development of assessment in their particular areas and consider the future, several larger trends begin to emerge. These meta-trends are well summarized in the book's closing chapter by Hundley, Kahn, and Jeffery Barbee, a colleague from the IU School of Medicine. Each of the chapters contained herein is worth reading by itself, but I hope that readers will take the time to consume all of the chapters in order to see these meta-trends taking shape in various settings—and to observe as well the growing sophistication of assessment practices as they evolve to fit the ever-changing contexts of higher education.

Trudy W. Banta
Professor of Higher Education and Vice Chancellor Emerita
Indiana University–Purdue University Indianapolis
February 2019

With Gratitude

I am immensely grateful to Karen Black, Angie Bergman, Michele Trent, Shirley Yorger, and Linda Durr, the members of my immediate staff who devoted many hundreds of hours to the details that made each annual event *seem* effortless. I am also indebted to the hundreds of assessment practitioners who have shared their experiences—both successes and failures—with conference audiences over the years. It has been such a privilege to count scores of IUPUI colleagues in that number. I appreciate the time and talent contributed by our keynote speakers, and I am especially thankful to Peter, Tom, Jeff, and George for their considerable knowledge, their willingness to share that, and their support and friendship.

Trudy W. Banta

Trends in Assessment draws its content, in part, from the Assessment Institute in Indianapolis, now the nation's oldest and largest event of its type. Founded in 1992 and sponsored by Indiana University–Purdue University Indianapolis (IUPUI), the Assessment Institute routinely attracts more than 1,000 participants from all 50 states and assorted foreign countries. Its principal purpose is to further the scholarship and practice of assessment in higher education. The program offers more than 200 sessions each year and includes tracks featuring special emphases in assessment and higher education, organized by leaders responsible for shaping the track themes. The Institute further benefits from partnerships with several national professional associations and research organizations, each of which makes a valuable intellectual contribution to the program.

We are both fortunate to have contributed to the Assessment Institute for the past 20 years by offering pre-Institute workshops and concurrent session presentations and leading tracks on specific assessment topics. Our involvement with the Institute has complemented our own professional responsibilities, because we have both held positions that required leadership for and use of assessment findings.

When the Assessment Institute's founding chair, Trudy W. Banta, retired from IUPUI in 2016, we assumed leadership responsibility within the campus's Office of Planning and Institutional Improvement (PAII), which serves as organizer of the Institute. We are honored to continue the Assessment Institute's valued traditions. One of our first tasks was to ask the track leaders to produce summaries of the major themes from their tracks based on recent Institute sessions. These summaries were subsequently developed into columns titled "Assessment Institute Insights" that appeared periodically in *Assessment Update*, a bimonthly publication with a national readership, for which we serve as editors.

Concurrently, we asked the student research team within PAII to analyze session abstracts from the past several years to find themes emerging from the overall Assessment Institute program offerings. The initial purpose was to enable us to plan for the future of the Institute. We soon realized, however, that the wealth of information contained in the analysis of session abstracts, along with information from the track summaries and "Assessment Institute Insights" columns, offered us an opportunity to identify trends that could be useful in advancing the understanding and practice of assessment. Hence, the idea for a book about trends in assessment was born.

Track leaders were also interested in exploring the assessment trends that appeared in their track summaries and in expanding their analyses of these trends by incorporating broader perspectives from the literature. We further reached out to the Assessment Institute partners to request contributions highlighting trends in assessment from their vantage points and discussing how their professional associations and research organizations were preparing to address those trends. Each partner readily agreed to this request. Finally, the enthusiastic response by David Brightman and his colleagues at Stylus Publishing to our proposal for the project enabled us to collaborate on *Trends in Assessment* and to debut this book at the 2019 Assessment Institute in Indianapolis.

We believe that readers will benefit in several ways from reading *Trends in Assessment*. First, the longevity and scope of the Assessment Institute provide a breadth of ideas not normally found in a single book on this topic. Second, the mix of assessment perspectives presented in one place offers readers the opportunity to identify and incorporate unique and cross-cutting themes and trends in assessment in their own contexts. Third, the reputations of the chapter authors and Assessment Institute partner contributors—all recognized longtime and emerging leaders in assessment and higher education—should signal to readers the value of the insights found in this volume.

Our intended audience for *Trends in Assessment* includes a broad and diverse mix of readers from all disciplines, institutional types, and levels of experience in assessment. Faculty, student affairs professionals, administrators, faculty developers, and those involved with accreditation, both regional and specialized, are among those we hope to reach with this book. We believe that higher education policymakers, leaders, researchers, and other influencers will also benefit from the ideas shared in this volume. Students of higher education administration and related disciplines will find the ideas and information presented in *Trends in Assessment* a useful complement to other books, articles, and resources on assessment and student learning. Further, this book is designed to be easily incorporated into such contexts as workshops, professional development programs, assessment committees, faculty and staff learning communities, and undergraduate- and graduate-level courses, with summaries of main trends and questions for consideration at the end of each track-focused chapter. Simply put, those who have an interest in or responsibility for assessment in higher education should find this volume useful in enhancing their understanding.

An undertaking such as this volume would not be possible without the willingness of many to contribute their time and talents. To our contributors, we are grateful to you for offering your energy and expertise to this book and for your dedication to the Assessment Institute. To the numerous Institute partners, we thank you for your contributions to the annual Institute program and to the ideas shared in this volume. Both are enriched by your unique, invaluable perspectives. This book would not be possible without Trudy W. Banta, the founding chair of the Assessment Institute in Indianapolis and a leading scholar on assessment in higher education. The Assessment Institute itself could not have achieved success if not for the early and ongoing contributions from renowned leaders and experts like Peter Ewell, George D. Kuh, Thomas A. Angelo, and Jeffrey A. Seybert. Our now retired colleague Karen E. Black also deserves thanks for her quiet leadership as executive director of the Assessment Institute for many years.

We thank our numerous IUPUI faculty and staff colleagues for their interest in this book and their continued support of the Assessment Institute. Chancellor Nasser Paydar and Executive Vice Chancellor Kathy Johnson exemplify the type of leadership required to make student learning and success an institutional priority, and we are fortunate to have both as IUPUI leaders. Special thanks to the PAII student researchers Yunah Kim, Zachary McDougal, Arthur Pearcy, and Shawn Peters and, in particular, to our PAII colleagues Angela Bergman, Linda Durr, Michele Trent, and Shirley Yorger for being wonderful friends and outstanding members of the PAII team. Finally, to David Brightman, McKenzie Baker, and their colleagues at Stylus Publishing, thank you for championing and supporting this project and for offering *Trends in Assessment* both to the 2019 Assessment Institute participants and wider audiences.

We hope that readers are inspired by this volume and that they find opportunities to incorporate in their own settings some of the trends presented in the chapters that follow. No one book can definitively and comprehensively inventory and document every assessment trend. Readers are likely aware of additional ideas and perspectives worthy of inclusion in our discussion of trends. We thus invite readers to engage with us by visiting assessmentinstitute.iupui.edu/trends to share and access resources related to trends, provide reactions to or suggestions for additional assessment trends, and learn about professional development opportunities related to assessment trends. We look forward to hearing from you, and we very much hope to see you at a future Assessment Institute in Indianapolis.

Stephen P. Hundley and Susan Kahn

INTRODUCTION

An Overview of Trends in Assessment

Stephen P. Hundley, Susan Kahn, and Karen E. Black

This volume explores current trends in the assessment of student learning in higher education. It is informed by recent sessions presented at the Assessment Institute in Indianapolis; the work of key Institute partner organizations; and the substantial bodies of literature on assessment, student learning, and higher education. In this introduction, we offer readers new to assessment some history and basic context on the purposes and principles of assessment. Following this brief overview of assessment and recent literature on the subject, we describe the Assessment Institute and preview the chapters on various assessment trends presented later in this volume.

A Brief Background on Assessment

Currently, nearly 20 million students are enrolled in institutions of higher education in the United States (National Center for Education Statistics, 2019). These students are embarking on their college or graduate/professional educations at a time when the higher education landscape is increasingly influenced by external forces reshaping the operations and very nature of higher education institutions. These forces include, among others: changing student characteristics and needs, technological advances, intensified competition for students, economic and competitive pressures, and public skepticism about educational quality (Kuh et al., 2015). This last force—skepticism about educational quality—raises the question, "What have students learned, not just in a single course, but as a result of their overall college experience?" (p. 3). This question has fueled the development of the assessment movement in American higher education for the past three decades.

Assessment *Defined*

What do we mean by *assessment*? A clearly understood, widely shared definition has always been one of the highest barriers to the advancement of the field (Terenzini, 1989). Many definitions of *assessment* exist, some emphasizing accountability and others emphasizing improvement of student learning as its principal purpose. Schilling and Schilling (1998) defined *assessment* as "a range of methods for investigating the phenomenon and outcomes of students' learning" (p. 12). Palomba and Banta (1999) viewed assessment as "the systematic collection, review, and use of information about educational programs undertaken for the purpose of improving student learning and development" (p. 4).

More recently, an updated volume by Banta and Palomba (2015) reviewed best practices in planning, implementing, and improving assessment. They defined *assessment as* the "measurement of what an *individual* knows and can do" (p. 1), adding that "the term *outcomes assessment* in higher education has come to imply aggregating individual measures for the purpose of discovering group strengths and weaknesses that can guide improvement actions" (p. 1). While assessment focuses mainly on student learning, broader definitions describe it as evaluation of institutional effectiveness. Thus, *assessment* can also be defined as the "process of providing credible evidence of resources, implementation actions, and outcomes undertaken for the purpose of improving the effectiveness of instruction, programs, and services in higher education" (Banta & Palomba, 2015, p. 2). Despite this lack of consensus about what assessment was, as early as 1989, Terenzini declared that "assessment is here to stay" (p. 644).

Assessment's Beginnings and Growth

A number of scholars have offered detailed histories of assessment's expansion in the United States. Most have noted that the "assessment movement" largely began in the 1980s as calls for greater accountability and transparency from the federal government, state governments, regional and specialized accreditors, and governing bodies of institutions themselves converged upon higher education (Astin, 2012; Banta & Palomba, 2015; Cumming & Miller, 2017; Kuh et al., 2015; Suskie, 2018). Three publications in the 1980s outlined the challenges confronting colleges and universities at the time: *A Nation at Risk* (Gardner, 1983), *Involvement in Learning* (National Institute of Education, 1984), and *The Self-Regarding Institution: Information for Excellence* (Ewell, 1984).

The president's National Commission on Excellence in Education produced *A Nation at Risk: The Imperative for Educational Reform* (Gardner,

1983), which argued that American schools were failing to produce graduates able to meet the national need for a competitive workforce. It recommended reforms across such areas as content, standards and expectations, teaching, leadership, and financial support. Although it focused primarily on the P–12 arena, the report called for all levels of education to assess the effectiveness of teaching and learning.

Involvement in Learning (National Institute of Education, 1984) emerged from the work of the Study Group on the Conditions of Excellence in American Higher Education. It outlined conditions of excellence that U.S. colleges and universities should strive to achieve, noting that "measures of educational excellence must thus be couched in terms of student outcomes— principally such academic outcomes as knowledge, intellectual capacities, and skills" (p. 27). The report further suggested that such excellence could be achieved through student involvement, high expectations, and assessment and feedback.

In *The Self-Regarding Institution*, also published in 1984, Ewell offered an additional rationale for the new calls for assessment of learning:

> Institutions have become larger, more specialized, and more public. Students have become more varied in background, preparation, and patterns of attendance. Curricula have evolved from the traditional liberal arts to a broad array of occupational, professional, and special-purpose programs. As a result of this diversity, the pattern of higher education outcomes has become almost bewilderingly complex. Thus, calls for accountability stem, at least in part, from a simple desire on the part of those who support higher education to *understand* what has occurred. (Ewell, 1984, p. 12)

At the same time, states were enacting accountability measures that accelerated what was becoming a national assessment movement. Tennessee, Colorado, New Jersey, and Virginia, for example, adopted performance funding for state-supported higher education institutions. Individual states were not the only stakeholders to apply external pressure; the federal government also began to require "all federally approved accreditation organizations to include in their criteria for accreditation evidence of institutional outcomes" (Banta & Palomba, 2015, p. 5). Now the onus shifted to the accreditors: "The primary external stimulus for assessment moved from states to regional associations as they began to issue specific outcomes assessment directives for institutional accreditation, and discipline-specific bodies created such guidelines for program accreditation" (Banta & Palomba, 2015, p. 5).

Throughout the 1990s, institutions responded to these external mandates by establishing assessment programs on campuses. Scholarship on assessment practices continued to emerge, as Cumming and Miller (2017) reported. One influential publication from this era, developed by the American Association for Higher Education (AAHE), set forth nine principles of good practice for assessing student learning. These principles, created by leading authorities on assessment, emphasized the need for clear educational goals, recognition of the multidimensionality of learning, the importance of tracking outcomes over time, and the need for involvement by a broad range of stakeholders (Astin et al., 1993).

In the early 1990s, Ernest L. Boyer's (1990) *Scholarship Reconsidered: Priorities of the Professoriate* catalyzed a reexamination of rewards and recognition for faculty teaching. Soon, "faculty roles and rewards" became the focus of an AAHE initiative and popular annual conference. With leadership from AAHE and the Carnegie Foundation for the Advancement of Teaching, the scholarship of teaching, which subsequently evolved into the current Scholarship of Teaching and Learning (SoTL) movement, emerged and spawned its own extensive literature. Hutchings and Shulman (1999) described the scholarship of teaching thus:

> Scholarship of teaching is *not* synonymous with excellent teaching. It requires a kind of "going meta," in which faculty frame and systematically investigate questions related to student learning—the conditions under which it occurs, what it looks like, how to deepen it, and so forth—and do so with an eye not only to improving their own classroom but to advancing practice beyond it. (p. 13)

Later in the 1990s, Barr and Tagg's (1995) influential article in *Change* magazine, "From Teaching to Learning: A New Paradigm for Undergraduate Education," offered a persuasive new *learning paradigm*, which focused on the design of powerful learning experiences and environments, rather than on delivery of instruction and information transfer. Their "learning paradigm" (p. 13), along with the SoTL movement and emerging scientific research on learning, provided further impetus for the assessment of student learning but emphasized internal improvement rather than external accountability.

Meanwhile, as Astin (2012) noted, two reports from the early 2000s exemplified the continued intensity of assessment activities. In 2000, the National Center for Public Policy in Higher Education issued *Measuring Up*, the first of a series of "biennial state grades on higher education performance," and found "all fifty states to be seriously lacking in the area of assessment of student learning" (Astin, 2012, p. 2). In 2006, the *Spellings*

Report on the Future of Higher Education further "criticized higher education for its limited demonstration of student learning and called for more sophisticated assessment in the name of public accountability" (Astin, 2012, p. 2).

Assessment Today

Although the assessment movement began with calls for external accountability—which have continued unabated—assessment in higher education today is increasingly focused on improving institutions' educational effectiveness. Scholars have emphasized transparency and use of assessment results to guide improvements in student learning and success (Kuh et al., 2015). Kuh and colleagues argued that the long-standing "culture of compliance has clouded the most important, actionable purpose for collecting evidence of student accomplishment—improving teaching and learning" (p. 22). The National Institute for Learning Outcomes Assessment (NILOA) developed its Transparency Framework in response to the needs for both transparency and improvement. The components of the framework—student learning outcomes statements, assessment plans, assessment resources, current assessment activities, evidence of student learning, and use of student learning evidence—have served as a guide to institutions' examination of "whether evidence of student accomplishment is readily accessible and potentially useful to intended audiences" (Kuh et al., 2015, p. 218).

Fulcher, Good, Coleman, and Smith (2014) similarly outlined standards for learning improvement and provided tools to elevate improvement conversations across higher education, while Jankowski and Marshall (2017) examined two recent initiatives, Tuning USA and the Degree Qualifications Profile, to argue that consensus, alignment, student centeredness, and communication are needed to support coherent learning experiences for students. Finally, involvement in assessment and improvement has broadened into institutional areas beyond the classroom, including student affairs (Henning & Roberts, 2016) and international education (Deardorff, 2015), among others, as subsequent chapters of this volume demonstrate.

Trends in Assessment draws on and incorporates these historic and recent scholarly perspectives. But we hope that it will also contribute to the literature by presenting ideas and information not found elsewhere. Our purpose in this volume is to offer readers information, strategies, and resources on assessment concepts and approaches that have endured and matured over the past quarter century, while also identifying emerging and future assessment ideas and opportunities drawn from the various tracks at the Assessment Institute and other sources.

The Assessment Institute in Indianapolis

Organized and hosted by Indiana University–Purdue University Indianapolis (IUPUI), the Assessment Institute in Indianapolis seeks to advance the scholarship and practice of assessment in higher education. Its mission, participants, partners, and content reflect the sustained growth and impact of assessment activity across higher education institutions. Visit assessmentinstitute .iupui.edu for information about the Assessment Institute, including downloadable resources from prior years' events.

Mission

The mission of the Assessment Institute is to

- offer opportunities for individuals and campus teams new to outcomes assessment to acquire fundamental knowledge about the field,
- enable assessment leaders to share and extend their knowledge and skills, and
- support the development of networks to provide ongoing support and expertise.

The Assessment Institute strives to be a valuable resource for faculty, administrators, policymakers, and others engaged in assessment. More than 200 sessions offered annually at the Institute address the full array of current and emerging assessment issues: methods, tools, processes, measures, design and implementation models, and assessment in a variety of contexts, as this volume demonstrates. The Institute welcomes and invites participants from all backgrounds, levels of experience in assessment, and higher education sectors.

Partners

The Assessment Institute has formed numerous partnerships with national higher education associations and organizations, who make important contributions to the annual program. Each of these partners brings a unique perspective to the program, offers attendees useful information and resources, and helps ensure that the Institute remains engaged with and informed by issues of interest to the broader higher education community. Our current partners include the following:

- Association for the Assessment of Learning in Higher Education (AALHE): AALHE is a professional association for assessment practitioners at colleges, universities, and higher education support organizations. It provides resources and a forum to support assessment practitioners' professional development and promotes assessment research, documentation, open discussion, strategies, policies, and practices to improve student learning and institutional effectiveness in fostering student success. Find AALHE at aalhe.org.

- Association for Authentic, Experiential, and Evidence-Based Learning (AAEEBL): AAEEBL is the professional association for ePortfolio researchers and practitioners. It offers an annual conference and occasional regional conferences; sponsors *The Field Guide to ePortfolio* and the *AAEEBL ePortfolio Review*, a peer-reviewed online journal; and cosponsors *The International Journal of ePortfolio*, also a peer-reviewed online journal, now published by the Association of American Colleges & Universities. Find AAEEBL at aaeebl.org.

- Association for General and Liberal Studies (AGLS): AGLS is a community of practitioner-scholars that offers strategic, effective, and innovative support for peers engaged in the day-to-day work of general and liberal learning in twenty-first-century higher education. Find AGLS at agls.org.

- Association for Institutional Research (AIR): AIR is a global association that empowers higher education professionals at all levels to use data, analytics, information, and evidence to make decisions and take actions that benefit students and institutions and improve higher education. Find AIR at airweb.org.

- Association of American Colleges & Universities (AAC&U): AAC&U advances the vitality and public standing of liberal education by making quality and equity the foundations for excellence in undergraduate education in service to democracy. Find AAC&U at aacu.org.

- Center for Assessment & Research Studies (CARS) at James Madison University: CARS provides high-quality assessment services to the university, offers applied graduate training in both assessment and measurement, increases the use of innovative technology in assessment practice, enhances the rigor of measurement and statistical techniques used in assessment practice, and produces valuable scholarship in assessment and measurement. Find CARS at jmu.edu/assessment.

- Center for Postsecondary Research (CPR)/National Survey of Student Engagement (NSSE): CPR, a research center of the Indiana University School of Education, investigates processes and practices that influence student success and institutional excellence in higher education and promotes those found to be effective. NSSE annually collects information from hundreds of four-year colleges and universities about first-year and senior students' participation in programs and activities that institutions offer to benefit their learning and personal development. The results provide an estimate of how undergraduates spend their time and what they gain from attending college. NSSE supplies participating institutions with a variety of reports that compare their students' responses with those of students at self-selected groups of comparison institutions. Find CPR at cpr .indiana.edu and NSSE at nsse.indiana.edu.

- Higher Education Data Sharing Consortium (HEDS): HEDS facilitates the exchange of data and professional knowledge among member institutions in a climate of trust, collegiality, and assured confidentiality. An independent not-for-profit corporation formed in 1983, HEDS is now located at the Center of Inquiry at Wabash College in Crawfordsville, Indiana. Find HEDS at hedsconsortium .org.

- Indiana Campus Compact: Formed in 1993, Indiana Campus Compact is a partnership of college and university presidents and chancellors who have committed themselves and their institutions to their communities through mutually beneficial and meaningful collaborations to create engaged citizens and vibrant communities. Indiana Campus Compact is the only organization in the state that works with public, independent, and two-year institutions of higher education. Find Indiana Campus Compact at indianacampuscompact. org.

- National Institute for Learning Outcomes Assessment (NILOA): The mission of NILOA, the Assessment Institute's signature partner, is to discover and disseminate ways in which academic programs and institutions can productively use assessment data internally to inform and strengthen undergraduate education and externally to communicate with policymakers, families, and other stakeholders. NILOA assists institutions and others in identifying and adopting promising practices in the assessment of college student learning outcomes—that is, documenting what students learn, know, and can do for the benefit of colleges and universities, accrediting groups, higher education associations, foundations, and others beyond campus, including students and their families, employers, and policymakers. Find NILOA at learningoutcomesassessment .org.

Assessment Institute Topics

Sessions at the Assessment Institute address a broad array of assessment topics. An analysis of presentation proposals and abstracts from the past several years reveals recurring themes of the annual program:

- Levels of assessment: Sessions have addressed assessment practices focused on individual students and groups or cohorts of students within classes, courses, programs, and disciplines in both academic and cocurricular units and across campuses, institutions, and systems of higher education.
- Assessment in various contexts: Contexts include general education and discipline-specific offerings; programs with specialized accreditation; cocurricular programs; student engagement, success, retention, and persistence interventions; learning activities in out-of-class settings like experiential, international, and virtual or online learning; and campus services.
- A variety of assessment methods: Assessment methods considered include both direct and indirect approaches; authentic assessments based on papers, projects, performances, and ePortfolios; observations of practice or simulated practice situations; paper-and-pencil and electronic tests; performance on locally developed or national tests; program reviews; signature assignments; surveys, interviews, and focus groups; syllabi or transcript analyses; and use of rubrics.
- Stakeholder involvement in assessment activities: Stakeholders discussed include students themselves; faculty, staff, and administrators; institutional governance bodies; employers and community members; P–12 institutions and higher education consortia; foundations and other grant-making organizations; regional and specialized accreditors; national organizations and associations; international partners; and publishers and commercial vendors.
- Integration with and linkage of assessment to other practices: Practices with important connections to assessment include curriculum planning and revision; faculty development; promotion and tenure processes; rewards and recognition for faculty and staff; strategic and annual planning; accreditation; institutional improvement and effectiveness strategies; data collection, storage, and analysis; resource identification, prioritization, and allocation; and technology and facilities planning, renovations, and upgrades.

- Uses of assessment findings: The various uses of assessment discussed include improving student learning in assorted contexts; designing assignments and learning activities; enhancing instructional environments, both physical and virtual; fostering internal improvement and development; demonstrating accountability or compliance with requirements and standards set by external stakeholders; communicating accomplishments to various audiences; and incorporating assessment findings into research and other scholarly pursuits.
- Emerging ideas in assessment: Institute sessions have addressed a wide range of emerging ideas over the years, including assessing assessment to ensure meaningful use of assessment findings; broadening assessment to include graduate and professional programs, cocurricular learning, and administrative functions; and improving assessment methods by responding to dynamic changes in institutional contexts and focusing on equitable, inclusive learning approaches and environments.

In addition to the breadth of general themes and topics, the Assessment Institute offers tracks focused on assessment in areas such as the following:

- Community engagement
- ePortfolios
- Faculty development
- Global learning
- Graduate and professional education
- High-impact practices
- Learning improvement and innovation
- NILOA
- Science, technology, engineering, and math (STEM) education
- Student affairs programs and services
- Diversity, equity, and inclusion (to be introduced at the 2019 Assessment Institute)

Assessment veterans and emerging assessment leaders take responsibility for organizing each of these tracks. This task includes generating and reviewing concurrent and poster session proposals and securing track-specific keynote presenters who raise important ideas or questions about the track's purpose or theme.

Trends From the Assessment Institute and Elsewhere

Although the Assessment Institute has a long record of growth and success, we have never published conference proceedings or produced a book addressing ideas or content from the Institute. Given the breadth and depth of the Institute, track leaders were enthusiastic about developing chapters highlighting assessment themes and trends from their tracks. The chapters that follow are organized into two main sections. Part One, "Trends in Assessment," comprises a series of chapters drawn from Assessment Institute tracks. Each of these chapters provides important background information with attention to the significance of the topic, describes trends from the Institute and elsewhere, offers ideas about emerging trends and their implications for higher education, and concludes with a summary of main trends and questions for discussion. Part Two, "Looking to the Future," offers three chapters that point to the future of assessment and identify several meta-trends that we see emerging from the preceding material.

Chapter 1: "Movement Afoot: Fostering Discourse on Assessment Scholarship"

Kicking off Part One of this book, this chapter by leaders of the Assessment Institute's signature partner, NILOA, sets the stage for the subsequent chapters by highlighting NILOA's own research on trends in several areas of assessment, including assessment methods, curriculum design, and equity in assessment, an issue that has recently attracted increasing discussion.

Chapter 2: "Becoming More HIP: Assessment Trends in High-Impact Learning Practices and Student Success"

Evidence continues to endorse the value of high-impact teaching and learning practices for supporting student learning, engagement, retention, and success. This chapter explores a range of trends related to high-impact practices (HIPs), with a particular focus on the quality and fidelity of HIPs' implentation, equitable access to HIPs, scaling HIPs, and authentic assessment of learning in HIP experiences.

Chapter 3: "Evolving Practices in the Development and Assessment of Global Learning"

This chapter explores trends in assessment of global learning and intercultural competence. Today, global learning goes beyond traditional study abroad to include curricular and cocurricular opportunities such as integration of global learning within courses and local experiences, community-based global learning, and study away. The chapter also describes the large number of assessment tools, including various authentic assessment measures, used to gauge achievement of outcomes such as intercultural competence and global citizenship.

Chapter 4: "Assessing Community Engagement"

Community engagement refers to collaborations between higher education institutions and their larger communities, including community-engaged learning and other university–community partnership activities. This chapter describes desired transdisciplinary learning outcomes of student community engagement and various assessment measures for them, and discusses assessment of other aspects of community engagement, including approaches to assessing the impact of these activities on the community.

Chapter 5: "Understanding Students Yesterday, Today, and Tomorrow: Trends in Student Affairs Assessment"

This chapter traces the history of student affairs assessment from early focuses on participation and satisfaction with cocurricular programs to the current assessment of student learning and developmental outcomes resulting from these activities. Emphases include the professionalization of student affairs assessment, equitable and inclusive assessment approaches, assessment of complex learning outcomes, and collaboration between student affairs and academic affairs.

Chapter 6: "STEM Education and Assessment: Evolving Through Evidence"

There is a growing need in the United States and internationally to educate STEM-literate graduates. This chapter addresses emerging trends in assessing student learning in STEM disciplines, with a focus on interventions and promising instructional practices that improve STEM learning of today's rapidly changing student population and assessment methods suited to the multifaceted STEM context.

Chapter 7: "Assessment at the Highest Degree(s): Trends in Graduate and Professional Education"

Disciplinary accreditation has historically driven assessment in graduate and professional programs. Today's graduate and professional students must attain more-difficult-to-assess competencies in interprofessional teamwork and other forms of collaboration, with assessment also focusing on professional formation. This chapter further proposes development of a set of national standards for graduate education.

Chapter 8: "Measuring Faculty Learning: Trends in the Assessment of Faculty Development"

The chapter contributors challenge faculty developers to move toward evidence-based practice in development interventions and discuss related needs for a theoretical foundation for faculty development activities, development of organizational cultures of learning, and methodologies for assessing learning outcomes of faculty who participate in faculty development.

Chapter 9: "Transforming Assessment, Assessing Transformation: ePortfolio Assessment Trends"

ePortfolios are both an assessment method and a HIP that can support powerful learning and yield actionable information for assessment. They are well suited to assessing complex learning outcomes, dispositional learning, and other so-called ineffable outcomes. This chapter explores approaches to ePortfolio assessment and proposes a more expansive view of assessment that considers students' personal, professional, and civic development.

Chapter 10: "Lots of Assessment, Little Improvement? How to Fix the Broken System"

Part Two of this volume opens with this chapter, which argues that we have overemphasized the mechanics of assessment to the detriment of genuine improvement. Focusing on program theory, fidelity, and sound measurement, and offering several examples, the contributors propose a revised model that views assessment as part of our improvement practices rather than improvement as a feature of assessment. Rethinking the faculty reward system will be crucial to the success of this new paradigm.

Chapter 11: "Using Assessment Trends in Planning, Decision-Making, and Improvement"

The diversity of students served by higher education institutions requires that faculty, staff, assessment professionals, and institutional leaders reconsider what we assess, how we assess, and how we leverage results. This chapter focuses on how to incorporate the assessment trends presented in this volume into planning, decision-making, and improvement, with an emphasis on holistic assessment of student gains through authentic, culturally responsive, and embedded approaches that account for student diversity and ensure equity.

Chapter 12: "Meta-Trends in Assessment: Perspectives, Analyses, and Future Directions"

Incorporating and drawing on brief contributions from the national associations and research organizations that partner with the Assessment Institute, this chapter highlights anticipated future trends and the ways in which our partner organizations are preparing to address them. The chapter concludes with 10 meta-trends in assessment that draw on the chapters in this volume and the contributors' observations of the assessment field.

Conclusion

The numbers of individuals, institutions, associations, and organizations involved in assessment evidences its prominence in American higher education. As a long-standing contributor to professional development and dissemination of assessment innovations and expertise, the Assessment Institute in Indianapolis has played a major role in advancing understanding of assessment practices. Assessment Institute partners, each bringing unique perspectives on assessment, also contribute to the widening influence of assessment on the higher education landscape. The chapters that follow, informed by the Assessment Institute and other sources, aim to enable readers to identify and incorporate cross-cutting and emerging assessment themes and ideas into their own contexts.

We want to hear from you about *Trends in Assessment*:

- Provide reactions or suggestions about trends.
- Share and access resources related to trends.
- Learn about professional development opportunities related to trends.

Visit assessmentinstitute.iupui.edu/trends

References

Astin, A. W., & Antonio, A. L. (2012). *Assessment for excellence: The philosophy and practice of assessment and evaluation in higher education* (2nd ed.). Lanham, MD: Rowman & Littlefield Publishers.

Astin, A. W., Banta, T. W., Cross, K. P., El-Khawas, E., Ewell, P. T., Hutchings, P., Marchese, T. J., McClenney, K. M., Mentkowski, M., Miller, M. A., Moran, E. T., & Wright, B. (1993). *American Association for Higher Education (AAHE) principles of good practice for assessing student learning.* Washington, DC: American Association for Higher Education.

Banta, T. W., & Palomba, C. A. (2015). *Assessment essentials: Planning, implementing, and improving assessment in higher education* (2nd ed.). San Francisco, CA: Jossey-Bass.

Barr, R. B., & Tagg, J. (1995). From teaching to learning: A new paradigm for undergraduate education. *Change: The Magazine of Higher Learning, 27*(6), 12–26.

Boyer, E. L. (1990). *Scholarship reconsidered: Priorities of the professoriate.* San Francisco, CA: Jossey-Bass.

Cumming, T., & Miller, M. D. (2017). *Enhancing assessment in higher education: Putting psychometrics to work.* Sterling, VA: Stylus.

Deardorff, D. K. (2015). *Demystifying outcomes assessment for international educators: A practical approach.* Sterling, VA: Stylus.

Ewell, P. (1984). *The self-regarding institution: Information for excellence.* Boulder, CO: National Center for Higher Education Management Systems.

Fulcher, K. H., Good, M. R., Coleman, C. M., & Smith, K. L. (2014). *A simple model for learning improvement: Weigh pig, feed pig, weigh pig* (Occasional Paper No. 23). Urbana, IL: University of Illinois and Indiana University, National Institute for Learning Outcomes Assessment.

Gardner, D. P. (1983). *A nation at risk: The imperative for educational reform. An open letter to the American people. A report to the nation and the secretary of education.* Washington, DC: U.S. Department of Education.

Henning, G. W., & Roberts, D. (2016). *Student affairs assessment: Theory to practice.* Sterling, VA: Stylus.

Hutchings, P., & Shulman, L. S. (1999). The scholarship of teaching: New elaborations, new developments. *Change: The Magazine of Higher Learning, 31*(5), 10–15.

Jankowski, N. A., & Marshall, D. W. (2017). *Degrees that matter: Moving higher education to a learning systems paradigm.* Sterling, VA: Stylus.

Kuh, G. D., Ikenberry, S. O., Jankowski, N., Cain, T. R., Hutchings, P., & Kinzie, J. (2015). *Using evidence of student learning to improve higher education.* San Francisco, CA: Jossey-Bass.

National Center for Education Statistics. (2019). *Fast facts: Postsecondary and beyond.* Retrieved from nces.ed.gov/FastFacts/

National Institute of Education. (1984). *Involvement in learning: Realizing the potential of American higher education. Final report of the Study Group on the Conditions of Excellence in American Higher Education.* National Institute of Education. Washington, DC: U.S. Department of Education.

Palomba, C., & Banta, T. W. (1999). *Assessment essentials: Planning, implementing, and improving assessment in higher education.* San Francisco, CA: Jossey-Bass.

Schilling, K. M., & Schilling, K. L. (1998). *Proclaiming and sustaining excellence: Assessment as a faculty role* (ASHE-ERIC Higher Education Report, Vol. 26, No. 3). Washington, DC: ERIC Clearinghouse on Higher Education.

Suskie, L. (2018). *Assessing student learning: A common sense guide.* San Francisco, CA: Jossey-Bass.

Terenzini, P. T. (1989). Assessment with open eyes: Pitfalls in studying student outcomes. *Journal of Higher Education, 60*(6), 644–664.

PART ONE

TRENDS IN ASSESSMENT

I

MOVEMENT AFOOT

Fostering Discourse on Assessment Scholarship

Natasha A. Jankowski and Gianina R. Baker

Assessment—the systematic collection, sense-making, and subsequent use of evidence of student learning to improve programs, institutions, and student learning—is an integral part of the work of U.S. colleges and universities. As institutions embed assessment processes into their organization and culture, questions proliferate about the current state of the field, about what other institutions are doing, and about what is working for whom and under what circumstances. While the assessment literature is historically practice driven with plentiful how-to manuals, assessment of student learning is also a disciplinary field with evolving directions, dialogues, and scholarly debates. For more than 30 years, considerable time and energy have been invested in advancing efforts to document and improve learning throughout a student's educational journey.

Among the various venues for sharing the state of the art of assessing student learning in higher education, the oldest and largest event is the Assessment Institute in Indianapolis. Since 2011, the National Institute for Learning Outcomes Assessment (NILOA) has partnered with the Institute, offering a conference track on national research, trends, and emerging practices (Kuh & Ikenberry, 2018). For NILOA, the Institute provides an opportunity to hear from the field, identify examples of assessment practice, connect with those doing the hard work of assessing student learning, and learn about resource needs and gaps. The NILOA track, in turn, offers a place for reflection on where we are and where we are going, for a national perspective on the state of the art of assessment, and for updates on emerging projects and national initiatives.

This chapter provides a brief introduction to the history of NILOA and the NILOA track at the Assessment Institute, reports on current challenges and debates in the field of assessment, discusses future directions, and concludes with final thoughts and reflective questions for the field.

History of NILOA and the NILOA Track

Established in 2008, NILOA serves as a research and resource-development organization, dedicated to documenting, advocating, and facilitating the systematic use of learning outcomes assessment to improve student learning. NILOA offers an evidence base of current practice, employing national surveys, focus groups, case studies, webscans, and document analysis, all openly shared on a regularly updated website (learningoutcomesassessment .org).[1]

The NILOA track at the Assessment Institute brings together NILOA scholars and researchers, presenting in partnership with institutional representatives and other national organizations, to provide an annual snapshot of current assessment practice, share resources and research, and learn from participants about their current and emerging needs. For example, track sessions have addressed faculty involvement in assessment (Hutchings, 2010) and preliminary findings from national surveys of program and institution-level assessment activity (Ewell, Paulson, & Kinzie, 2011; Jankowski, Timmer, Kinzie, & Kuh, 2018). Each year, we sponsor sessions on transparency and effective communication, building on NILOA's (2011) Transparency Framework, and discussions on how to better use evidence (Blaich & Wise, 2011). We have held sessions on national efforts such as the Degree Qualifications Profile (Lumina Foundation, 2011, 2014), Tuning, and the work of the Valid Assessment of Learning in Undergraduate Education (VALUE) Institute (McConnell & Rhodes, 2017); assignment design and assignment charrettes (Hutchings, Jankowski, & Ewell, 2014); and culturally responsive assessment—focusing on the relationship between equity and assessment (Montenegro & Jankowski, 2015, 2017).

Each year, we bring in partners leading forward-looking conversations on topics such as documenting learning in the form of comprehensive learner records or competency-based education, outlining approaches to using rubrics to engage in cross-institution comparisons, and considering the entire body of learning that adds up to a degree. We also seek to broaden the engagement of diverse institutional approaches to assessing student learning through conversations with Historically Black Colleges and Universities (HBCUs; Orr, 2018) and Minority-Serving Institutions

(Montenegro & Jankowski, 2015) and the multifaceted approaches to assessment undertaken by Excellence in Assessment designees.[2]

National Trends in Assessment

On a four-year cycle, NILOA surveys the landscape of institution-level assessment activity at all regionally accredited, undergraduate degree–granting institutions in the United States by asking provosts about assessment efforts on their campuses. In the third iteration of our nationwide survey, we found that assessment continues to take new forms and revise old ones.

Movement Toward Authentic Assessment

Institutions are moving toward greater use of authentic measures of student learning such as class assignments, capstones, and rubrics, with the evidence of student learning derived from these embedded approaches deemed most valuable for improving that learning (Jankowski et al., 2018).

NILOA's efforts to support use of well-designed assignments as assessments, underway since 2013, have focused on assignment charrettes. The assignment charrette process (NILOA, 2018a), which has been field-tested with more than 1,000 faculty and staff at more than 400 institutions (including statewide events in coordination with the Multi-State Collaborative to Advance Quality Student Learning), has been instrumental for faculty development on assessment, addressing questions such as the following:

- Does the assignment address the intended learning outcomes?
- Are the activities, pedagogies, and scaffolding in place to support meaningful student engagement in completing the assignment?
- Do the evaluative criteria or rubric, if used, align with the assignment tasks and intended learning outcomes?

The *charrette*—a term borrowed from architecture education, denoting a collaborative design process—brings together groups of faculty for a peer-review, faculty-driven, collaborative process that examines the design and use of the various tasks, projects, papers, and performances we set for our students (NILOA, 2018a). Our goal in this work has been to promote an embedded, faculty-driven approach to assessment built on the authentic demonstrations of learning that emerge from well-designed assignments. The assignments that faculty require of their students are integral to the teaching and learning process and, therefore, more likely to lead to improvements in student learning than add-on, compliance-driven approaches. For faculty, working together on the design of assignments has turned out to be a powerful professional development experience that has elevated the intellectual rigor of assignment design. Findings from follow-up surveys with charrette participants indicate the following:

- Ninety-seven percent of assignment charrette participants reported that the event gave them a new way to think about their assignments and better see their assignments through the eyes of their students.
- Ninety-five percent of participants indicated that they are more aware of aligning their assignment with institutional outcomes. Six months after the charrette, 95% are looking at other assignments more critically and carefully in partnership with other faculty.
- Seventy-two percent have consistently, over time, better aligned their assignment to the agreed-on evaluative criteria. These findings hold for participants who have responded a year, and a year and a half, out from the charrette experience.
- Six months after the event, 82% of survey respondents reported that they more actively involved students in assignment design and prompts and clearly stated the learning expected from an assignment in a way they had not before.
- Seventy-two percent of participants indicated that the experience changed their thinking about assessment, and 6 months later, 75% had made substantial changes in their approach to teaching.

Assignment design conversations continue, with 62% of provosts reporting that their campuses are currently facilitating faculty work on assignment design (Jankowski et al., 2018). Furthermore, a focus on assignments provides a mechanism for launching other discussions; for example, a review of aligning not only assignments but also courses and learning experiences with desired learning outcomes (Hutchings, 2016; Jankowski & Marshall, 2017). The work of the VALUE Institute has been instrumental in this shift, as has technology, which allows course-level assessments to be rolled up to the institution level (Harrison & Braxton, 2018; Richman & Ariovich, 2013).

The use of assignments can connect assessment with teaching and learning, professional development, and faculty roles and responsibilities. But this approach also brings up questions about sampling, comparability, fitness, alignment, and fidelity, and organizational issues of undertaking embedded assessment approaches at scale. Authentic measures are being employed, but the implications of this trend for design, measurement, and implementation as part of institution-level assessment structures are still being debated. Furthermore, assignment conversations serve as an entry point to discussions of additional educational design issues, such as the contexts in which evidence from assignments can be documented and used and the use of portfolios to document and capture the developmental nature of attainment of desired learning.

Focus on Improvement and Equity

As we move toward more authentic measures of learning such as assignments, interest is also shifting to more authentic assessment drivers and processes of assessment. While accreditation remains a primary driver of assessment practice, improvement and equity are becoming increasingly important drivers (Jankowski et al., 2018). The emerging dialogues on the relationship between equity and assessment (Montenegro & Jankowski, 2015, 2017), real-time assessment that is responsive to individual learners (Maki, 2017), issues of social justice (Zerquera, Hernández, & Berumen, 2018), and inclusive assessment are advancing our understanding of the role assessment plays in supporting or hindering our diverse learners. New understandings of culturally responsive assessment, as well as better data on assessment within institutions serving unique populations and missions, like HBCUs and Minority-Serving Institutions, should be shared with the field to inform our collective practice. Lessons learned about equity and assessment from organizations such as the Historically Black Colleges and Universities' Collaboration for Excellence in Educational Quality Assurance (Orr, 2018) and issues of equity and measurement—beyond fairness in measurement—need to be explored as counterpoints to compliance-driven assessment approaches.

Embedded, culturally responsive approaches also align with the growth of partnerships between assessment professionals and faculty development staff, integration of assessment with teaching and learning and student success, and the use of assessment results to inform changes at the program or course level—all in support of sustainable and authentic assessment.

Challenges and Debates

Over the years, assessment scholarship has grown and developed, and while some things stay the same—like the delicate balance between compliance and improvement (Ewell, 2009), the need for effective communication to particular audiences, and larger issues of measurement within assessment approaches—we have noticed some additional points of contention in the past 10 years. Specific areas of interest include aligning learning throughout an institution, expanding the roles of partners involved in assessment, diversifying models of how to assess, and questioning the value and worth of assessment overall.

Alignment of Learning Throughout an Institution

Institutions are moving to align learning outcomes internally throughout the institution and across academic and student affairs (NILOA, 2018b), with 77% of provosts reporting current efforts to map curricula (Jankowski et al., 2018). Areas of continued challenge and growth include mapping, alignment, and understanding of our work as part of a larger system focused on learning from various perspectives, and growing awareness and acceptance that demonstration of learning can take various forms and that learning occurs in many settings. Integration between academic and student affairs remains elusive, however, and while alignment is beginning to take hold, only 50% of survey respondents indicated that all of their programs align in some manner with institutional learning outcomes, with 20% indicating that there is no alignment, and another 30% indicating some alignment (Jankowski et al., 2018). Furthermore, what is classified as *alignment* or *mapped* learning is not well defined or easily agreed on (Jankowski & Marshall, 2017).

Expansion of Partners Involved in Assessment

In the past 10 years, professional positions and organizational structures dedicated to assessment of student learning have increased (Nicholas & Slotnick, 2018). But these years have also brought increasing awareness that meaningful, sustainable assessment cannot be done in isolation or by a single office; while assessment is (ideally) led by faculty, effective assessment efforts must involve multiple institutional constituencies. Partnerships between assessment professionals and faculty have thus emerged, as have closer connections with student affairs staff (Schuh & Gansemer-Topf, 2010), institutional researchers (Volkwein, 2011), and librarians (Gilchrist & Oakleaf, 2012; Malenfant & Brown, 2017), to name a few. More institutional units are engaged in supporting assessment, including centers for teaching and learning, which serve a vital professional development role. The roles and responsibilities of these groups and the strategies for aligning and connecting learning from different kinds of experiences within an institution are still evolving, as are the roles and required competencies of assessment professionals themselves (Jankowski & Slotnick, 2015). Finally, the most effective approaches to engaging students as partners in assessment, while developing, have yet to fully emerge.

Diversification of Models of How to Assess

The past decade has also seen increased differentiation among the various models used to assess student learning. As folks have moved from denial to acceptance that assessment is here to stay (Miller, 2012), conversations have focused on when to employ which approach and to what end, with different models emerging to inform practice (e.g., Fulcher, Good, Coleman, & Smith, 2014) and research devoted to exploring differences (Kuh et al., 2014). As we debate what exactly we are doing, why, and for whom, institutions are moving away from approaches, processes, and structures built for reporting results toward new strategies that aim to support student learning and success. Yet these different approaches rely on different models, organizational structures, and schools of thought (Jankowski, 2017; Kinzie & Jankowski, 2014), some of which are in misalignment with each other. As models diversify, so too will demarcation of different schools of thought about student learning and its assessment.

Questions About the Value and Worth of Assessment

NILOA was formed in response to questions about the quality and worth of higher education emerging from the Spellings Commission on the Future of Higher Education. Today, questions about the value of assessment remain. Is it worth the cost? Should faculty, as some might say, "waste their time on such nonsense"? Do students learn more as a result of assessment? In the shift from assessment driven by compliance to assessment driven by faculty interest in educational design, higher education has lagged in making the case for meaningful assessment and clearly connecting assessment to student learning and success. Furthermore, responses to critiques of assessment have too often been reactive in nature and done little to explore the assumptions about the purpose(s) and design of assessment motivating such critiques.

Yet, without a clear purpose, we are in no position to make an argument for our value and worth. While assessment practitioners and the field have responded to recent commentary on the roles and uses of assessment, little has been done to argue clearly for the value of assessment in its own right. Without a concerted proactive response, it is unlikely that questions of the merit of assessment will go quietly into the night, especially in a time of paradigm shifts within the field itself (Jankowski & Marshall, 2017).

Future Directions

While much is in flux and there are many areas of interest, when we look to future directions of the field of assessment, we find three we want to comment on.

Conversations and Debates Within the Field of Assessment Will Continue and Mature

We will see further delineation within the field of assessment of schools of thought, philosophies underlying our work, issues of measurement, and models for assessing student learning. The movement of prior learning assessment into mainstream practice and the uptake of assessment of learning within student employment—particularly on-campus employment (McClellan, Creager, & Savoca, 2018), work-based learning, and internships (Grose, 2017)—will emerge as a space of dialogue and practice. The ability of institutions to work with evidence of learning from external sources and connect it to learning within, based on growing awareness that learning occurs throughout students' lives and beyond the curriculum, will foster new approaches and assessment-related organizational structures (Jankowski & Marshall, 2017). The roles of additional partners, including students, educational developers, instructional designers, faculty developers, and adjunct faculty (Kezar & Maxey, 2014), as integral parts of assessment will solidify.

These additional layers, roles, and stakeholders will broaden assessment scholarship and bring into relief various points of contention about process, practice, and measurement. New thought leaders will gain ground as others step down, widening the conversation and connecting assessment to other literatures and models, such as learning improvement (Fulcher et al., 2014). In addition, we will continue efforts to assess so-called ineffable outcomes, including noncognitive outcomes, and development of ethics, creativity, and other capacities. Finally, discussions about the competencies needed by assessment professionals and the roles they play will be more clearly defined as we strive to support meaningful and sustainable assessment.

Technology Will Continue to Influence the Practice of Assessment

Technology will play a fundamental role in shaping assessment work, whether through integration of assessment data with other sources of student data throughout our institutions, research focused on the intersection of assessment with retention and graduation, or exploration of other connections between assessment and student success efforts. Research on the use, applicability, and equity implications of predictive analytics and models related to student learning will increase, and we will continue to seek new connections between assessment data and data on teaching and learning. Discussions on data interoperability standards, the ethical use of predictive analytics, and ways to embed learning demonstrations into electronic information transfers will help empower learners to control their learning records, while also raising questions about the design and validation of learning experiences from multiple providers. The potential for artificial intelligence, blockchain, and other technology solutions to assist with assessment will be explored, and we will see continued examination of the role of technology vendors in supporting (as opposed to driving) assessment efforts.

We Will Get Better at Telling Our Story

Higher education badly needs to better and more clearly tell its story about student learning and assessment practice to multiple audiences. Some examples of how best to share what we do, why we do it, and what we have learned from it are emerging, but they are scarce, and we have much to discover. Currently, NILOA is building a tool kit for evidence-based storytelling, following tests of a narrative development and review process with various groups throughout 2018. By unpacking institutional history, student demographics, and data collected throughout the institution and from other sources, institutions can now write rich histories of their institutional assessment efforts and philosophies. Furthermore, practitioners like institutional researchers, faculty, and assessment professionals are working to "count" and "recount" stories using effective narrative and data visualization techniques to provide relevant and timely data to stakeholders for decision-making (Shulman, 2007). This process, when well designed, sets up the conditions needed for the learning systems paradigm shift described next.

Conclusion

As we examine how assessment has changed over NILOA's 10 years and look to the future, it becomes plain that we need different ways of thinking about and envisioning our work. When paradigms shift, so too does practice. In *Degrees That Matter*, Jankowski and Marshall (2017) presented a learning systems paradigm that brings together the various elements of change seen in more than 800 institutions attempting to alter processes, practices, structures, and culture. Through these efforts to meaningfully document learning from a systems perspective, four elements of a paradigm shift became apparent: Assessment efforts must be consensus based; without knowing what we are striving toward, we will not be able to get there. Whether consensus means shared understanding of desired learning outcomes or of other purposes, conversation among the responsible stakeholders is key. Through those conversations emerges alignment, the examination of the relationships among different elements of the educational enterprise. What are the roles of particular learning experiences? How does this course connect to or support learning in another? By examining points of relationship or disconnection, stakeholders begin to understand their roles within the larger educational system. These efforts are for naught, however, if learners are not squarely in the center—meaning that we are not only thinking of them when examining our practice but also actively involving them in the exploration and review of our educational designs. And, finally, if we understand the points of connection, agree on where we are going and how different elements of the system help us get there, we must communicate our efforts broadly and often. In some ways, the field of assessment is moving between and among each of these elements as a scholarship—seeking spaces where we have consensus or need further conversation, raising questions about relationships and alignment among various elements, rethinking the role of the learner, and reworking the ways we communicate about how we assess student learning. Our hunch is that no single paradigm will emerge but many will, leading to exciting discussions at future Assessment Institutes, with which NILOA is delighted to partner.

Summary of Main Trends

- The assessment field is increasingly emphasizing authentic assessment, and NILOA is focusing on improving assignment design to support the use of authentic measures.
- Improvement and equity are becoming increasingly important drivers of assessment, although accreditation continues to be a primary driver.
- Institutions are seeking greater alignment of learning outcomes across programs and between the curriculum and the cocurriculum. New partnerships between and among units are supporting this focus.
- Models for assessment practice are diversifying, with emphases shifting from reporting on outcomes to supporting student learning and success.
- Debates about the value of assessment are continuing; the field needs clearer and more proactive arguments to support the position that assessment is worthwhile.

Questions for Discussion

- In what ways has individual institutional history with assessment influenced current assessment efforts?
- What are the implications of our decisions about assessment design for issues of equity and theories of student learning?

- What assumptions about learners are built into assessment processes and practices? Which of those assumptions need to be reexamined and unpacked?
- Who should be involved in assessment conversations to advance student learning and success throughout an institution, in all the spaces learning happens?

We want to hear from you about *Trends in Assessment*:

- Provide reactions or suggestions about trends.
- Share and access resources related to trends.
- Learn about professional development opportunities related to trends.

Visit assessmentinstitute.iupui.edu/trends

Notes

1. The history of NILOA and its origins and signature work are highlighted in *NILOA at Ten: A Retrospective*, written by our cocreators Kuh and Ikenberry (2018). They eloquently described trends from NILOA's national perspective and offered the context for the creation of NILOA, along with its ongoing need.
2. The Excellence in Assessment (EIA) program recognizes institutions for their efforts in intentional integration of institution-level learning outcomes assessment. The EIA designations focus on processes and uses of assessment outcomes, rather than on student performance or accomplishment. Building on the foundation of reporting both student learning outcomes assessment results and processes established in the Voluntary System of Accountability (VSA), the EIA designation evaluation process is directly and intentionally built from NILOA's (2011) Transparency Framework. The Excellence in Assessment Designation is cosponsored by the VSA, NILOA, and the Association of American Colleges & Universities (AAC&U). VSA is a joint initiative of the American Association of State Colleges and Universities (AASCU) and the Association of Public and Land-grant Universities (APLU).

References

Blaich, C. F., & Wise, K. S. (2011, January). *From gathering to using assessment results: Lessons from the Wabash National Study* (Occasional Paper No. 8). Urbana,

IL: University of Illinois and Indiana University, National Institute for Learning Outcomes Assessment.

Ewell, P. T. (2009, November). *Assessment, accountability, and improvement: Revisiting the tension* (Occasional Paper No. 1). Urbana, IL: University of Illinois and Indiana University, National Institute for Learning Outcomes Assessment.

Ewell, P. T., Paulson, K., & Kinzie, J. (2011). *Down and in: Assessment practices at the program level.* Urbana, IL: University of Illinois and Indiana University, National Institute for Learning Outcomes Assessment.

Fulcher, K. H., Good, M. R., Coleman, C. M., & Smith, K. L. (2014, December). *A simple model for learning improvement: Weigh pig, feed pig, weigh pig* (Occasional Paper No. 23). Urbana, IL: University of Illinois and Indiana University, National Institute for Learning Outcomes Assessment.

Gilchrist, D., & Oakleaf, M. (2012, April). *An essential partner: The librarian's role in student learning assessment* (Occasional Paper No. 14). Urbana, IL: University of Illinois and Indiana University, National Institute for Learning Outcomes Assessment.

Grose, A. W. (2017, July). *Internships, integrative learning and the Degree Qualifications Profile (DQP)* (Occasional Paper No. 30). Urbana, IL: University of Illinois and Indiana University, National Institute for Learning Outcomes Assessment.

Harrison, J. M., & Braxton, S. N. (2018, September). *Technology solutions to support assessment* (Occasional Paper No. 35). Urbana, IL: University of Illinois and Indiana University, National Institute for Learning Outcomes Assessment.

Hutchings, P. (2010, April). *Opening doors to faculty involvement in assessment* (Occasional Paper No. 4). Urbana, IL: University of Illinois and Indiana University, National Institute for Learning Outcomes Assessment.

Hutchings, P. (2016, January). *Aligning educational outcomes and practices* (Occasional Paper No. 26). Urbana, IL: University of Illinois and Indiana University, National Institute for Learning Outcomes Assessment.

Hutchings, P., Jankowski, N. A., & Ewell, P. T. (2014). *Catalyzing assignment design activity on your campus: Lessons from NILOA's assignment library initiative.* Urbana, IL: University of Illinois and Indiana University, National Institute for Learning Outcomes Assessment.

Jankowski, N. A. (2017). Moving toward a philosophy of assessment. *Assessment Update, 29*(3), 10–11.

Jankowski, N. A., & Marshall, D. W. (2017). *Degrees that matter: Moving higher education to a learning systems paradigm.* Sterling, VA: Stylus.

Jankowski, N. A., & Slotnick, R. (2015). The five essential roles of assessment practitioners. *Journal of Assessment and Institutional Effectiveness, 5*(1), 78–100.

Jankowski, N. A., Timmer, J. D., Kinzie, J., & Kuh, G. D. (2018). *Assessment that matters: Trending toward practices that document authentic student learning.* Urbana, IL: University of Illinois and Indiana University, National Institute for Learning Outcomes Assessment.

Kezar, A., & Maxey, D. (2014, July). *Student outcomes assessment among the new non-tenure-track faculty majority* (Occasional Paper No. 21). Urbana, IL: University of Illinois and Indiana University, National Institute for Learning Outcomes Assessment.

Kinzie, J., & Jankowski, N. A. (2014). Making assessment consequential: Organizing to yield results. In G. D. Kuh, S. O. Ikenberry, N. A. Jankowski, T. R. Cain, P. Hutchings, & J. Kinzie (Eds.), *Using evidence of student learning to improve higher education* (pp. 73–94). San Francisco, CA: Jossey-Bass.

Kuh, G. D. (2016). Foreword. In T. W. Banta, P. T. Ewell, & C. A. Cogswell, *Tracing assessment practice as reflected in Assessment Update* (Occasional Paper No. 28, p. 3). Urbana, IL: University of Illinois and Indiana University, National Institute for Learning Outcomes Assessment.

Kuh, G. D., & Ikenberry, S. (2018, October). *NILOA at ten: A retrospective.* Urbana, IL: University of Illinois and Indiana University, National Institute for Learning Outcomes Assessment.

Kuh, G. D., Ikenberry, S. O., Jankowski, N. A., Cain, T. R., Hutchings, P., & Kinzie, J. (2014). *Using evidence of student learning to improve higher education.* San Francisco, CA: Jossey-Bass.

Lumina Foundation. (2011). *Degree Qualifications Profile.* Indianapolis, IN: Author.

Lumina Foundation. (2014). *Degree Qualifications Profile.* Indianapolis, IN: Author.

Maki, P. L. (2017). *Real-time student assessment: Meeting the imperative for improved time to degree, closing the opportunity gap, and assuring student competencies for 21st-century needs.* Sterling, VA: Stylus.

Malenfant, K. J., & Brown, K. (2017, November). *Creating sustainable assessment through collaboration: A national program reveals effective practices* (Occasional Paper No. 31). Urbana, IL: University of Illinois and Indiana University, National Institute for Learning Outcomes Assessment.

McClellan, G. S., Creager, K. L., & Savoca, M. (2018). *A good job: Campus employment as a high-impact practice.* Sterling, VA: Stylus.

McConnell, K. D., & Rhodes, T. L. (2017). *On solid ground: VALUE report 2017.* Washington, DC: Association of American Colleges & Universities.

Miller, M. A. (2012, January). *From denial to acceptance: The stages of assessment* (Occasional Paper No. 13). Urbana, IL: University of Illinois and Indiana University, National Institute for Learning Outcomes Assessment.

Montenegro, E., & Jankowski, N. A. (2015, April). *Focused on what matters: Assessment of student learning outcomes at minority-serving institutions.* Urbana, IL: University of Illinois and Indiana University, National Institute for Learning Outcomes Assessment.

Montenegro, E., & Jankowski, N. A. (2017, January). *Equity and assessment: Moving towards culturally responsive assessment* (Occasional Paper No. 29). Urbana, IL: University of Illinois and Indiana University, National Institute for Learning Outcomes Assessment.

National Institute for Learning Outcomes Assessment. (2011). *Transparency framework.* Urbana, IL: University of Illinois and Indiana University, National

Institute for Learning Outcomes Assessment. Retrieved from http://www
.learningoutcomesassessment.org/TransparencyFramework.htm

National Institute for Learning Outcomes Assessment. (2018a, February). *The
assignment charrette toolkit.* Urbana, IL: University of Illinois and Indiana University, National Institute for Learning Outcomes Assessment.

National Institute for Learning Outcomes Assessment. (2018b, March). *Mapping
learning: A toolkit.* Urbana, IL: University of Illinois and Indiana University,
National Institute for Learning Outcomes Assessment.

Nicholas, M. C., & Slotnick, R. C. (2018, April). *A portrait of the assessment professional in the United States: Results from a national survey* (Occasional Paper No.
34). Urbana, IL: University of Illinois and Indiana University, National Institute
for Learning Outcomes Assessment.

Orr, V. F. (2018, October). *Assessment, accountability, and student learning outcomes
at historically Black colleges and universities.* Urbana, IL: University of Illinois and
Indiana University, National Institute for Learning Outcomes Assessment.

Richman, W. A., & Ariovich, L. (2013, October). *All-in-one: Combining grading,
course, program, and general education outcomes assessment* (Occasional Paper No.
19). Urbana, IL: University of Illinois and Indiana University, National Institute
for Learning Outcomes Assessment.

Schuh, J. H., & Gansemer-Topf, A. M. (2010, December). *The role of student affairs
in student learning assessment* (Occasional Paper No. 7). Urbana, IL: University of
Illinois and Indiana University, National Institute for Learning Outcomes Assessment.

Shulman, L. S. (2007). Counting and recounting: Assessment and the quest for
accountability. *Change, 39*(1), 20–23.

Volkwein, J. F. (2011, September). *Gaining ground: The role of institutional research
in assessing student outcomes and demonstrating institutional effectiveness* (Occasional Paper No. 11). Urbana, IL: University of Illinois and Indiana University,
National Institute for Learning Outcomes Assessment.

Zerquera, D., Hernández, I., & Berumen, J. G. (Eds.). (2018). [Special issue]. *New
Directions in Institutional Research: Assessment and Social Justice: Pushing Through
Paradox, 2018*(177), 1–144.

2

BECOMING MORE HIP

Assessment Trends in High-Impact Learning Practices and Student Success

Jennifer Thorington Springer, Amy A. Powell,
Steven Graunke, Thomas W. Hahn, and Julie A. Hatcher

For more than a decade, high-impact practices (HIPs) have been recognized on college campuses as powerful strategies for supporting student learning and success. HIPs are "active learning practices . . . that educational research suggests increase rates of student retention and student engagement" (Kuh, 2008, p. 9) and promote deeper learning, higher grades, and other desirable student outcomes (Kuh & Kinzie, 2018). A common feature of all HIPs is that they offer students opportunities to make "their own discoveries and connections, grapple with challenging real-world questions, and address complex problems—all necessary skills if students are to become engaged and effective members of their communities" (Kinzie, 2012, para. 1). Since George Kuh (2008) identified the original set of HIPs more than a decade ago, institutional leaders, faculty, staff, and administrators have intentionally incorporated them into strategic plans, woven them into the curriculum and cocurriculum, and provided faculty and staff opportunities for professional development to design and implement them. As the implementation of HIPs continues to spread, it is important to ensure that they are done effectively and that students derive maximum benefit from these experiences. In this chapter, we thus explore current and future directions of HIPs assessment.

Discussions of how best to assess HIPs, given their importance and potential to support student achievement, have been unfolding over the past decade at the Assessment Institute in Indianapolis, at the various conferences and summer institutes sponsored by the Association of American Colleges

& Universities (AAC&U), on college campuses, and elsewhere. In this chapter, we offer a definition of and some foundational background on HIPs as context for a discussion of current HIPs assessment trends and strategies in higher education. We then address approaches to five key questions about HIPs assessment: How do institutions assess HIP implementation for quality? How do we track and document participation in HIPs? How do we leverage HIPs assessment to address issues of access and equity? How do we assess the impact of HIPs on student success? How do we assess student learning from HIP experiences? Throughout this chapter, we note specific tools and practical ways in which various institutions are effectively planning, implementing, and assessing HIPs to improve student learning and success.

History

In the following, we review the history of HIPs.

The Practice of HIPs: A Legacy for Student Learning and Success

Through the Liberal Education and America's Promise (LEAP) program, the AAC&U has endorsed research that identifies teaching and learning strategies that have substantial educational benefits for all students as "high impact." The initial list of 10 practices appeared in the AAC&U's 2007 report *College Learning for the New Global Century* (National Leadership Council for Liberal Education and America's Promise, 2007). Kuh fully delineated the concept of HIPs, drawing on research from the National Survey of Student Engagement (NSSE), in the 2008 AAC&U monograph *High-Impact Educational Practices: What They Are, Who Has Access to Them, and Why They Matter* (Kuh, 2008). The 10 HIPs he discussed were First-Year Seminars and Experiences, Common Intellectual Experiences, Learning Communities, Writing-Intensive Courses, Collaborative Assignments and Projects, Undergraduate Research, Diversity/Global Learning, Service/Community-Based Learning, Internships and Field Placements, and Capstone Courses and Projects (Kuh, 2008). In 2017, ePortfolios were added as an 11th HIP (Kuh, 2017; Kuh, Gambino, Bresciani Ludvik, & O'Donnell, 2018).

The research carried out by Kuh and his colleagues at Indiana University's Center for Postsecondary Research (CPR) indicated that "students who reported doing one or more of these practices benefited in various desired ways. In fact, the differences between those who did a HIP and those who did not were so large that we reanalyzed the data" (Kuh & Kinzie, 2018, para. 5). On the basis of CPR's research findings, Kuh (2008) recommended that universities "make it possible for every student to participate in *at least two high-impact activities* during his or her undergraduate program, one in the first year, and one taken later in relation to the major field" (p. 19, emphasis in original). He added, "The obvious choices for incoming students are first-year seminars, learning communities, and service learning" (p. 19). More recent scholarship has revealed that students who participate in five to six HIPs have higher gains in all areas than students who do not participate in any or who participate in one to two or three to four HIPs (Finley & McNair, 2013). Finally, there is even more impact when students participate in combined HIP opportunities—for example, a first-year seminar with a community-engagement focus or a study abroad experience with a service-learning component.

Kuh and O'Donnell (2013) attributed the impact of HIPs to the following common characteristics: (a) expectations set at appropriately high levels; (b) significant investment of time and effort over an extended period of time; (c) increased interaction with faculty and peers about substantive matters; (d) experiences with diversity, wherein students interact with others different from themselves; (e) frequent, timely, and constructive feedback from instructors and peers; (f) periodic, structured opportunities for students to reflect on and integrate learning; (g) opportunities to discover relevance of learning through real-world applications; and (h) public demonstration of competence. The more of these markers are present in a HIP experience, the more students are likely to achieve.

Current Trends: What's Trending in HIPs Assessment?

The efficacy of HIPs continues to be validated by practitioners, champions, and extant research. A guiding value for HIPs is that they must be "done well" to lead to deep learning and other benefits (Kuh & O'Donnell, 2013). One important assessment trend is thus examination of the quality and fidelity of HIP practice. Finley and McNair (2013) further challenged us to examine who is participating in HIPs and to leverage findings to address inequities. Tracking and disaggregating participation data to determine who has access and how HIPs can be offered equitably to all students is thus another key trend. Recent sessions at the Assessment Institute have also addressed questions of how to scale HIPs opportunities to achieve equity and maximize participation. Finally, institutions are developing authentic approaches to assessing what students learn from participating in HIPs. We will discuss each of these trends, with examples drawn from Assessment Institute presentations and elsewhere.

Assessing HIPs' Quality and Fidelity

Assessment can help us ascertain whether or not we are offering our students genuinely valuable HIP experiences. As McNair (2017) argued, HIPs offered without attention to fidelity and quality are empty promises. And as use of HIPs continues to increase across all institutional types, it becomes even more important to ensure that they are being done well. To address this issue, several institutions have developed fidelity measures or "taxonomies" to track consistency of implementation. California State University, Dominguez Hills, for example, designed taxonomies to describe the most effective practices for such experiences and programs as early alert, first-year experience, intrusive advising, learning communities, peer mentoring, supplemental instruction, summer bridge programs, orientation, and undergraduate research (O'Donnell, 2015).

The 2018 inaugural HIPs in the States Conference at California State University, Dominguez Hills, included notable presentations from other campuses that had created taxonomies for assessment purposes. At the University of Wisconsin Colleges, a multidisciplinary team developed scalable taxonomies to incorporate HIPs into a new degree program. For the undergraduate research taxonomy, presenters reported aligning undergraduate research experiences with best practices across disciplines, types of research opportunities, and student achievement levels. At Indiana University–Purdue University Indianapolis (IUPUI), each unit with responsibility for a HIP constructed a taxonomy to serve as a framework to guide course design, implementation, assessment, and improvement (Indiana University–Purdue University Indianapolis, n.d.). The Learning Communities program developed a pre-semester planning document and post-semester reflection survey aligned with the taxonomy; these were distributed to all faculty teaching learning community sections. Collecting pre- and post-semester plans and reflections provided additional dimensions of feedback to both faculty and the program to guide professional development and program improvements.

As HIP programs are taken to scale to address issues of equity and access, tools like taxonomies can help ensure that high-quality experiences are developed and delivered. Taxonomies can identify the most effective aspects of HIPs to guide their design and implementation. When coupled with additional assessment tools and professional development, fidelity assessment can support the consistency and effectiveness of HIPs.

Tracking and Documenting Participation in HIPs

Determining best practices for accurately collecting, documenting, and disaggregating data on HIP participation can help us understand which students are benefiting from these experiences. Kuh's (2008) initial research on HIPs caused a number of institutions to merge and expand existing programs to encourage greater participation. Unfortunately, these efforts frequently occurred without consideration for tracking participation at an institutional level. Having inaccurate or inaccessible data on participation in HIPs makes it particularly difficult to assess the impact of HIPs on student learning, as Kuh, O'Donnell, and Schneider (2017) noted. Because HIPs are rarely recorded on traditional transcripts, they can be untraceable by traditional tools of institutional research, like federally reported Integrated Postsecondary Education Data System (IPEDS) data or campus-based student information systems. Sara Finney (2018) addressed a similar issue when discussing implementation fidelity during her track keynote at the 2018 Assessment Institute. Determining the effectiveness of an intervention, such as an orientation program, is impossible if the student did not receive the intervention. Similarly, we cannot assess attainment of specified learning outcomes of a service-learning experience or learning community if no documentation exists that the student actually participated.

Many institutions use NSSE to both track the frequency of student participation in HIPs and understand the effects of engagement on student success. NSSE asks respondents about their participation in six HIPs, enabling campuses to correlate levels of student participation in HIPs to a variety of student outcomes (see Hahn & Hatcher, 2013). California State University, San Marcos, for example, used NSSE data to identify groups of students less likely to participate in HIPs (National Survey of Student Engagement, 2017). Similarly, the University of Toronto developed a series of dashboards demonstrating that students who participated in the recommended number of HIPs reported greater engagement in quantitative reasoning and student–faculty interaction (National Survey of Student Engagement, 2017).

Other institutions have developed their own instruments that allow students to self-report HIP participation. Sweat, Jones, Han, and Wolfgram (2013) used an internally developed self-report instrument to collect data for their study of student participation in HIPs by ethnicity. But the use of self-report measures as a means to collect data on participation in HIPs has been called into question. Kolek (2013) found that about half of students who self-reported that they had completed a service-learning course or program had not enrolled in any of the university's designated community-based learning courses. Many plausible explanations exist for such a discrepancy, including student misunderstanding of survey items or miscoded information in an institutional database.

While self-report instruments are one method of documenting student participation in HIPs, several other methods might provide more accurate records. In a presentation at the Assessment Institute, Croxton and Moore (2018) discussed a comprehensive effort at the University of North Carolina, Charlotte, to collect data from the university library, student affairs, and other campus offices. This data-collection initiative was designed to connect engagement in cocurricular activities, including HIPs, with outcomes such as GPA and retention. Coordinated institution-wide data-collection initiatives such as these may become more popular as a way to obtain the information necessary for the assessment of HIPs.

Many institutions are also implementing cocurricular transcripts, which document learning activities that occur outside the classroom. Indiana State University offered an example of a cocurricular transcript at the Assessment Institute. The university's locally developed system receives data from a wide variety of programs across the campus, stores engagement data with other student metrics, and provides data visualizations to help internal stakeholders understand the relationship between engagement and other outcomes (Dalrymple, Ferguson, & Miklozek, 2018). Cocurricular transcripts could be one method to both document students' participation in HIPs and collect data necessary to begin assessing student learning outcomes.

Tracking participation is a necessary step in the institution-wide assessment of HIPs. At the very least, institutions that set goals for expanding the number of participants may be satisfied by exploring growth over time. Institutions often begin HIP initiatives with much broader goals, however, such as improving retention rates or enhancing student learning (Kuh et al., 2017). Those responsible for program or institution-wide assessment, therefore, should aim to move beyond simply tracking participation in HIPs and toward more meaningful assessment of implementation and learning outcomes.

Leveraging HIPs Assessment for Equity and Access

When we assess participation in HIPs, questions of equity and access are critical. Where do the disparities lie? Finley and McNair (2013) found that historically minoritized and underserved students significantly benefit from participating in HIPs and that participating in multiple HIPs had cumulative, intensifying effects. The unfortunate reality, however, is that these communities of students do not participate at high levels. Intentional efforts are necessary to engage traditionally underserved and underrepresented students and to build in equitable access and opportunity. In the 2017 Assessment Institute HIPs track keynote address, *Becoming a Student-Ready College: High-Impact Practices and Intentionality by Design,* McNair (2017) shared the AAC&U's important work on becoming a "student-ready" college. This publication reinforced the need for campus leadership to escape deficit-minded thinking about incoming students, specifically those we have historically considered "underprepared." Rather than embrace such thinking, McNair recommended that we equip ourselves to meet our students' needs. Instead of asking what students are lacking, she advised, we should identify the barriers to student success for underserved and underrepresented students and determine what we can offer proactively.

If HIPs can indeed narrow achievement gaps and improve the effectiveness of students' educational experiences, what then might we consider as ways to intervene to support equity and inclusive excellence? Institutions are beginning to mount intentional efforts to create equal access to HIPs. For example, some campuses offer financial aid to first-generation students who might not participate equally in study abroad experiences (Kinzie, 2012). Introducing transfer and underserved students to HIPs early and often and exploring and debunking myths that may impede student participation in HIPs can also assist in equity efforts (Hansen & Kahn, 2018). Combining curricular and cocurricular experiences where student affairs and academic affairs collaborate to make HIPs more widespread and readily available (Hansen & Kahn, 2018) and disaggregating data to identify those who need encouragement to participate can aid in setting and attaining equity goals (McNair, 2017; Thorington Springer, Hatcher, & Powell, 2018).

Scaling HIPs

Scaling individual HIPs to serve more students can increase participation and further address issues of equity and access. When we use this approach, it is important to ensure that students who will benefit the most and/or are less likely to participate in HIPs are included. For example, at IUPUI students with high levels of unmet financial need, a risk indicator, can receive institutional aid in the form of a Pledge Grant if they agree to participate in a first-year learning community or the Summer Bridge program. Several early orientation sessions are reserved for Pledge Grant recipients to ensure that seats in learning communities and Summer Bridge are available. Gaps in Pledge Grant enrollment can be identified by disaggregating HIP tracking data by markers relevant to the institution's student population such as race and ethnicity, gender, first-generation status, and Pell status. Outcomes assessment data should be similarly disaggregated to identify groups that benefit at high levels from HIP participation. Such analyses can identify and guide actions to reduce inequities.

Disaggregating HIPs assessment data to identify gaps in student participation, along with strategies to support traditionally underserved populations, is an assessment trend that can help to ensure equity in higher education. Better understanding the barriers to participation and offering incentives and rewards for underserved populations to participate is an institutional tactic that can support student success. Providing resources for scaling HIPs to allow greater access, paired with mechanisms for encouraging underserved students to participate in HIP experiences, can help reduce equity gaps.

Direct Assessment of HIP Learning

In addition to indirect measures of student gains like NSSE, institutions are using authentic assessment approaches and direct measures of student learning to determine the impact of HIPs. ePortfolios, for example, are both a HIP and a direct, authentic assessment tool that provides opportunities for students to engage in a "meta-high-impact practice" (see Kahn, chapter 9, volume). With thoughtful guidance, students can bring together evidence of learning from multiple HIPs in their ePortfolios and engage in metacognitive reflection to deepen and integrate their learning. Those assessing ePortfolios can thereby gain insight into not only *what* students learn from HIPs participation but also *how* they learn (Kahn, chapter 9, this volume). Tools like the AAC&U Valid Assessment of Learning in Undergraduate Education (VALUE) rubrics can also provide important insight into student learning from HIPs. The VALUE Institute, a partnership between the AAC&U and the CPR, provides direct measures of student learning using the VALUE rubrics (Association of American Colleges & Universities, n.d.). Under a fee-for-service model similar to the NSSE, institutions can submit student artifacts that are scored by trained reviewers and receive reports by rubric dimension, comparison with institutions participating nationally, and disaggregation by demographic variables.

Future Trends: What's in the Pipeline?

Emerging trends in HIPs assessment are beginning to answer some important questions. The most pressing issue currently discussed at the Assessment Institute and nationally is how we can implement high-quality HIPs at scale and provide equitable access to all students. Other new questions tie into this theme: How can we embed HIPs into all levels of the institution so students participate in at least one HIP each year, whether in the curriculum or the cocurriculum? How can institutions best support HIPs at scale? Taking HIPs to scale is resource intensive, making it important to identify the variables that influence student learning outcomes. As they incorporate these variables, programs and institutions may need to restructure and redesign HIPs.

Using HIP taxonomies to assess quality and fidelity and connect specific attributes to student learning outcomes is one approach to consider. Once key HIP attributes that increase student success outcomes are identified, HIP programs and practices can be combined and redesigned to maximize impact while making efficient use of resources.

To support this work, some institutions are rethinking organizational structures, sometimes bringing together HIP units that are distributed across a campus. IUPUI, for example, has recently launched an Institute for Engaged Learning in its Division of Undergraduate Education to bring together all campus HIP units under one organizational structure.

Any discussion of future trends in HIPs assessment would be incomplete without consideration of professional development. If we are to bring HIPs to scale with quality, investment in and development of faculty and staff are key. If we are to successfully respond to employers' needs for graduates who have more than classroom experience, and if we believe that HIPs can help prepare our students for job opportunities, we will need professional development to ensure that HIPs are done well—with intentionality, fidelity, and quality.

Faculty participation in the assessment of HIPs is another future trend that supports HIP quality. Involving faculty in the assessment of learning outcomes associated with HIPs, using a tool like a VALUE rubric, can help faculty gain insight into student learning experiences. Through this understanding, faculty can make ongoing, incremental changes that deepen student learning. For such work to succeed, however, institutions must prioritize, incentivize, and reward participation in HIPs and HIPs assessment.

Conclusion

The value and effectiveness of HIPs have been recognized by researchers and practitioners. When done well, HIPs contribute to deepen learning, student engagement, retention, timely degree completion, and satisfaction and also prepare students for life after graduation. As we work to continually improve the delivery of HIPs, assessment should aim to ensure fidelity, quality, and access; to build in equity models; and to look closely at the impact on student success and learning outcomes. Simply tracking HIPs to determine student participation may be a thing of the past. Continuing to create and expand our HIP assessment methods and tools is essential. Using the various assessment strategies discussed in this chapter can help us design, implement, and improve HIPs with attention to institutional cultures and needs.

Summary of Main Trends

- Institutions are developing tools for assessment of the fidelity of HIP implementation to ensure that they are "done well."
- Tracking and documenting participation in HIPs is key to assessing learning outcomes and identifying who has access and who lacks access.
- Institutions are moving to address inequities in access to and participation in HIPs.
- Institutions are going beyond indirect measures of HIP outcomes and are beginning to use authentic assessments like ePortfolios and VALUE rubrics.
- Institutions are reconsidering organizational structures and practices, including professional development, to ensure that HIPs are being implemented in intentional ways campus-wide.

Questions for Discussion

- How might we better understand how variables related to HIP quality and fidelity influence student learning outcomes?
- How might we use data collected on HIPs to determine the institutional support needed?
- Would institutions benefit from assembling campus-wide assessment teams to identify improvements that might enhance the effectiveness of HIPs for student learning?
- What might intentional efforts to improve access to and equity in HIPs on your campus look like?

We want to hear from you about *Trends in Assessment*:

- Provide reactions or suggestions about trends.
- Share and access resources related to trends.
- Learn about professional development opportunities related to trends.

Visit assessmentinstitute.iupui.edu/trends

References

Association of American Colleges & Universities. (n.d.). The VALUE Institute: Learning outcomes assessment at its best. Retrieved from https://www.aacu/org/VALUEInstitute

Croxton, R. A., & Moore, A. C. (2018, October). *From matriculation to graduation: A university-wide assessment of student engagement and success.* Paper presented at the 2018 Assessment Institute, Indianapolis, IN.

Dalrymple, M., Ferguson, L., & Miklozek, H. (2018, October). *Gauging engagement: Tracking, reporting, and assessing student engagement.* Paper presented at the 2018 Assessment Institute, Indianapolis, IN.

Finley, A. P., & McNair, T. (2013). *Assessing underserved students' engagement in high-impact practices.* Washington, DC: Association of American Colleges & Universities.

Finney, S. J. (2018, October). *Showcasing the utility of implementation fidelity data when evaluating program effectiveness.* Paper presented at the 2018 Assessment Institute, Indianapolis, IN.

Hahn, T. W., & Hatcher, J. A. (2013). Service learning and deep learning. *Research Brief,* Issue 1. Indianapolis, IN: IUPUI Center for Service and Learning. Retrieved from http://hdl.handle.net/1805/18104

Hansen, M., & Kahn, S. (2018, February). *Maximizing student success in high-impact practices.* Workshop presented at the University of North Carolina–Wilmington, Wilmington, NC. Retrieved from https://uncw.edu/universitystudies/

Indiana University–Purdue University Indianapolis (n.d.) Rise Initiative: Taxonomies. Retrieved from rise.iupui.edu/taxonomies

Kinzie, J. (2012). High-impact practices: Promoting participation for all students. *Diversity and Democracy, 15*(3). Retrieved from https://www.aacu.org/publications-research/periodicals/high-impact-practices-promoting-participation-all-students

Kuh, G. D., & Kinzie, J. (2018, May 1). What really makes a "high-impact" practice high impact? *Inside Higher Ed.* Retrieved from https://www.insidehighered.com/views/2018/05/01/kuh-and-kinzie-respond-essay-questioning-high-impact-practices-opinion

Kolek, E. A. (2013). Can we count on counting? An analysis of the validity of community engagement survey measures. *International Journal on Service-Learning and Community Engagement, 1,* 92–108. Retrieved from https://journals.sfu.ca/iarslce/index.php/journal/article/view/23/17

Kuh, G. D. (2008). *High-impact educational practices: What they are, who has access to them, and why they matter.* Washington, DC: Association of American Colleges & Universities.

Kuh, G. D. (2017). Foreword: And now there are 11. In B. Eynon & L. M. Gambino, *High-impact ePortfolio practice* (pp. vii–xi). Sterling, VA: Stylus.

Kuh, G. D., Gambino, L. M., Bresciani Ludvik, M., & O'Donnell, K. (2018, February). *Using ePortfolio to document and deepen the impact of HIPs on learning dispositions* (Occasional Paper No. 32). Urbana, IL: University of Illinois and Indiana University, National Institute for Learning Outcomes Assessment. Retrieved from http://learningoutcomesassessment.org/occasionalpaperthirtytwo.html

Kuh, G. D., & O'Donnell, K. (2013). *Ensuring quality and taking high-impact practices to scale.* Washington, DC: Association of American Colleges & Universities.

Kuh, G. D., O'Donnell, K., & Schneider, C. G. (2017, November). HIPs at ten. *Change: The Magazine of Higher Learning, 49*(5), 8–16. doi:10.1080/00091383.2017.1366805

McNair, T. (2017, October). *Becoming a student-ready college: High-impact practices and intentionality by design.* Paper presented at the 2017 Assessment Institute, Indianapolis, IN.

National Leadership Council for Liberal Education and America's Promise. (2007). *College learning for the new global century.* Washington, DC: Association of American Colleges & Universities. Retrieved from https://www.aacu.org/sites/default/files/files/LEAP/GlobalCentury_final.pdf

National Survey of Student Engagement. (2017). *Lessons from the field: Digging deeper to focus and extend data use* (Vol. 4). Bloomington, IN: Center for Postsecondary Research, Indiana University School of Education.

O'Donnell, K. (2015, October). *Strengthening student success foundations through assessment.* Paper presented at the 2015 Assessment Institute, Indianapolis, IN.

Sweat, J., Jones, G., Han, S., & Wolfgram, S. M. (2013). How does high-impact practice predict student engagement? A comparison of White and minority students. *International Journal for the Scholarship of Teaching and Learning, 7*(2), 1–24. doi:10.20429/ijsotl.2013.070217

Thorington Springer, J., Hatcher, J. A., & Powell, A. A. (2018). High-impact practices: The call for a commitment to quality educational experiences and inclusive excellence. *Assessment Update, 7*(4), 6–7.

EVOLVING PRACTICES IN THE DEVELOPMENT AND ASSESSMENT OF GLOBAL LEARNING

Leslie A. Bozeman, Dawn M. Whitehead, Darla K. Deardorff, and Gil Latz

G lobal learning, a recently developed subfield within international higher education, prepares students to analyze complex problems in local and global communities and engage with people from diverse disciplinary and cultural backgrounds. Historically, global learning has been most closely associated with study abroad, but it has evolved over the years to include many other educational practices: meaningful engagement with international students, interactive videoconferences, community-based global learning, globally focused internships and capstones, and study away—educational experiences within the home country in communities that are culturally different from one's own (Carter, Latz, & Thornton, 2010; Whitehead, 2016). Each can be implemented on and off campus, in local and global communities, to address curricular and cocurricular learning goals. Global learning can be further described as an educational process that prepares students for citizenship and work in a diverse and interconnected world (Hovland, 2006) and an experience that involves both theory and a variety of educational practices.

Global Learning and Assessment: Historical Context

Institutions define and integrate the various aspects of global learning in complex ways, and assessment approaches are similarly diverse. In the past, assessment of global learning typically took the form of pre– and/or post–self-report assessments, and results were used mainly for program improvement rather than for improving student learning and development. In the 1970s, a more concerted scholarly effort invested in quantitative techniques to ascertain students' intercultural effectiveness (Ruben, Askling, & Kealey, 1977) and propensity for cross-cultural adaptation (Hammer, Gudykunst, & Wiseman, 1978; Ruben & Kealey, 1979). Additional assessment tools were developed during the 1980s and 1990s. By the early 2000s, more than 140 assessment tools were in use for measuring various elements of intercultural and global learning (Deardorff, 2017). These techniques and tools drew on literature that can be traced back to the 1930s in the United States, including the work of Edward Hall, Rachel DuBois, and others (Arasaratnam-Smith, 2017). In 2018, the construct of global competence was measured worldwide through the Program in International Student Assessment (PISA) test by the Organization of Economic Development and Cooperation (2018).

Current Trends in Global Learning Assessment

While global learning includes a number of skills and competencies, intercultural competence dominates the field. Intercultural competence is the ability to communicate and behave effectively and appropriately in intercultural situations, drawing on one's intercultural knowledge, skills, and attitudes (Deardorff, 2006). The development of intercultural competence is a lifelong process; thus, students need multiple opportunities to practice these skills both in and out of the classroom. Intercultural competence is not limited to global learning, however; these skills apply to all situations that involve engaging with new or unfamiliar people or situations, whether in local or international settings. Employers today seek these types of skills in recent graduates entering the workforce (Hart & Associates, 2015).

Global Learning Trends

Important current trends in global learning reflect various conceptions of global engagement for today's college student. *Global citizenship*, *global perspectives*, and *community-based learning* are just a few of the terms that colleges and universities use to refer to institutional global engagement and shape their own narratives on global learning.

By exploring the role of global citizenship in global learning (Nussbaum, 2002; Reimers, 2014; UNESCO, 2018), institutions seek to graduate students with skills and attitudes that enable them to engage globally and locally as members of both communities. Students are challenged to see the world through the eyes of others and to consider both their own perspectives and those of people they have never met as they make decisions (e.g., about voting) that may affect others near and far. They are also challenged to consider how global interconnectivity raises complicated issues of social responsibility (Reimers, 2014). Hartman, Kiely, Boettcher, and Friedrichs (2018) further argued for a critical approach to global citizenship; this perspective emphasizes human dignity and an understanding, rooted in values, reflection, and action, of historical and contemporary systems of oppression. Students are thus asked to examine their own place in the world as they consider their responsibilities and roles in society.

Other institutional efforts are intended to help students develop *global perspectives*. This framing pushes students to think critically about their views of others and themselves throughout all of their experiences. As a result, they learn to think and interact skillfully with people from backgrounds different from their own (Braskamp, 2015) and to consider diverse perspectives on their own actions. Over the course of an educational program, a global perspectives framework enables students to explore from various angles a number of intercultural and global situations and consider how their actions affect local, regional, national, and/or global communities.

Community-based learning, which draws on the rich legacy of service-learning, international service, and global service-learning, is another important approach to global learning. Community-based global learning (CBGL) is a "community-driven learning and/or service experience that employs structured, critically reflective practices to better understand global citizenship, positionality, power, structure, and social responsibility in a global context" (Hartman et al., 2018, p. 21). CBGL captures, in particular, the importance of structured reflection in guiding students' understanding of hierarchy and power as they engage with global and local communities that represent the world's cultural diversity (Hatcher, Price, Whitehead, & Latz, 2015).

As reviewed here, international education and the newer field of global learning are inextricably linked, establishing a strong foundation for considering intercultural competence, global citizenship, and global perspectives as central trends in both fields. Recent research by Landorf, Doscher, and Hardrick (2018) observed that the term *global learning* can be traced to ideas articulated by the United Nations University; global learning aims to "enable people to understand and determine solutions to global problems. To accomplish this, people's diverse perspectives are essential. Global problems transcend borders, so participation in global problem-solving must do so as well" (p. 31). This concept is at the heart of global learning, defining what students should know and be able to do, in collaboration with diverse communities, to solve problems that cross borders and disciplines.

Global Learning Assessment Trends

Because global learning is connected to multiple educational practices and structures, its assessment tends to be context specific and not limited to a single practice. Within international higher education, education abroad has led the way in propagating the use of pre- and post-assessment measures, often to demonstrate that such programs lead to desired student outcomes. Increasingly, though, global learning assessment is included in curricular and cocurricular programs other than study abroad and is moving beyond the use of pre- and post-assessment measures. For example, the use of electronic portfolios (ePortfolios) in international education has increased over the past decade in the United States as well as in other countries. The Association of American Colleges & Universities' (AAC&U) Valid Assessment of Learning in Undergraduate Education (VALUE) project includes a rubric for and definition of *global learning* as "a critical analysis of and an engagement with complex, interdependent global systems and legacies (such as natural, physical, social, cultural, economic, and political) and their implications for people's lives and the earth's sustainability" (AAC&U, n.d.). The VALUE rubric is now considered an important standard for assessment of global learning.

Based on the case studies in Deardorff and Arasaratnam-Smith (2017), the use of peer assessments and authentic assessments is increasing. These approaches are changing the paradigm for assessment of global learning (Deardorff, 2015)—moving from a focus on outcomes to a focus on process, from pre- and post-measures to formative assessments (direct evidence collected during the learning experience), from standardized tools to customized and tailored ones (e.g., ePortfolios). These newer approaches rely on direct and indirect evidence aligned to specific learning outcomes and focus on changes in the learner's knowledge, attitudes, and skills.

Evolving Practices in the Development and Assessment of Global Learning

Trends in the field of global learning assessment call for clear articulation of overarching strategies and terminology definitions, measurement of intercultural competence, pedagogies for global citizenship, ePortfolios centered on deepened student self-reflection, customized tools for specific curricular or institutional contexts, and the challenges to implementation of innovative assessment approaches. Each is discussed in the following sections.

Clear Articulation of Strategies and Terminology
As noted earlier, a clear overarching strategy can help ensure a collaborative, inclusive approach to assessing global learning institution-wide. Researchers and practitioners increasingly recognize the importance of such strategies.

The application of comprehensive strategic thinking to global learning assessment must transcend boundaries, integrate units and missions, and develop practices that are meaningful to the broad institution and appropriate to organizational cultures (Kahn, 2016). Such strategies should reflect five elements: faculty leadership, a culture of inquiry rather than compliance, sufficient support for assessment, manageability, and utility (Green, 2017). Strategies are predicated on agreement about terminology, so that students, faculty, staff, and administrators understand the nature and scope of a global learning activity. Assessment terminology should define precisely what is being measured. Clarifying terminology is often critical to facilitating dialogue and moving work forward (Bozeman & Hansen, 2017). Such stage setting is essential to implementing assessment and empowering it to influence policy and meet higher education's obligation to students in an age of globalization (Charles, 2015).

Measurement of Intercultural Competence
Measuring intercultural competence is challenging, as attempts over the past decade have shown. Research has indicated that it is important to use a multimethod, multiperspective approach to measuring this complex construct (Deardorff, 2015). Some of the many existing assessment tools aligned with global learning assessment goals thus continue to be used. But while such tools may be part of an assessment approach to measuring global learning, practice is evolving beyond the sole use of such instruments. One existing tool for pre- and post-measures that is garnering increasing attention is the Kozai Group's Intercultural Effectiveness Scale (IES). This tool focuses on three dimensions of intercultural effectiveness: continuous learning, interpersonal engagement, and hardiness (Kozai Group, 2017).

Miami University of Ohio administers the IES in its course on global and strategic issues in information technology to help students accomplish three objectives: deconstruct their own cultural identities and unique worldviews, compare and contrast the values underpinning their own and other cultural perspectives, and apply cultural competencies and global learning in interactions and coursework effectively and appropriately. Instructors use initial IES scores to form groups for a semester-long, culture-related, collaborative project. Then they review written self-reflections and peer assessment to assess each student group's ability to function in a constructed environment. Students use IES's comprehensive guide for self-reflection and personal action planning to assist them in developing critical intercultural competencies. In this case, post-IES results showed progress from the low end of the effectiveness scale to the high end of the scale.

The School of Physical Education and Tourism Management (now the School of Health and Human Sciences) at Indiana University–Purdue University Indianapolis (IUPUI) uses concepts from Deardorff's Process Model of Intercultural Competence (Deardorff, 2006) to gauge student intercultural learning in an internship component of its Global Tourism Seminar (Fu & Vaughan, 2016). The course is designed to provide students with an international perspective on the key issues facing tourism in a global market and to help them become better critical thinkers on tourism-related issues. Over the course of 3 seminar offerings, instructors use the IES to survey 3 groups of students on their perceptions of 15 concepts outlined in the process model.

Jacobs University in Bremen, Germany, offers a peer-learning and reflection-based course on intercultural competence in practice, also based on Deardorff's Process Model of Intercultural Competence. Instructors use a multiple method approach to assessment (Binder, 2017), including the short version of the Test to Measure Intercultural Competence (TMIC-S) as a pre-/post-measure, to assess intercultural competence and direct evidence of achievement of learning outcomes from student assignments in a portfolio.

Pedagogies for Global Citizenship
Exemplary approaches to enabling students to learn the global dimensions of civic responsibilities are occurring at a number of universities.

Florida International University's (FIU's) Global Learning for Global Citizenship initiative, with more than 160 global learning courses and 250 global learning activities, ensures that "every corner of the university is touched by global learning" (Landorf, Doscher, & Hardrick, 2018). FIU has identified existing tools that align closely with its global learning outcomes, including the Global Perspective Inventory (GPI), developed at Iowa State University (2015–2019), for institution-level assessment and the AAC&U global learning VALUE rubric for individual assignments (Doscher, 2018). The GPI is a Web-based assessment of global learning experiences and perspectives. It emphasizes cognitive, intrapersonal, and interpersonal dimensions, providing a holistic approach to assessing learning and development. By administering the GPI to a minimum 10% sample of incoming freshmen, transfer students, and graduating seniors, FIU is able to assess achievement of its goal to increase cocurricular opportunities for integrative global learning. The GPI's cocurricular scale enables FIU to demonstrate an increase in cocurricular activities offered by student affairs and track the number of faculty integrating a globally focused, cocurricular activity into a foundational or discipline-specific global learning course (Landorf et al., 2018).

At Texas Christian University (TCU), the Discovering Global Citizenship program seeks to explore global engagement by providing international and comparative experiences for its students. To evaluate student work, TCU faculty use the IES, the AAC&U intercultural knowledge and competence VALUE rubric, and self-reflections. TCU students develop, collect, and display self-reflections and artifacts in an ePortfolio called FrogFolio created with the Digication ePortfolio platform. The self-reflections include blogs written during education abroad programs in which students respond to prompts and analyze their experiences through theoretical models. Students begin their FrogFolios in the campus's Introduction to University Life course, where an assessment team also begins to debrief the results of the IES with them (Hightower, 2017a, 2018). TCU's use of multiple methods captures an important evolving trend in global learning assessment: refining criteria for assembling and evaluating student ePortfolios and blogs (Hightower, 2017b; Mansilla & Jackson, 2011).

ePortfolios and Other Reflective Practices

Another evolving trend is the development of ePortfolios centered on deepening student self-reflection. Several universities are engaged in this practice. For example, in its Global Engagement Scholars Program, the University of North Carolina at Charlotte, uses ePortfolios to demonstrate student global learning through multiple assessment methods. The program features three pillars: academic, cocurricular, and international experience. It employs a program-specific rubric developed in collaboration with faculty and staff from different departments to assess artifacts and reflections, such as photos and videos, that students curate for their ePortfolios. Students' ePortfolios include references to the three pillars of the Global Engagement Scholars Program and demonstrate skills in analysis and reflection. Finally, they participate in a poster session showcasing their ePortfolios during the campus's International Education Celebration.

The use of critical reflection as an assessment method is becoming more commonplace as we have already seen. In IUPUI's two-semester-long program with Newcastle University, American and British dental students meet electronically to exchange understandings of different approaches to health care. Both student groups read and research the same subjects and then discuss them via video link. The students keep reflective, evidence-based journals as they prepare for and participate in the program. Instructors conduct a thematic analysis to address central questions about students' cultural competencies and overall professional outcomes (Kowolik & Scharder, 2018). At the departmental level, the University of Hawai'i at Manoa's undergraduate communication program uses ePortfolios featuring written reflection for assessment of seven student learning outcomes, including demonstration of "global awareness, including an awareness of cultures in the Hawai'i-Pacific region and issues related to cross-cultural communication" (Buente, Sunrise Winter, & Kramer, 2015, p. 172).

At Virginia Commonwealth University (VCU), the VCU Globe program, a global education living-learning community, prepares students to navigate within and between global communities at home and abroad and in professional and personal contexts. The program uses ePortfolios as a repository of students' program-related work. The ePortfolio represents the students' developing professional identities and features five to seven of their most significant learning experiences, with reflections on their educational or career aspirations that explain how program participation has promoted their personal growth and distinguished them from other graduates (C. Marino, personal communication, January 10, 2019).

These are just a few of many universities in the United States and abroad that use ePortfolios for assessment of global learning and as sites for student reflection on their own global learning experiences (Deardorff & Arasaratnam-Smith, 2017).

Customized Tools for Specific Curricular or Institutional Contexts

Another evolving trend in global learning assessment is the design of course- or program-specific surveys that combine discipline-specific items with items on cultural knowledge. Such instruments are part of the changing paradigm of international education assessment (Deardorff, 2015).

At Bentley University, in addition to the IES, courses use the instructor-designed Intercultural Effectiveness Context Model (Berdrow, 2017), along with self-reflection assignments, to measure progress toward the objective of demonstrating personal competencies associated with environments where there are cultural norms and behaviors different from their own. In their sophomore year, Bentley students take the IES and complete a written self-reflection assignment. They take the IES again in their senior year. The self-reflection assignment includes students' perceptions of their IES scores. The instructor-designed Intercultural Effectiveness Context Model is used to analyze student demographics and international education experiences prior to enrolling at Bentley (inputs) and the international education opportunities

(IEOs) in which students participate while at Bentley (environment) to determine whether engagement in IEOs correlates with IES scores.

At IUPUI, instructors developed customized surveys blending cross-cultural and information technology questions for assessing a spring break study abroad course in China featuring discipline-specific collaborative international projects. The survey collects information on concerns about working with students from a foreign university, including language differences and nonverbal communication differences, as well as attitudes toward the course's IT projects (Elliot & Luo, 2018).

Ohio State University designed its own assessment survey customized to its large, land-grant university context. The instrument assesses the university's agreed-on five global competencies. The initiative brought together faculty, students, and staff for two years to build and pilot the survey, hold focus groups, and test the survey for validity and reliability (Gottlieb, Lawther, & Bozeman, 2018). VCU Globe similarly began its assessment efforts with a customized assessment tool. Staff designed a program-specific survey to collect pre- and post-data on students' global engagement behaviors, intercultural communication skills, and knowledge of theoretical concepts from the program curriculum. Some questions were based on concepts from the GPI. While producing valuable information, the survey had limitations and posed challenges that are discussed later in this chapter. The program subsequently adopted the Intercultural Development Inventory.

Challenges Associated With Innovative Approaches.

As might be expected, attempts to create innovative approaches to assessing student global learning bring with them a variety of challenges. As is often the case with assessment, these challenges include attracting faculty participation in assessment; ensuring that faculty and staff understand the purpose of assessment; determining what to assess, including clearly articulating learning outcomes; designing effective assessment plans; understanding various assessment methods and aligning methods to outcomes; determining when unique tools specific to the program or course context need to be developed; in some cases, addressing limited confidence in the effectiveness of newly created tools; and using assessment data appropriately (Bozeman, 2018). For example, while assessment instruments used in the aforementioned IUPUI Computer and Information Technology course yielded helpful information, their design posed challenges for the instructors, including concerns about the validity of the surveys (R. Elliott, personal communication, November 12, 2018) and an inability to collect completed surveys from the Chinese students, resulting in a small sample size. The University of North Carolina at Charlotte found designing self-reflection prompts challenging; as a result, the course instructors are now exploring ways to refine the next iteration of these prompts (J. Hoff, personal communication, November 13, 2018).

Similarly, VCU Globe has experienced challenges in its effort to assess intercultural competence with a customized survey and its attempts to engage students in meaningful self-reflection. Custom-made surveys tend to face challenges such as lack of benchmarks outside the particular program context and low response rates, which make drawing statistical inferences difficult. The program's decision to move to the Intercultural Development Inventory (IDI) was partly influenced by the availability of the IDI's national data set. The IDI, however, comes with a financial commitment that institutions need to consider (C. Marino, personal communication, January 10, 2019). In the case of ePortfolios and self-reflection, program staff report that levels of student effort in writing reflections were often less than expected.

Future Trends in Global Learning Assessment

Effective assessment instrument design represents a particularly important, although challenging, frontier for the field of global learning assessment, as it seeks more holistic assessment methods. For example, research by Doscher (2018) notes the challenge and opportunity confronting FIU as it attempts to adopt a systems-thinking approach to assessing global learning. Systems thinking, as described in the FIU context, analyzes the relationships among the system's parts to understand the potential for better decision-making (Mestenhauser, 2003). Various parts of the university support global learning and can be sources of information for determining how and why students benefit from it (Doscher, 2018). Offices of residential life and housing, international affairs, and institutional research, as well as individual academic schools each facilitate and assess learning in different ways, resulting in different insights into how, what, and when students learn. Essential to a comprehensive, systems thinking approach is recognition that there are different stakeholders, contexts, and motivations for global learning assessment. Continued capacity building and dissemination of models for effective global learning practices will be necessary to further guide the higher education community as it seeks to prepare students for a globally focused future.

The systems-thinking approach suggests several directions for future research into assessment of global learning. These include the holistic development of the learner, so that global learning is not viewed in isolation; the degree to which cultural and conceptual biases interfere with data collection and analysis; assessment of global learning in real-world contexts; and the role of multiple perspectives in assessing global learning.

Conclusion

The literature on global learning, with its emphasis on intercultural competence, can be traced back to the 1930s in the United States and continues to flourish today. In addition to broad, continuing interest in intercultural competence, ideas and questions that illustrate evolving trends in global learning assessment include the need to clearly articulate overall strategies and terminology definitions, more holistic measurement of intercultural competence, innovative pedagogies for global citizenship, the use of ePortfolios centered on deepened student self-reflection, development of customized tools for specific curricular or institutional contexts, and the challenges of implementing innovative approaches to global learning assessment.

In theory and practice, international educators increasingly recognize that overarching strategies are essential to ensuring collaborative and inclusive approaches to developing and implementing institution-wide assessment of global learning. Comprehensive strategic thinking about global learning and its assessment must transcend institutional boundaries, integrate a variety of units and missions, and develop practices meaningful to the whole institution and to organizational subcultures. Strategies, in turn, are predicated on agreement about terminology and definitions, so that students, faculty, staff, and administrators understand the nature and scope of a learning activity, along with the stated learning outcomes defining precisely what is being measured. Such strategies and stage-setting work are essential to implementing and empowering assessment to influence higher education policy and meet higher education's obligation to student learning in an age of globalization.

Systems thinking may grant new insights into the field, especially when combined with research on holistic development of the learner, so that global learning is not viewed in isolation from a university's mission, values, and vision. Overall, a framework of accountability defined by academic strategic thinking will continue to emphasize assessment of the knowledge, attitudes, and skills that compose global learning.

Summary of Main Trends

- Intercultural competence, which includes the concepts of global citizenship, global perspectives, and community-based global learning, dominates the field of global learning and is the main focus of assessment.
- The global learning field is recognizing the importance of using multiple methods to assess student achievement, and assessment

practice is moving beyond the sole use of traditional pre- and post-measures.
- Many programs and institutions are developing their own context-specific assessment approaches and instruments.
- Reflection and ePortfolios are increasingly widely used, but some institutions and programs have had difficulty eliciting meaningful reflection from students.
- The field is seeking assessment methods that treat global learning as part of the holistic development of the learner.

Questions for Discussion

- What is global learning, and how do colleges and universities seek to advance students' ability to engage with and navigate local and global communities?
- What kinds of approaches and tools are used to assess global learning and intercultural competence outcomes? What are the advantages and disadvantages of the various types of tools available?
- What are the barriers to developing and implementing innovative approaches to the assessment of global learning?
- How might systems thinking help improve our approaches to assessing global learning?

We want to hear from you about *Trends in Assessment*:

- Provide reactions or suggestions about trends.
- Share and access resources related to trends.
- Learn about professional development opportunities related to trends.

Visit assessmentinstitute.iupui.edu/trends

References

Arasaratnam-Smith, L. A. (2017). Intercultural competence: An overview. In D. K. Deardorff & L. A. Arasaratnam-Smith (Eds.), *Intercultural competence in higher education* (pp. 7–18). New York, NY: Routledge.

Association of American Colleges & Universities. (n.d.). Global learning VALUE rubric. Retrieved from https://www.aacu.org/value/rubrics/global

Berdrow, I. (2017, October). *What do I think about what the mirror tells me? Experiential and empirical outcomes of a transformative learning assignment focused on self-reflection and intercultural effectiveness.* Paper presented at the 2017 Assessment Institute, Indianapolis, IN.

Binder, N. (2017). Intercultural competence in practice: A peer-learning and reflection-based university course to develop intercultural competence. In D. K. Deardorff & L. Arasaratnam-Smith (Eds.), *Intercultural competence in higher education: International approaches, assessment and application* (pp. 151–155). London, UK: Routledge.

Bozeman, L. A. (2018, October). *Global learning roundtable.* Paper presented at the 2018 Assessment Institute, Indianapolis, IN.

Bozeman, L. A., & Hansen, M. (2017, October). *The language of global learning and assessment.* Paper presented at the 2017 Assessment Institute, Indianapolis, IN.

Braskamp, D., Braskamp, L. A., & Glass, C. R. (2015). Belonging: The gateway to global learning for all students. *Liberal Education, 101*(3), 22–29.

Buente, B., Sunrise Winter, J., & Kramer, H. (2015). Program-based assessment of capstone ePortfolios for a communication BA curriculum. *International Journal of ePortfolio, 5*(2), 169–179.

Carter, D., Latz, G., & Thornton, P. (2010). Through a new lens: Assessing international learning at Portland State University. *Journal of General Education, 59*(3), 172–181.

Charles, H. (2015, October). *Global learning assessment: Key to institutionalizing the global education agenda.* Paper presented at the 2015 Assessment Institute, Indianapolis, IN.

Deardorff, D. K. (2006). Identification and assessment of intercultural competence as a student outcome of internationalization. *Journal of Studies in International Education, 10*(3), 241–266.

Deardorff, D. K. (2015). *Demystifying outcomes assessment for international educators: A practical approach.* Sterling, VA: Stylus.

Deardorff, D. K. (2017). The big picture of intercultural competence assessment. In D. K. Deardorff & L. Arasaratnam-Smith (Eds.), *Intercultural competence in higher education: International approaches, assessment and application* (pp. 124–134). London, UK: Routledge.

Deardorff, D. K., & Arasaratnam-Smith, L. (2017). *Intercultural competence in higher education: International approaches, assessment and application.* London, UK: Routledge.

Doscher, S. (2018, October). *A systems thinking approach to assessing all students' global learning.* Paper presented at the 2018 Assessment Institute, Indianapolis, IN.

Elliott, R., & Luo, X. (2018, October). *Evaluating multi-institution student collaboration via study abroad.* Paper presented at the 2018 Assessment Institute, Indianapolis, IN.

Fu, Y., & Vaughan, A. (2016, October). *Assessing significance and implications of intercultural competence from the perspectives of students and employers.* Paper presented at the 2016 Assessment Institute, Indianapolis, IN.

Gottlieb, E., Lawther, M., & Bozeman, L. A. (2018). *Assessing students' global competencies: Why and how.* Paper presented at NAFSA Region 6 Annual Conference, Columbus, OH.

Green, M. (2017, October). *Are we there yet? The long (and winding) road to global learning for all.* Paper presented at the 2017 Assessment Institute, Indianapolis, IN.

Hammer, M. R., Gudykunst, W. B., & Wiseman, R. L. (1978). Dimensions of intercultural effectiveness: An exploratory study. *International Journal of Intercultural Relations, 2*(4), 382–393.

Hart & Associates. (2015). *Falling short? College learning and career success.* Washington, DC: Association of American Colleges & Universities.

Hartman, E., Kiely, R., Boettcher, C., & Friedrichs, J. (2018). *Community-based global learning: The theory and practice of ethical engagement at home and abroad.* Sterling, VA: Stylus.

Hatcher, J. F., Price, M. A., Whitehead, D. M., & Latz, G. (2015). Using a partnership approach in study abroad: Implications and strategies for program design and assessment. In V. Savicki & B. Brewer (Eds.), *Assessing international learning: Theory and practice* (pp. 277–293). Sterling, VA: Stylus.

Hightower, C. (2017a, October). *Campus-wide assessment at an internationalizing institution.* Paper presented at the 2017 Assessment Institute, Indianapolis, IN.

Hightower, C. (2017b). Intercultural competence at Texas Christian University. In D. K. Deardorff & L. Arasaratnam-Smith (Eds.), *Intercultural competence in higher education: International approaches, assessment and application* (pp. 192–196). London, UK: Routledge.

Hightower, C. (2018, October). *Using ePortfolio as a direct measure for global learning.* Paper presented at the 2018 Assessment Institute, Indianapolis, IN.

Hovland, K. (2006). *Shared futures: Global learning and liberal education.* Washington, DC: Association of American Colleges & Universities.

Iowa State University. (2015–2019). Global Perspective Inventory. Retrieved from http://www.gpi.hs.iastate.edu/

Kahn, H. (2016, October). *Going beyond boundaries with global learning assessment.* Paper presented at the 2016 Assessment Institute, Indianapolis, IN.

Kowolick, J., & Scharder, S. (2018, October). *Student perspective of community dental care in England: A study abroad experience.* Paper presented at the 2018 Assessment Institute, Indianapolis, IN.

Kozai Group. (2017). Intercultural Effectiveness Scale (IES). Retrieved from http://www.kozaigroup.com/intercultural-effectiveness-scale-ies/

Landorf, H., Doscher, S., & Hardrick, J. (2018). *Making global learning universal.* Sterling, VA: Stylus.

Mansilla, V. B., & Jackson, A. (2011). *Educating for global competence: Preparing our youth to engage the world.* Council of Chief State School Officers' EdSteps Initiative and Asia Society Partnership for Global Learning. Retrieved from https://asiasociety.org/files/book-globalcompetence.pdf

Mestenhauser, J. (2003). In search of a comprehensive approach to international education: A systems perspective. In W. Grünzweig & N. Rinehart (Eds.), *Rockin' in Red Square: Critical approaches to international education in the age of cyberculture* (pp. 330–358). Münster, Germany: Lit Verlag.

Nussbaum, M. (2002). Education for citizenship in an era of global connection. *Studies in Philosophy and Education, 21*, 289–303.

Organization of Economic Development and Cooperation. (2018). PISA: Programme for International Student Assessment. Retrieved from http://www.oecd .org/pisa/

Reimers, F. M. (2014). Bringing global education to the core of the undergraduate curriculum. *Diversity and Democracy, 17*(2). Retrieved from https://www.aacu .org/diversitydemocracy/2014/spring/reimers

Ruben, B. D., Askling, L. R., & Kealey, D. J. (1977). Cross-cultural effectiveness. In D. S. Hoopes, P. B. Pedersen, & G. Renwick (Eds.), *Overview of intercultural education, training, and research*: Vol 1. *Theory* (pp. 92–105). Washington, DC: Society for Intercultural Training, Education, and Research.

Ruben, B. D., & Kealey, D. J. (1979). Behavioral assessment of intercultural competency and the prediction of cross-cultural adaptation. *International Journal of Intercultural Relations, 3*(1), 15–47.

UNESCO. (2018). *Global citizenship education: Taking it local*. Paris, France: Author. Retrieved from https://bridge47.org/sites/default/files/2018-12/21_unesco_ taking_it_local.pdf

Whitehead, D. M. (2016). *Essential global learning*. Washington, DC: Association of American Colleges & Universities.

ASSESSING COMMUNITY ENGAGEMENT

Kristin Norris and H. Anne Weiss

The notion of education as a public good has been rooted in American higher education since its inception. Campus mission statements and the Morrill Acts of the nineteenth century (1862, 1890) serve as evidence of our public purpose. This social charter of higher education involves commitments to develop research to improve society, train leaders and the workforce, educate citizens for democracy, foster economic development, and inform public policy. Americans, however, report growing skepticism that higher education truly benefits society (Pew Research Center, 2017), perhaps because both the media and higher education institutions themselves tend to emphasize the benefits, especially the economic benefits, of higher education to the individual student (Kezar, Chambers, & Burkhardt, 2005). Distrust in higher education may also be related to a broader societal trend of distrust in institutions, which recently recorded the largest-ever drop in U.S. history (Edelman Trust Barometer, 2018).

According to a national survey, senior academic leaders believe that "colleges and universities must more clearly and persuasively communicate relevant, timely, and contextualized information on their impact on students and *value to society*" (Jankowski, Timmer, Kinzie, & Kuh, 2018, p. 4; emphasis added). Furthermore, "institutions must find ways to use assessment data internally to inform and strengthen education, and *externally to communicate with policy makers, families, and other stakeholders*" (Jankowski et al., 2018, p. 7; emphasis added). These needs have contributed to increased attention to assessment of the impact of higher education institutions' community engagement in recent years. Such assessments require that institutions collect more robust information about how faculty, staff, and students are working in and with communities to address societal issues and the subsequent impacts of such activities.

Two nationwide recognitions have provided campuses with frameworks for developing more systematic ongoing approaches to assessing community engagement: the president's Higher Education Community Service Honor Roll (referred to here as The Honor Roll) and the Carnegie Foundation for the Advancement of Teaching's elective Community Engagement Classification. The Honor Roll, which recognized institutions that supported exemplary service programs and effective practices in campus–community partnerships, was established in 2006, sending institutions a strong signal that community engagement in higher education was worth tracking and assessing. The annual award application required institutions to monitor service engagement (e.g., number of students, service hours, faculty involved) and collect robust stories of impact. The Honor Roll was discontinued, however, in 2017.

Today, the primary external driver of assessment of community engagement is the Community Engagement Classification, established in 2006. The application for the classification requires evidence of institutional mission, identity, and commitments to community engagement, drawing on information from systematic campus-wide tracking and assessment. Institutions are asked specifically for documentation of student engagement (curricular and cocurricular), community perceptions of institutional engagement, the process for tracking and monitoring engagement locations, and the degree to which partnerships are mutually beneficial and reciprocal.

The purposes of the two recognitions are distinct and relevant to this chapter. The Honor Roll focused on ranking institutions, whereas the Community Engagement Classification adheres to the values and purpose of assessment—to improve practice. The intention of the classification is to encourage an institutional self-assessment *process*, a means of improving or developing effective and equitable infrastructure for community engagement in alignment with best practices and institutional priorities (Driscoll, 2008; Giles, Sandmann, & Saltmarsh, 2010).

Community Engagement and *Community-Engaged Learning* Defined

Community engagement is defined as "the collaboration between institutions of higher education and their larger communities (local, regional/state, national, global) for the mutually beneficial exchange of knowledge and resources in a context of partnership and reciprocity" (Carnegie Foundation for the Advancement of Teaching, 2011). Here *community* is not defined by sector, such as private or public, for profit or nonprofit. Rather, *community* is broadly defined to include individuals, groups, and organizations external to campus that use collaborative processes for the purposes of contributing to the public good (Driscoll & Sandmann, 2011). *Reciprocity* is defined as "the recognition, respect, and valuing of the knowledge, perspectives, and resources that each partner contributes to the collaboration" (Saltmarsh, Hartley, & Clayton, 2009).

Community-engaged learning has not been consistently defined in prior scholarship. For the purpose of this chapter, we rely on the work of Janke and Shelton (2011), who described it as "those activities that 1) honor principles of community engagement (reciprocal partnerships, public purpose), and 2) provide opportunities for students to collaborate with faculty and community members for the dual—and integrated—purposes of learning" (p. 7). Community-engaged learning may occur in a variety of academic and cocurricular experiences, including, but not limited to, service-learning, project-based learning, clinical experiences, professional internships, community-based research or creative activities, collaborative programs, study abroad courses and alternative break experiences, international instruction, and distance education courses. It is community-engaged learning when these practices involve reciprocal partnerships with community members, groups, or organizations and contribute to the public good and student learning.

Historical Context of Assessing Community-Engaged Learning

The primary focus in assessment of community engagement has been on student learning in community-engaged learning contexts, as well it should be, given that we are, first and foremost, institutions of higher education. Assessment of teaching and learning has focused on discipline-based outcomes within service-learning courses and community service activities (Gelmon, Holland, Driscoll, Spring, & Kerrigan, 2001; Jacoby, 2015). Decades of assessment of student learning tied to service-learning have been fundamental to positioning service-learning as a high-impact practice (Kuh, 2008) and, thus, legitimized it as an instructional method that yields significant gains in students' academic or discipline-based learning (Celio, Durlak, & Dymnicki, 2011; Conway, Amel, & Gerwien, 2009; Eyler & Giles, 1999; Novak, Markey, & Allen, 2007; Warren, 2012; Yorio & Ye, 2012).

Disciplinary learning outcomes, however, are not the only outcomes of interest to many educators and members of society. Service-learning gained attention within the academy because of its potential to generate transdisci-plinary learning. We define *transdisciplinary* to include cognitive, affective, and kinesthetic outcomes that transcend single disciplines or areas of study. Mitchell (2005) argued, "True transdisciplinarity goes beyond simply drawing together concepts from the disciplines in that it creates new frameworks that break down (transgress) the traditional boundaries of the discipline" (p. 332).

The most widely recognized areas of transdisciplinary learning within community-engaged learning contexts are related to the civic realm: civic identity, civic literacy, civic agency, development of democratic values, and others. One such construct developed at Indiana University–Purdue University Indianapolis (IUPUI) and empirically tested and validated is the Civic-Minded Graduate (CMG; Steinberg, Hatcher, & Bringle, 2011): "The civic-minded graduate is a person who has completed a course of study and has the capacity and desire to work with others to achieve the com-mon good" (p. 20). The CMG integrates cognitive, affective, and kinesthetic aspects of transdisciplinary outcomes into one construct that can be meas-ured by asking students to complete a self-report scale or an interview proto-col or by applying a rubric to a student's artifact of learning (e.g., essay, oral presentation, ePortfolio, capstone project). This construct, as represented by the Civic-Minded Rubric 2.0 (Weiss, Hahn, & Norris, 2017), takes into account aspects of civic-mindedness that *any* subject or discipline might wish to foster in a course or program (Figure 4.1).

In summary, assessment of community engagement is rooted in students' discipline-based and transdisciplinary civic learning outcomes. As Gelmon and colleagues (2001) indicated many years ago, when new programs and pedagogies—such as service-learning—are introduced into higher education, they must "endure institutional examination to prove their value . . . and their contribution to student learning" (p. 19). Research on community-engaged learning still holds great potential to inform practices and transform institu-tions of higher education. The following section illustrates several trends in assessing community engagement that go beyond examination of the peda-gogy of service-learning.

Current Trends in Assessment of Community Engagement

The following section describes three trends in assessment of community engagement and their importance for the future of higher education:

1. A focus on developing more direct evidence of transdisciplinary outcomes that align with our public missions. For many campuses, this focus is at the heart of education for democracy (Campus Compact, n.d.).

Figure 4.1. Civic-Minded Graduate Rubric 2.0.

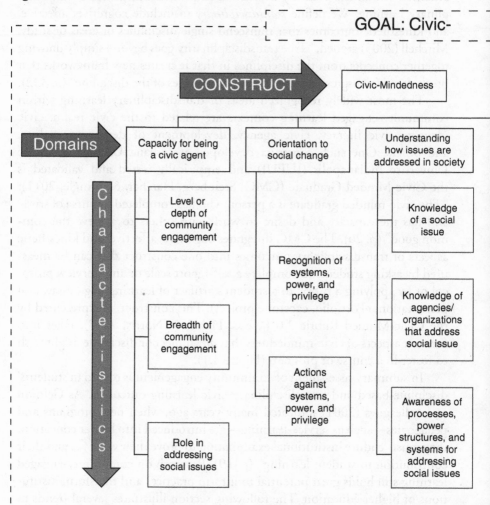

Note. An example of the civic realm of transdisciplinary learning outcomes during college. Reprinted/adapted with permission from "Civic-Minded Rubric 2.0," by H. A. Weiss, T. W. Hahn, and K. E. Norris, 2017. Retrieved from https://scholarworks.iupui.edu/handle/1805/13367

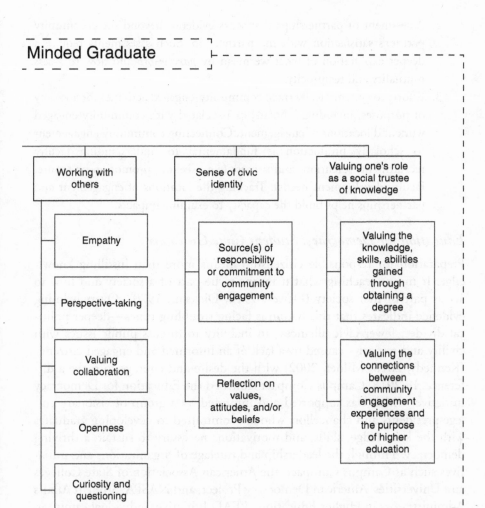

Minded Graduate

Working with others

- Empathy
- Perspective-taking
- Valuing collaboration
- Openness
- Curiosity and questioning

Sense of civic identity

- Source(s) of responsibility or commitment to community engagement
- Reflection on values, attitudes, and/or beliefs

Valuing one's role as a social trustee of knowledge

- Valuing the knowledge, skills, abilities gained through obtaining a degree
- Valuing the connections between community engagement experiences and the purpose of higher education

2. Assessment of partnerships that seeks evidence beyond the community partner's satisfaction with the partnership. Such assessments require a deeper exploration of what we mean by *partnership* and how to assess mutuality and reciprocity.
3. Efforts to systematically track community-engaged activities for a variety of purposes, including scholarship associated with community-engaged work and locations of engagement. Connecting community engagement to scholarly production is fundamental to understanding faculty recruitment, retention, and success (e.g., seeking promotion or tenure, faculty development needs). Tracking the locations of engagement and partnerships helps build the capacity to examine impacts.

Education for Democracy: Student Civic Outcomes

Preparation for responsible citizenship means more than instilling knowledge: It means teaching what it means to be part of a society and how to act as part of that society (Dewey, 1916; Dickson, 1979). Overwhelming evidence indicates that this nation is facing troubling times—deeper political divides, fewer civic alliances, an inability to discuss public issues with civility and respect—caused by a lack of an informed and engaged citizenry (Kennedy, 2016; Milner, 2002) with the desire and courage to make a difference. In 2018, Campus Compact launched the Education for Democracy initiative, which was supported and informed by a group of visionary college presidents and chancellors who are committed to developing graduates with the knowledge, skills, and motivations necessary to sustain a thriving democracy. Through the leadership and tutelage of organizations and initiatives such as Campus Compact, the American Association of State Colleges and Universities' American Democracy Project, and NASPA: Student Affairs Administrators in Higher Education's LEAD Initiative, individual campuses across the country and in a variety of place-based contexts are reimagining their core curricula, developing pathways for engaged learning, and identifying campus-wide civic outcomes.

In addition, the community engagement movement has called for more robust and rigorous measures of student learning outcomes, including direct measures. Direct measures of civic learning, for example, include test or quiz scores. (See the Civic Literacy Exam from the Intercollegiate Studies Institute or questions from the U.S. Naturalization Exam.) Assessment tools continue to evolve, including more rubrics (see the Civic-Minded Graduate Rubric 2.0, the Valid Assessment of Learning in Undergraduate Education [VALUE] rubric for civic engagement) and HEIghten, the first-ever direct assessment of civic competence and engagement, as well as global learning, offered by the Educational Testing Service (ETS; Torney-Purta, Cabrera, Roohr, Liu, & Rios, 2015).

Indirect measures can also be useful in providing a proxy of student learning, based on students' perceptions and feedback. Examples of indirect measures of civic learning include local or nationally developed student surveys. (See the National Survey of Student Engagement's Civic Engagement Module and Iowa State's Personal and Social Responsibility Inventory.) The ETS report, *Assessing Civic Competency and Engagement in Higher Education* (Torney-Purta et al., 2015), offers an in-depth discussion of direct measures versus indirect measures of transdisciplinary outcomes of civic engagement.

Finally, evidence of transdisciplinary learning from participation in high-impact practices (HIPs) suggests a need to scale up the number of opportunities. Research also demonstrates that not all students have equal access or opportunities to engage in HIPs (Finley & McNair, 2013). Many institutions are working to ensure that students of all backgrounds, but especially first-generation and students from minoritized or racialized groups, are able to participate. Assessing community engagement is important for scaling up HIPs, because community partners play a role in many high-impact experiences. Assessment of community engagement, including identifying where a campus has existing partnerships, the types of faculty engagement, and the use of best practices, can inform a scaling-up strategy that also takes into consideration the community's needs, capacity, and resources required.

Mutually Beneficial and Reciprocal Partnerships

Assessing partnerships is not a new trend, but how and why we assess partnerships are changing. Historically, campuses have solicited feedback from employers and community partners through a variety of mechanisms like advisory boards, town halls, and memberships on neighborhood association boards. In addition, many centers or offices responsible for service-learning or cocurricular engagement conduct partnership assessments for purposes of informing faculty development and, sometimes, for documenting the benefits of engagement for the community partner. The current trend is to broaden assessment of partnerships through activities like community-engaged research, P–20 engagement programs, sustained initiatives, volunteerism, and others, and to examine the partnership process—how and the extent to which partnerships are mutually beneficial and reciprocal.

Assessing partnerships as just described can be challenging. For instance, to examine a *representative* sample of partnership types across courses, research projects, and other community-based initiatives requires systematic, institution-wide tracking and monitoring. Furthermore, the tracking process requires knowing not only who your partners are but also the nature of the partnership, who is involved, the goals for both the university and the community, and so on. The methods for systematically tracking partnerships are complicated because of the layers of interactions and diversity of people and purposes, but tracking is a necessary first step toward any assessment endeavor.

We recommend that institutions developing plans to assess partnerships consider a number of factors. Who is willing to participate in an assessment and why? How does the community benefit by participating? How do we build trust so that participants feel comfortable and are honest with us? How do we ensure that we conduct assessments to improve practice rather than to earn campus awards or recognitions? How do we ensure that community voices are accurately represented? Finally, are we interested in learning from partners who are not satisfied with the university's engagement, and how do we capture that information in a systematic way? Inherent biases and limitations of partnership assessments should be addressed in the methods employed. Again, such assessments are challenging because of the interrelatedness of issues; layers of interactions; and diversity of people, purposes, and processes (Janke, 2018).

In summary, partnership principles are central to community engagement, and we recognize the need to understand how reciprocity and mutual benefit are actually enacted among various university constituents and community partners. The current trend is toward increased efforts to examine the partnership process: how (a) community voice is represented, (b) power is distributed, (c) staff and resources are leveraged, and (d) diverse perspectives and experiences are valued among all participants, to name a few considerations. These efforts have led to a need to better define *partnership*—when is it more than a partner, a relationship, or a collaboration?—and develop methods of examining these issues.

Documenting Engagement and Scholarship

As we have just seen, robust documentation systems and processes are required to fully examine partnerships. Many campuses have improved such tracking, which initially gained momentum in the early 2000s as the need grew to designate courses for assessment and awards purposes (e.g., the Community Engagement Classification, accreditation). As systems and processes have evolved, however, so has our desire to understand the effects of teaching and learning practices on student learning and success (Finley, 2011; Kuh, 2008).

The ultimate goal of tracking engagement is to be able to examine how students, faculty, and staff are working with the community—its people, problems, organizations, issues, and assets—to achieve a variety of outcomes. For example, how are faculty recognized and rewarded for community-engaged work? And how do we capture the outputs and outcomes of engagement to examine policies (e.g., promotion and tenure guidelines), implement best practices, and help to attract and support the next generation of engaged scholars and practitioners? Ultimately, how does community engagement contribute to the institution's performance of its public mission or its institutional effectiveness in areas like fund-raising, job placement, alumni engagement, recruitment, and enrollment? Improving systems and processes for documenting faculty engagement and, subsequently, their scholarship is imperative for determining how institutions can create campus cultures that live up to their public missions and tell stories of impact.

Answering these questions calls for complex data collection processes that go beyond traditional academic practices. Institutions need information about community organizations, geographic locations, populations served, social issues being addressed, nature of engagements, and goals for the institution and the community. Of great importance are the outputs and scholarship related to community-engaged work (research, teaching, and service). Community engagement encompasses the myriad ways in which the institution is working in and with the community in areas such as research and creative activity, recruitment of students, diversity and inclusion, economic growth and development, and purchasing. Assessing such engagement requires robust planning for assessment and improved systems and processes for gathering information in alignment with the institution's mission and goals.

Future Trends

Current trends in assessment of community engagement illustrate the need for institutions to be able to demonstrate how we are achieving our public missions, in addition to assessing student learning. The goal is to collect information that enables us to look internally at policies, systems, and practices that support community-engaged activities and examine how they align with best practices. As we look to the future, we have identified three trends that also highlight the tensions inherent in this work.

Community Impact

We will continue to see increasing interest in understanding the impacts of engagement on communities: residents, organizations, neighborhoods, and broader societal issues. This trend aligns with the survey of senior academic leaders, which indicated that institutions need to demonstrate their "value to society" and to better "communicate with policy makers, families, and other stakeholders" (Jankowski et al., 2018, pp. 4, 7). Those "other stake-holders" include alumni, funding agencies, and donors—who are also asking these questions of our institutions. The trends we have discussed, particularly tracking and monitoring, must be addressed for campuses to examine the collective impact of engagement. Assessment of community engagement will never replace or change the need for the evaluation of specific programs. Instead, we see opportunities in the future to beget community impact when we combine program evaluation with systematic tracking and monitoring processes that are aligned with institutional priorities.

Communications, Assessment, or Both

The primary purpose of assessment has been to improve practice and inform decision-making. As such, it has largely been an internal function of the university. As noted earlier, however, a growing distrust of societal institutions and pressures of accountability to stakeholders have elevated the importance of communications and management of public perception. Tensions exist between assessing community engagement to improve practice and using the same information to tell a story—a story that can sometimes turn communities back into "beneficiaries" of the institution and not reciprocal partners. We must be more cognizant of the tensions between our desire for public recognition and perceived value to society and statements or claims of impact that (re)position the institution as impact-maker rather than community contributor.

When the information collected can be used for multiple purposes, how are we attending to who may give permission to use data to tell a story? In the future, we see an opportunity for campus assessment and communications units to work together. Together, we can consider how results are disseminated and to whom and who is considered an investigator. We can also involve community perspectives earlier in the planning process.

Collaboration Between Assessment and Community Engagement Professionals

Community engagement values collaboration and the cocreation of knowledge. The best program evaluators stand with and beside their stakeholders to help clarify values and interests, keep those interests in check, help them deliberate effectively, and help assess the extent to which the public good and goals have been addressed. We value community members' expertise and their deep understanding of the community. Communities thus have important roles in the stories we tell and in the purposes of assessment. Rarely does the community play a role in institution-level assessment, however, and community engagement professionals tend to approach assessment differently, which may cause tension. We encourage the examination of our assumptions and an exploration of the axiological, ontological, and epistemological approaches to conducting assessment (Mertens & Wilson, 2012). The Competency Model for Community Engagement Professionals (Dostilio et al., 2017) may be useful as well, because it highlights the responsibilities that community engagement staff assume for assessment. In the future, we envision greater collaboration between community engagement and assessment professionals. Such collaboration has the potential to transform higher education and demonstrate its public mission.

Conclusion

In today's higher education environment, community engagement can be a crucial component of institutional success, effectiveness, and advancement. Assessment of community engagement focuses on accomplishment of institutional priorities, both disciplinary and transdisciplinary student learning, the nature and quality of relationships between institutions and community partners, and impact of community engagement activities. Disseminating outcomes of engagement may be one strategy for restoring public confidence in the value of higher education to society.

Assessment of community engagement brings with it some complex issues, however, including lack of a commonly accepted definition of *assessment* in this context (for stakeholders as well as scholars in the field), scarcity of robust measures of student learning outcomes of engagement, difficulty of tracking engagement initiatives across an institution, and the need for more comprehensive planning for assessment. Future trends are likely to include increased focuses on community impact, strategies for communicating about engagement in concert with internal and external partners, and collaboration between assessment units and community engagement offices within institutions.

Summary of Main Trends

- Community engagement is a strategy for institutional success. Assessment should demonstrate how we are advancing such institutional priorities as research and creative activity, enrollment management, student learning and success, faculty diversity, economic growth and development, and equity and access.
- We encourage assessment that examines the relationship between best practices in community–university engagement and institutional processes like faculty rewards, promotion and tenure, and annual reporting. All of these processes require systematic tracking.
- Public trust in higher education is declining because we lack robust stories of impact, especially about our place-based nature. Tensions between our need for a national reputation and the local value of our institutions must be reconsidered. Our stories must reposition the role of community partners as valued experts and contributors.

Questions for Discussion

- What data on community engagement are you collecting? How are data used to improve practice? To improve processes (e.g., promotion and tenure)?
- How and when do we embody the values of community engagement when conducting assessment? How are we managing tensions? With whom or from where are the tensions arising?
- How are we operationalizing our mission statements or strategic plans? What are the metrics and what systems, processes, and practices support (or hinder) alignment? Does our assessment result in evidence for our campuses' strategic plans?
- What data are necessary to examine the quality of community–university partnerships? Could those data also inform faculty development, enrollment management, global learning, general education, and so on?

We want to hear from you about *Trends in Assessment*:

- Provide reactions or suggestions about trends.
- Share and access resources related to trends.
- Learn about professional development opportunities related to trends.

Visit assessmentinstitute.iupui.edu/trends

References

Campus Compact. (n.d.). Education for democracy. Retrieved from https:// compact .org/education-for-democracy/

Carnegie Foundation for the Advancement of Teaching. (2011). Classification description: Community engagement elective classification. Retrieved from http:// classifications.carnegiefoundation.org/descriptions/community_engagement .php?key=1213

Celio, C. I., Durlak, J., & Dymnicki, A. (2011). A meta-analysis of the impact of service-learning on students. *Journal of Experiential Education, 34*(2), 164–181.

Conway, J. M., Amel, E. L., & Gerwien, D. P. (2009). Teaching and learning in the social context: A meta-analysis of service learning's effects on academic, personal, social, and citizenship outcomes. *Teaching of Psychology, 36*(4), 233–245.

Dewey, J. (1916). *Democracy and education: An introduction to the philosophy of education.* New York, NY: Macmillan. Retrieved from http://www.ilt.columbia .edu/publications/dewey.html

Dickson, A. (1979). Altruism and action. *Journal of Moral Action, 8*, 147–155.

Dostilio, L. D., Benenson, J., Chamberlin, S., Crossland, S., Farmer-Hanson, A., Hernandez, K....Weaver, L. (2017). Preliminary competency model for community engagement professionals. In L. D. Dostilio (Ed.), *The community engagement professional in higher education: A competency model for an emerging field* (pp. 46–51). Boston, MA: Campus Compact.

Driscoll, A. (2008). Carnegie's community-engagement classification: Intentions and insights. *Change: The Magazine of Higher Learning, 40*(1), 38–41.

Driscoll, A., & Sandmann, L. (2011). Evaluation criteria for the scholarship of engagement. Retrieved from http://www.scholarshipofengagement.org/ evaluation/evaluation_criteria.html

Edelman Trust Barometer. (2018). 2018 Edelman Trust Barometer reveals record-breaking drop in trust in the U.S. Retrieved from https://www.edelman.com/news-awards/2018-edelman-trust-barometer-reveals-record-breaking-drop-trust-in-the-us

Eyler, J., & Giles, D. E., Jr. (1999). *Where's the learning in service-learning?* San Francisco, CA: Jossey-Bass.

Finley, A. (2011). Assessment of high-impact practices: Using findings to drive change in the compass project. *Peer Review, 13*(2), 29–33. Retrieved from http://ulib.iupui.edu/cgibin/proxy.pl?url=http://search.proquest.com/docview/1081339892?accountid=7398

Finley, A., & McNair, T. (2013). *Assessing underserved students' engagement in high-impact practices.* Washington, DC: Association of American Colleges & Universities.

Gelmon, S. B., Holland, B. A., Driscoll, A., Spring, A., & Kerrigan, S. (2001). *Assessing service-learning and civic engagement: Principles and techniques.* Boston, MA: Campus Compact.

Giles, D., Sandmann, L., & Saltmarsh, J. (2010). Engagement and the Carnegie classification system. In H. E. Fitzgerald, C. Burack, & S. Seifer (Eds.), *Handbook of engaged scholarship: Contemporary landscapes, future directions: Community-campus partnerships* (vol. 2) (pp. 161–176). East Lansing, MI: Michigan State University Press.

Jacoby, B. (2015). *Service-learning essentials: Questions, answers, and lessons learned.* San Francisco, CA: Jossey-Bass.

Janke, E. M. (2018). *Rethinking what we need to know about partnerships.* Paper presented at the 2018 Assessment Institute, Indianapolis, IN. Retrieved from http://assessmentinstitute.iupui.edu/overview/institute-files/2018-institute/monday-2018/janke-2018.pdf

Janke, E., & Shelton, T. (2011, March 1). Community engagement: Terms and definitions for promotion and tenure guidelines. Retrieved from https://communityengagement.uncg.edu/wp-content/uploads/2014/07/here.pdf

Jankowski, N. A., Timmer, J. D., Kinzie, J., & Kuh, G. D. (2018, January). *Assessment that matters: Trending toward practices that document authentic student learning.* Urbana, IL: University of Illinois and Indiana University, National Institute for Learning Outcomes Assessment.

Kennedy, S. S. (2016). *Talking politics? What you need to know before opening your mouth.* Washington, DC: Georgetown University Press.

Kezar, A. J., Chambers, T. C., & Burkhardt, J. (2005). *Higher education for the public good: Emerging voices from a national movement.* San Francisco, CA: Jossey-Bass.

Kuh, G. D. (2008). *High-impact educational practices: What they are, who has access to them, and why they matter.* Washington, DC: Association of American Colleges & Universities.

Mertens, D., & Wilson, A. (2012). *Program evaluation theory and practice: A comprehensive guide.* New York, NY: Guilford Press.

Milner, H. (2002). *Civic literacy: How informed citizens make democracy work.* Hanover, NH: University Press of New England.

Mitchell, P. H. (2005). What's in a name? Multidisciplinary, interdisciplinary, and transdisciplinary. *Journal of Professional Nursing, 21*(6), 332–334.

Novak, M., Markey, J., & Allen, M. (2007). Evaluating cognitive outcomes of service learning in higher education: A meta-analysis. *Communication Research Reports, 24,* 149–157.

Pew Research Center. (2017). Republicans skeptical of colleges' impact on U.S., but most see benefits for workforce preparation. Retrieved from http://www .pewresearch.org/fact-tank/2017/07/20/republicans-skeptical-of-colleges -impact-on-u-s-but-most-see-benefits-for-workforce-preparation/

Saltmarsh, J., Hartley, M., & Clayton, P. (2009). *Democratic engagement white paper.* Boston, MA: New England Resource Center for Higher Education. Retrieved from http://futureofengagement.wordpress.com/

Steinberg, K., Hatcher, J. A., & Bringle, R. G. (2011). Civic-minded graduate: A north star. *Michigan Journal of Community Service Learning, 18*(1), 19–33.

Torney-Purta, J., Cabrera, J. C., Roohr, K. C., Liu, O. L., & Rios, J. A. (2015). Assessing civic competency and engagement in higher education: Research background, frameworks, and directions for next-generation assessment. *ETS Research Report Series, 2015*(2), 1–48.

Warren, J. L. (2012). Does service-learning increase student learning? A meta-analysis. *Michigan Journal of Community Service Learning, 18*(2), 56–61.

Weiss, H. A., Hahn, T. W., & Norris, K. E. (2017). Civic-minded rubric 2.0. Retrieved from https://scholarworks.iupui.edu/handle/1805/13367

Yorio, P. L., & Ye, F. (2012). A meta-analysis on the effects of service-learning on the social, personal, and cognitive outcomes of learning. *Academy of Management Learning and Education, 11*(1), 9–27.

5

UNDERSTANDING STUDENTS YESTERDAY, TODAY, AND TOMORROW

Trends in Student Affairs Assessment

A. Katherine Busby and A. Sonia Ninon

The college experience for students extends well beyond the classroom. It includes programs, activities, and cocurricular learning experiences, many of which are provided by divisions of student affairs. The learning and development that take place as a result of these experiences have not gone unnoticed by students and their families, employers, and higher education professionals. Student affairs assessment efforts provide opportunities to improve understanding of the skills and knowledge students gain, and for this reason, student affairs assessment plays a critical role in higher education today.

Background

Student affairs plays an important and evolving role in higher education. In recent years, assessment in student affairs has emerged and developed into a key component in understanding student learning and development and in informing institutional decisions.

Student affairs assessment professionals assess programs and services designed to enhance the student experience. Results of these assessment efforts not only benefit the departments within student affairs offices but also contribute to university-wide efforts to demonstrate student learning and development; improve programs and services; and report student achievements to federal, state, and accrediting organizations.

This chapter provides a brief history of the role of student affairs in higher education and the emergence of student affairs assessment and examines current and future trends observed in student affairs assessment. These trends include managing student affairs assessment activities, applying assessment best practices to understand the student experience holistically, and collaborating with campus partners to improve the college experience for students.

Brief History of Student Affairs Assessment in Higher Education

The history of student affairs reflects the evolution of higher education itself. It includes changing student populations, expanding curricula and cocurricular programming, advancing technology, and a continuing need to improve understanding of student learning and development. Throughout this history, individuals who sought to guide and support students through advising, mentorship, programs, and services, while using institutional data and student development research, founded and advanced the field of student affairs (Rhatigan, 2009).

Student Affairs in Higher Education

Early student affairs positions included deans of men and deans of women. These positions developed in the late nineteenth century as faculty interest in monitoring student behavior decreased and the number of colleges and universities admitting women increased (Hevel, 2016). Initially, these deans were responsible primarily for discipline and housing, but the duties of student affairs professionals grew to include mentoring, academic advising, career guidance, student employment, scholarships and financial aid, student organizations, and orientation (Caple, 1998; Hevel, 2016; Schwartz, 2010). These areas are among the many programs and services still provided by student affairs divisions. Many student affairs divisions also encompass enrollment management, community engagement, service-learning, campus recreation, student health, and diversity and inclusion (Garland & Grace, 1993).

Student affairs educators today prioritize holistic student development, taking into consideration not only students' intellectual development but also their physical, emotional, social, and identity development (American Council on Education, 1937, 1949). Over several decades, studies of student affairs in higher education have demonstrated an enduring commitment to holistic student development, individual differences, and initiatives rooted in research and practice (Evans & Reason, 2001). A deeper look at the history of student affairs and its role in higher education can be found in the higher education literature (e.g., Caple, 1998; Evans, Forney, & Guido-DiBrito, 1998; Evans & Reason, 2001; Long, 2012; McClellan, Stringer, Lamb, & Michaelis, 2009; Nuss, 2003).

As the field of student affairs developed, faculty and staff began using student demographic characteristics, health records, results of psychological tests, and other data to develop a "mechanical record" that was used as an advising tool (Schwartz, 2010, p. 99). These practices were early examples of the programs and processes used by faculty and student affairs professionals today. The need to understand students' experiences and personal development continues to underpin the work of student affairs assessment. Currently, campus professionals use myriad software programs, including customer relationship management (CRM) software, retention and persistence tools, and dashboard visualizations to gather, store, and interpret data about students in an effort to encourage and engage them in campus life, often with the goal of supporting their persistence to graduation. Professionals engaged in student affairs assessment also play a key role in analyzing such data to inform student learning theory and practice.

Role of Student Affairs Assessment

Early student affairs professionals who gathered and used student information and applied student development research to inform their work set the trend for many in the field to follow. Whether those data were gathered before desktop computing or mobile devices were commonplace or more recently with the aid of nationally administered surveys and visualization software, assessment has been an important part of student affairs. Indeed, assessment has been recognized by the profession as a critical need for more than 80 years. The *Student Personnel Point of View* (American Council on Education, 1937) called for student affairs professionals to evaluate and improve activities, programs, and services and to better understand the student experience outside the classroom. This call has been reiterated and refined over time (ACPA: College Student Educators International, 1994; American Council on Education, 1949; Keeling, 2004).

Notably, the development of student affairs assessment has paralleled that of the student affairs profession and of higher education assessment in the United States (Henning & Roberts, 2016) and includes the continuing need to understand the whole student, changing approaches to assessment, evolving student development research, and advancing technology.

Student affairs educators have long believed that, overall, their programs and services support student learning and development. Professional expertise and anecdotal data from current and former students shaped early student affairs professionals' understanding of the impact of programs and services on students. These anecdotal data resonated with internal and external stakeholders, but they were not sufficient for making decisions or demonstrating learning and development. Understanding that well-executed programs and services can improve student achievement measures such as retention, graduation, and job placement, as well as the student experience itself, student affairs educators began employing more rigorous data collection and analysis techniques.

With a focus on student services, assessment in student affairs began with measures that focused primarily on participation and student satisfaction (Schuh & Gansemer-Topf, 2010). Professionals developing and administering programs and services wanted to ensure that these efforts met the expectations of participants and were considered valuable—that is, that participation in the program or service was worth the cost of implementation. The availability of user-friendly, cost-effective survey software enabled practitioners to evaluate their own programs and services. These measures of student participation and satisfaction provided actionable information to student affairs educators, who used the data gathered through surveys to shape their activities and make more strategic planning and budgeting decisions (Busby, 2017). These surveys, however, were often administered in isolation, without consideration of broader campus learning outcomes. But while satisfaction and participation data are important, student affairs educators have a far greater story to tell.

As student affairs educators emphasized student development and learning through cocurricular programs, they began assessing student learning, using approaches similar to those used by academic programs. These approaches included the development of student learning outcomes at the outset of a program and the use of robust measurement techniques to assess that learning. Student affairs professionals also began identifying and using established measures of student development grounded in student development theory. Today, administration of participation and satisfaction surveys also includes better rigor and coordination with broader campus initiatives. Assessment efforts in student affairs inform division-wide decision-making and contribute to university-wide efforts to demonstrate student learning, development, and achievement (Busby, 2017).

Trends

The field of student affairs assessment has expanded over the past decade, and the practice of assessing the student experience has evolved rapidly. Over this period of time, several trends have emerged, including establishment of student affairs assessment as a profession, holistic assessment of student development, and student affairs–academic affairs collaboration to advance assessment.

Professionalizing Student Affairs Assessment

Many student affairs educators entered the profession because they had a strong desire to work with students and offer a positive cocurricular learning experience (Henning & Roberts, 2016). Often, these professionals benefited from the mentorship they received as students and wanted a career that afforded them the opportunity to engage in that work. Previously, student affairs educators were not formally prepared to participate in assessment activities by their graduate education programs or their professional development activities.

In the early 2000s, divisions of student affairs began investing in offices and/or full- and part-time positions dedicated to student affairs assessment. Texas A&M University's Department of Student Life Studies and The Ohio State University's Center for the Study of Student Life are offices within student affairs divisions dedicated to executing assessment activities focused on student affairs programs as well as the student experience more broadly. Institutions such as Indiana University–Purdue University Indianapolis, the University of Mississippi, DePaul University, and Western Michigan University all have dedicated director positions for student affairs assessment. Positions and/or offices of student affairs assessment have been established, but institutions are also investing in professional development opportunities for many student affairs educators.

The two primary professional organizations for student affairs educators, NASPA: Student Affairs Administrators in Higher Education and ACPA: College Student Educators International, support student affairs assessment practices independently and jointly. Both organizations have special interest groups dedicated to assessment in student affairs. NASPA formed the Assessment, Evaluation, and Research Knowledge Community to advance assessment efforts through professional education and dissemination of research and best practices (NASPA: Student Affairs Administrators in Higher Education, 2019). The ACPA Commission for Assessment and Evaluation promotes assessment skills and knowledge among student affairs professionals at all levels (ACPA: College Student Educators International, 2019).

Both ACPA's and NASPA's annual meeting programs include sessions dedicated to the topic of assessment. In addition, both organizations sponsor conferences specifically designed to advance student affairs assessment. In particular, ACPA's Student Affairs Assessment Institute and NASPA's Assessment, Persistence, and Data Analytics Conference are focused on student affairs assessment.

Although the primary student affairs professional organizations offer myriad opportunities for assessment education, professional development for student affairs educators is not limited to these meetings. Professional meetings such as the Association for the Assessment of Learning in Higher Education (AALHE) annual conference (www.aalhe.org/page/AnnualConference) and the Assessment Institute in Indianapolis (assessmentinstitute.iupui.edu/) also offer sessions on student affairs assessment. For more than 15 years, the Assessment Institute has sponsored a program track aimed at meeting the needs of student affairs professionals and others interested in assessment of student development and student affairs programs and services (Busby, 2017).

The trend of professionalizing student affairs assessment can be seen in other contexts as well. Literature on the development of student affairs assessment has emerged. In 2006, ACPA developed the *ASK Standards: Assessment, Skills, and Knowledge Content Standards for Student Affairs Practitioners and Scholars* to help student affairs educators better understand the knowledge and skills student affairs professionals needed to successfully carry out assessment activities (ACPA: College Student Educators International, 2006). Together ACPA and NASPA (2010) developed the *Professional Competency Areas for Student Affairs Educators.* These competency areas represent the "essential knowledge, skills, and dispositions expected of all student affairs educators" (p. 7); assessment, evaluation, and research make up 1 of the 10 competency areas outlined in this document.

In December 2009, a small group of student affairs assessment professionals founded Student Affairs Assessment Leaders (SAAL). The organization grew from a shared desire to turn a group of directors of student affairs assessment on various college campuses into a thriving network of professionals dedicated to advancing the scholarship and practice of student affairs assessment (studentaffairsassessment.org/). Through professional networks and long-standing professional associations, conferences, and publications, student affairs assessment professionals have embraced and advanced their profession. They have set an example that has caught the attention of student affairs educators and assessment practitioners alike by accepting the challenge of assessing the whole student, including complex outcomes such as leadership, cultural competence, critical thinking, and ethical reasoning.

Holistic Assessment of Student Development

Student affairs educators have prioritized a holistic view of the student experience, including both student learning and student development, throughout the history of the profession (ACPA: College Student Educators International, 1994; American Council on Education, 1937, 1949; Keeling, 2004). Although the student affairs focus on providing programs and services to meet the students' desires has not changed, the student population and its needs certainly have. Similarly, student affairs assessment professionals have remained focused on assessing student learning and development but have employed different assessment methods for understanding students' knowledge, skills, and attitudes.

Institutions of higher education strive to prepare students to become well-rounded, thoughtful, and engaged leaders. Student affairs professionals work with campus and community partners to offer services and programs that address the challenges students face, recognizing the importance of cocurricular experiences to a holistic educational experience. Engaging activities such as leadership roles in student organizations, alternative break trips, community-engaged initiatives, and peer health educator programs provide opportunities for students to apply the skills and knowledge they develop in the classroom. Palomba and Banta (1999) referenced George Kuh's "seamless learning" (p. 269), the result of a good marriage between in-class and out-of-class experiences as a way to maximize student learning and development. These authors also argued that "activities such as studying, using learning resources, interacting with faculty and peers, participating in campus programs, and utilizing on-campus services and facilities should support in-class activities and help students gain as much as possible from their college experiences" (p. 269). Research indicates that these engaging curricular and cocurricular activities, often referred to as high-impact practices (HIPs), are beneficial for students, particularly for historically underserved students, who receive a greater benefit from participating in such activities (Kuh, 2008).

Student affairs assessment professionals pay close attention to changes in demographics and enrollment trends, as well as to the influences of those factors on students' sense of belonging and engagement. The student population has become more diverse, and this diversity is already evident on many college campuses. First-generation college students, students from low socioeconomic status backgrounds, and minoritized students may initially lack the social capital to navigate the postsecondary system and often retreat to safe spaces on campus. Students coming to college questioning their gender, sexual identity, and sexual orientation also seek supportive campus communities. Postsecondary institutions must respond by offering programs, services, and assessment methods that are inclusive and welcoming of a diverse student body.

D-L Stewart (2018) challenged student affairs professionals and researchers to take a deep dive into their data, checking their inherent biases, to ensure that they engage in inclusive assessment practices. Critical questions need to be asked: (a) Who is not coming to our programs and why? (b) How do we treat students when they come to our programs? (c) Do we make accommodations for students with hearing or visual impairments? and (d) Do we intersect the data when conducting our analyses? Stewart further argued that minoritized students have different experiences than their White peers.

Student affairs educators strive to meet the needs of diverse students by providing programs, services, and activities to support their identity development and afford them cross-cultural experiences. Student affairs assessment professionals thus must seek innovative approaches to designing inclusive learning outcomes and assessment methods. While they are well positioned to do so, they must work in partnership with other on- and off-campus stakeholders, because the college experience includes both curricular and cocurricular programs. As Elise Newkirk-Kotfila (2018) said, "our institutional knowledge and commitment to student success, combined with partners' expertise and point of view, can coalesce to make great things happen for our students." Newkirk-Kotfila (2018) further argued that we must have open and sincere discussions with our partners aimed at reaching a clear understanding of outcomes and expectations and mutual agreement regarding time, resources, and program management. Student affairs educators and, in particular, student affairs assessment professionals are therefore forging intentional and strategic partnerships with on- and off-campus partners to better understand the needs of diverse students and to help all students succeed.

Student Affairs Collaborations

The student experience is multifaceted and is best understood through academic, social, and cocurricular perspectives. Collaboration between student affairs and academic affairs is necessary to understand, assess, and improve students' experiences.

The importance of cocurricular learning is recognized across the academy, and faculty and academic leaders want to understand the impact of cocurricular learning. Unfortunately, on many college campuses, coordination across units is lacking, and cocurricular programs often operate in silos (Suskie, 2014). This siloed culture can lead to duplication of effort and wasted financial and human resources. Darby M. Roberts, director of student life studies at Texas A&M University, emphasized the need for collaboration in her Assessment Institute track keynote address *Academic and Student Affairs Sides of the House: Can We Have an Open Concept Learning Design?* (Roberts, 2016). Comparing campus interactions to home design, she challenged attendees to expand beyond their "side of the house" and create an "open concept" to foster student learning. Schuh and Gansemer-Topf (2010) also called for such partnerships because "it is important to find opportunities where faculty and student affairs can work together in assessing student learning so that the students' total experience can be understood" (p. 8).

Partnerships between academic affairs and student affairs can support student learning and development and foster assessment of such skills as critical thinking, teamwork, and ethical reasoning. At some institutions, student affairs educators and faculty pursue strategic partnerships through first-year seminars, health and wellness presentations in classes, service-learning opportunities, career services, and living-learning communities. Where such partnerships exist, student affairs assessment professionals have the opportunity to share assessment methods such as paper portfolios or electronic portfolios and performance-based assessments, results, and uses of those results. Suskie (2015), for example, called on institutional researchers to include student affairs in institutional program review processes so that institutional outcomes and effectiveness could be measured.

Future Trends

The future is bright for student affairs assessment. Recent trends in the field have laid a firm foundation for the student affairs assessment profession, holistic student assessment, and campus partnerships. Many of the current trends described in this chapter will continue to be an important part of assessing student learning and development. In addition, student affairs educators and assessment professionals should keep an eye on the following emerging trends.

Student Affairs Assessment Profession

Student affairs graduate programs are now offering more courses focused on assessment. Some programs offer these courses as electives, whereas other programs include the assessment courses as core requirements. These courses not only provide an overview of the skills and knowledge expected of student affairs educators but also offer opportunities for emerging professionals to practice those skills. Higher education faculty are sharing the results of experiential learning pedagogies and best practices to ensure that coming generations of student affairs educators are prepared properly to perform assessment activities on their campuses. Programs at the University of South Carolina (Newton, Maher, & Smith, 2015) and Murray State University (Bourke, 2017) offer service-learning graduate courses in assessment.

The role of graduate students in the practice of assessment has also emerged as a trend in the student affairs track at the Assessment Institute, highlighting the need for well-executed experiential learning opportunities in assessment classes to benefit students and departments or divisions of student affairs. Satterfield and Schiller (2017) demonstrated the power of cocurricular assessment through the leadership of the chief academic officer, the chief student affairs officer, and graduate faculty. They enabled graduate students in the student affairs/higher education program at Missouri State University to carry out assessment projects across the division of student affairs, applying the skills they learned in their assessment course and inspiring a shift in division culture to use assessment results for improvement. Winslow-Edmonson, Agrawal, and Snow (2017) also described the impact of graduate experiential learning on the students themselves by sharing the stories of graduate students who applied their assessment skills to programs in the division of student affairs at Indiana University-Bloomington. We can expect that student affairs educators entering the profession will engage in assessment of student learning and development and will advance the processes used to complete these efforts. We can also expect student affairs assessment professionals to make scholarly contributions to higher education and assessment literature and become an integral part of assessment practice not only within divisions of student affairs but also across college and university campuses.

Holistic Assessment of a Diverse Student Population

Student affairs educators are committed to developing not only the whole student but also *all* students regardless of their identities, including race, ethnicity, gender, sexual orientation, age, and ability. As the college student population changes with respect to race and ethnicity, attitudes, beliefs, behaviors, and abilities, student affairs assessment professionals are positioned to lead efforts to advance culturally responsive assessment. Montenegro and Jankowski (2017) defined *culturally responsive assessment* as assessment that is mindful of the student populations the institution serves, using language that is appropriate for all students when developing learning outcomes, acknowledging students' differences in the planning phases of an assessment effort, developing and/or using assessment tools that are appropriate for different students, and being intentional in using assessment results to improve learning for all students. (p. 10)

We can anticipate that student affairs assessment professionals will contribute significantly to efforts to develop robust, culturally responsive assessment measures by pairing research on student identity development with assessment best practices.

Key Collaborations With Institutional Partners

Although many student affairs assessment efforts are focused on undergraduates, holistic student assessment also includes graduate and professional students. Both student affairs educators and faculty recognize the importance of experiential learning to graduate and professional students, and they take advantage of opportunities to assess learning that occurs through research opportunities, clinical experiences, and paraprofessional career involvements (Busby, 2017). Including these populations in student affairs assessment efforts is a growing trend, as evidenced by the increasing number of graduate student–focused sessions at the Assessment Institute in Indianapolis.

Faculty and staff members coordinating cocurricular programs within professional schools, in particular, are applying innovative assessment techniques. Hughes, Fuentes, Cleven, and Ross (2016) demonstrated the processes used to document and assess discipline-specific cocurricular learning experience and use assessment results to improve curricula and satisfy professional accreditation standards. Student affairs assessment professionals have important opportunities to establish collaborative partnerships with assessment coordinators and academic leaders focused on student affairs within individual colleges and schools, and we anticipate that these types of collaborations will increase and develop.

We further expect that collaborations among student affairs assessment professionals and institutional research (IR) and information technology (IT) professionals will increase. Opportunities to share institutional and experiential data between student affairs assessment and IR professionals will enable all stakeholders to enrich their understanding of student learning, development, and experiences. Including IT professionals in these efforts will ensure that data are stored securely, allowing for appropriate use. Effective communication between student affairs and IT can also engender cost savings for purchases of software, computers, and other technology. Such collaborative partnerships will support assessment professionals across campuses in collecting better data on their institutions and the students they serve. But such joint projects can grow only if the leadership of student affairs; academic affairs; enrollment management; IR; IT; and other units, divisions, and departments are committed to breaking down the silos.

Conclusion

Student affairs assessment professionals work tirelessly to assess the cocurricular learning and development of a diverse student population. Understanding students and their experiences has been a key component of student affairs work throughout the history of higher education. From a few individuals assessing cocurricular experiences to offices of student affairs assessment and professional conferences and journals, student affairs assessment has grown and developed as a field, and student affairs assessment professionals have become integral participants in higher education and assessment. From working within a division to establishing partnerships across campus, these professionals contribute to the broader assessment of institutional student learning outcomes and provide key information used to answer calls for student achievement and accountability. Through student affairs assessment, higher education stakeholders have the opportunity to better understand the college experience of former, current, and future students.

Summary of Main Trends

- Student affairs assessment professionals have a robust professional network and make notable contributions to higher education and assessment research and practice.
- Student affairs assessment focuses on assessing the whole student, including complex outcomes such as leadership, cultural competence, critical thinking, and ethical reasoning.
- Today's highly diverse and constantly changing student population requires culturally responsive assessment methods.
- Assessment efforts in student affairs inform division-wide decision-making and contribute to university-wide efforts to demonstrate student learning, development, and achievement.

Questions for Discussion

- How is student affairs assessment managed on your campus? Is there an individual or office responsible for these efforts?
- What partnerships exist between student affairs and other campus units? Do these partnerships advance assessment of student learning and development?
- How well has your campus examined the characteristics and needs of your student population? Are the assessment methods used appropriate for your population?

We want to hear from you about *Trends in Assessment*.

- Provide reactions or suggestions about trends.
- Share and access resources related to trends.
- Learn about professional development opportunities related to trends.

Visit assessmentinstitute.iupui.edu/trends

References

ACPA: College Student Educators International. (1994). *The student learning imperative: Implications for student affairs.* Washington, DC: Author.

ACPA: College Student Educators International. (2006). *ASK standards: Assessment, skills, and knowledge content standards for student affairs practitioners and scholars.* Washington, DC: Author.

ACPA: College Student Educators International. (2019). Commission for assessment and evaluation. Retrieved from http://www.myacpa.org/commae

ACPA: College Student Educators International & NASPA: Student Affairs Administrators in Higher Education. (2010). *Professional competency areas for student affairs educators.* Washington, DC: Author.

American Council on Education. (1937). *Student personnel point of view.* Washington, DC: Author.

American Council on Education. (1949). *Student personnel point of view* (rev. ed.). Washington, DC: Author.

Bourke, B. (2017). Using a CAS self-study to teach assessment practice. *Research and Practice in Assessment, 12*(1), 47–52.

Busby, A. K. (2017). Assessing student affairs programs and services: Trends and strategies. *Assessment Update, 29*(6), 6–7. Retrieved from https://doi.org/10.1002/au.30115

Caple, R. B. (1998). *To mark the beginning: A social history of college student affairs.* Washington, DC: American College Personnel Association.

Evans, N. J., Forney, D., & Guido-DiBrito, F. (1998). *Student development in college: Theory, research, and practice.* San Francisco, CA: Jossey-Bass.

Evans, N. J., & Reason, R. D. (2001). Guiding principles: A review and analysis of student affairs philosophical statements. *Journal of College Student Development, 42*(4), 359–377.

Garland, P. H., & Grace, T. W. (1993). *New perspectives for student affairs professionals: Evolving realities, responsibilities, and roles* (ASHE-ERIC Higher Education Report No. 7). Washington, DC: George Washington University, School of Education and Human Development.

Henning, G. W., & Roberts, D. (2016). *Student affairs assessment: Theory to practice.* Sterling, VA: Stylus.

Hevel, M. S. (2016). Toward a history of student affairs: A synthesis of research, 1996–2015. *Journal of College Student Development, 57*(7), 844–862. Retrieved from https://doi.org/10.1353/csd.2016.0082

Hughes, J. A., Fuentes, D. G., Cleven, A. J., & Ross, J. (2016, October). *Revealing the hidden curriculum through documentation, tracking, and assessment strategies.* Paper presented at the 2016 Assessment Institute, Indianapolis, IN.

Keeling, R. (Ed.). (2004). *Learning reconsidered: A campus-wide focus on the student experience.* Washington, DC: ACPA: College Student Educators International and NASPA: Student Affairs Administrators in Higher Education.

Kuh, G. D. (2008). *High-impact educational practices: What they are, who has access to them, and why they matter.* Washington, DC: Association of American Colleges & Universities.

Long, D. (2012). The foundations of student affairs: A guide to the profession. In L. J. Hinchliffe & M. A. Wong (Eds.), *Environments for student growth and development: Librarians and student affairs in collaboration* (pp. 1–39). Chicago, IL: Association of College & Research Libraries.

McClellan, G. S., Stringer, J., Lamb, D. C., & Michaelis, J. (Eds.). (2009). *The handbook of student affairs administration* (3rd ed.). San Francisco, CA: Jossey-Bass.

Montenegro, E., & Jankowski, N. A. (2017, January). *Equity and assessment: Moving towards culturally responsive assessment* (Occasional Paper No. 29). Urbana, IL: University of Illinois and Indiana University, National Institute for Learning Outcomes Assessment.

NASPA: Student Affairs Administrators in Higher Education. (2019). Assessment, evaluation, and research. Retrieved from https://www.naspa.org/constituent-groups/kcs/assessment-evaluation-and-research

Newkirk-Kotfila, E. (2018, September 20). I'm not here to help: Three lessons for academics who want to be better partners [Blog post]. Retrieved from https://www.naspa.org/rpi/posts/im-not-here-to-help-three-lessons-for-academics-who-want-to-be-better-partn

Newton, A. R., Maher, M. A., & Smith, D. A. (2015). Practical collaborations for positive impact. *Research and Practice in Assessment, 10*(1), 57–59.

Nuss, E. M. (2003). The development of student affairs. In S. R. Komives, D. B. Woodard, Jr., & Associates (Eds.), *Student services: A handbook for the profession* (4th ed., pp. 65–88). San Francisco, CA: Jossey-Bass.

Palomba, C. A., & Banta, T. W. (1999). *Assessment essentials: Planning, implementing, and improving assessment in higher education.* San Francisco, CA: Jossey-Bass.

Rhatigan, J. J. (2009). From the people up: A brief history of student affairs administration. In G. S. McClellan, J. Stringer, D. C. Lamb, & J. Michaelis (Eds.), *The handbook of student affairs administration* (3rd ed., pp. 3–20). San Francisco, CA: Jossey-Bass.

Roberts, D. M. (2016, October). *Academic and student affairs sides of the house: Can we have an open concept learning design?* Paper presented at the 2016 Assessment Institute, Indianapolis, IN.

Satterfield, J., & Schiller, J. (2017, October). *Leveraging the power of co-curricular assessment.* Paper presented at the 2017 Assessment Institute, Indianapolis, IN.

Schuh, J. H., & Gansemer-Topf, A. M. (2010, December). *The role of student affairs in student learning assessment* (Occasional Paper No. 7). Urbana, IL: University of Illinois and Indiana University, National Institute for Learning Outcomes Assessment.

Schwartz, R. A. (2010). *Deans of men and the shaping of modern college culture.* New York, NY: Palgrave Macmillan.

Stewart, D.-L. (2018, June). *Giving voice: Designing inclusive assessment.* Paper presented at the Student Affairs Assessment and Research Conference, Columbus, OH.

Suskie, L. (2014). *Five dimensions of quality: A common sense guide to accreditation and accountability.* San Francisco, CA: Jossey-Bass.

Suskie, L. (2015). Introduction to measuring co-curricular learning. *New Directions for Institutional Research, 164,* 5–14.

Winslow-Edmonson, C., Agrawal, M., & Snow, L. (2017, October). *Other duties as assigned: Why graduate students in student affairs programs need assessment projects.* Paper presented at the 2017 Assessment Institute, Indianapolis, IN.

6

STEM EDUCATION AND ASSESSMENT

Evolving Through Evidence

Anthony Chase, Gabrielle Kline, and Stephen P. Hundley

S cience, technology, engineering, and mathematics (STEM) disciplines comprise a diverse set of academic programs, typically requiring prerequisite foundational knowledge in mathematics and science and usually incorporating laboratory components. STEM courses and programs help college students master complex discipline-specific concepts, prepare students for preprofessional degree requirements, and educate students to become STEM-literate graduates. In recent years, these disciplines have been active in developing programs to attract underserved students and offering experiences to engage students in research, including opportunities at the undergraduate level.

As a term, *STEM* had its origins in the 1990s at the National Science Foundation (NSF) and has been used to describe any event, policy, program, or practice that involves one or several of the STEM disciplines (Bybee, 2010). As a set of disciplines, STEM has attracted significant investment from the federal government; annual federal appropriations for STEM education are typically in the range of $2.8 billion to $3.4 billion. More than half of federal STEM education funding is intended to serve the needs of postsecondary institutions and students (Gonzalez & Kuenzi, 2012). One reason for such federal interest in STEM is the need to ensure that the United States is prepared to adequately address such challenges as health-care improvement, national production capacity, and research excellence (National Research Council [NRC], 2011a, 2011b).

Despite considerable and long-standing federal investment, the U.S. leadership position in STEM faces increasing challenges. Concerns center on academic achievement gaps among various demographic groups, STEM teacher quality, the rankings of U.S. students on international STEM assessments, increased educational attainment in STEM fields in other countries, and the ability of the U.S. educational system to meet demand for STEM labor. Other challenges include promoting public awareness of STEM issues, expanding the STEM pipeline, enhancing professional preparation of STEM college students, and improving student learning in STEM (Fairweather, 2008). Poor preparation for college-level mathematics and science, coupled with high rates of attrition among STEM majors, are also significant challenges for undergraduate STEM education in the United States. Collectively, these are among the many reasons for increased interest in assessing and improving STEM education outcomes (Gonzalez & Kuenzi, 2012).

History

Many STEM disciplinary societies can trace their origins to the 1800s and have made important contributions to STEM research and education. Similarly, the federal government has always had a keen interest in STEM, evidenced, for example, by the 1862 passage of the Morrill Act, which established land-grant universities focusing on agriculture and the mechanic arts, and by intensive STEM-oriented research during World Wars I and II. The creation of the NSF in the early 1950s enabled the federal government to play a more pivotal role in guiding the nation's focus on STEM education. The launch of the Russian satellite *Sputnik* in the late 1950s served as a powerful call to action in the United States to leverage capabilities in STEM to compete with international peers in what was referred to as the Space Race (Mohr-Schroeder, Cavalcanti, & Blyman, 2015).

Since then, the government has continued to invest considerable resources in STEM-oriented policy, curricula, and research. The NSF and other federal agencies funded programs to engage students in STEM activities, while STEM disciplinary associations created programs aimed at improving the educational experiences and outcomes of students in both P–12 and collegiate settings. One national leader has been Project Kaleidoscope (PKAL), established in 1989 as an independent organization and now part of the Association of American Colleges & Universities. PKAL (2017) seeks to "competitively train and liberally educate *every* STEM undergraduate" (p. 2, emphasis in original) through a series of programs, projects, and initiatives aimed at "catalyzing the reform of undergraduate STEM teaching" (p. 2).

Some STEM disciplines, notably engineering, have long-standing histories of discipline-specific accreditation and licensure of professionals through which quality standards for both higher education and the professions have been articulated, implemented, and evaluated. The 1990s saw an increased emphasis on assessing the educational outcomes of students in STEM, as was the case in other disciplines. Prior to that time, outcomes assessment had been relatively foreign to the STEM academic culture, leading to much discomfort at first. Although the development of effective programs of outcomes assessment and continuous improvement required an investment of effort, once established, such programs have become part of the academic culture and have been embedded into educational processes (Prados, Peterson, & Lattuca, 2005). Smith, Douglas, and Cox (2009) discussed the importance of cultivating an assessment-centered culture in *all* STEM disciplines, not just those subject to specialized accreditation. Such a culture provides multiple opportunities to monitor and make visible students' progress from initial understandings to the ultimate learning goals for those completing a course or program.

Assessment and improvement in STEM are vital to the ability to attract and retain students in these disciplines. Well-prepared students have been found to leave STEM because of what they saw as poor instruction, undesirable curricular structure, overreliance on lectures, and faculty who valued their research above teaching (Seymour & Hewitt, 1997). Despite several studies citing empirical evidence of effectiveness, numerous reforms have not led to the hoped-for magnitude of change in STEM student learning or retention. Some resistance to adopting more effective teaching strategies derives, in part, from the perception of STEM faculty that research is viewed as more valuable than teaching at their institutions (Fairweather, 2008).

Many national STEM associations are also increasingly expressing dissatisfaction with the rate of implementation and adoption of research-based instructional strategies. Borrego and Henderson (2014) noted that STEM education leaders and researchers are just beginning to view change as a scholarly endeavor that can and should be informed by the educational research literature. These researchers identify several approaches to facilitating change, ranging from *diffusing and integrating* instructional practices to *valuing scholarly teaching and the Scholarship of Teaching and Learning* to *developing the faculty and administrative leadership capacities and cultures* to sustain STEM innovations over time.

Against this backdrop, the Assessment Institute in Indianapolis recently introduced a STEM education track. Presentations provided the fundamentals of STEM educational research and offered insights into assessment practices in the field. Many of the innovations shared were designed to more effectively reach a changing student population. Presentation topics emphasized broadening participation in STEM, collaborations between and among institutions, validity and reliability in assessment methods, and evidence-based STEM pedagogies. The trends that follow are informed by presentations in the STEM education track, as well as scholarly publications and national reports on STEM education interventions.

Current Trends

Assessment trends in STEM education draw on several decades of investment and attention to improving the student experience and preparing students for employment, scientific literacy, advanced study, and lifelong learning. Trends include enhancing goals for STEM learning and connecting them to assessment and quality practices, promoting promising practices through evidence-based pedagogy and changes in STEM curricula, and recruiting and retaining students by expanding and diversifying the STEM talent pipeline.

Enhancing Goals for STEM Learning and Connecting Them to Assessment and Quality Practices

All college graduates, regardless of major, should be STEM-literate and possess certain STEM competencies. These include the ability to identify STEM issues, explain these issues from STEM perspectives, and use STEM information to make conclusions based on evidence (Organisation for Economic Co-operation and Development, 2006). Bybee (2010) identified several additional elements of STEM literacy that all students should achieve. For example, college graduates should be able to acquire scientific, technological, engineering, and mathematical knowledge; apply that knowledge to STEM-related issues; recognize how STEM disciplines shape our material, intellectual, and cultural world; and, as concerned and constructive citizens, engage issues through the STEM disciplines.

Students in STEM academic programs have learning goals more specific to their disciplines, and, as Labov, Singer, George, Schweingruber, and Hilton (2009) noted, such learning goals vary considerably within STEM courses. These may include understanding a particular STEM concept, mastering a few major principles in depth, building a mental framework that serves as a foundation for future learning, developing and integrating the higher order analytical skills and judgment needed to use scientific information in a given context, and ultimately finding satisfaction in engaging with real-world issues requiring STEM knowledge.

Kennedy and Odell (2014) outlined components needed for academic programs in STEM to achieve these disciplinary goals. Such programs should provide students the opportunity to integrate technology and engineering into science and math curricula and promote scientific inquiry and engineering design. They should offer collaborative approaches to learning by connecting students and educators with STEM professionals, while also stressing global and multiperspective viewpoints. Finally, STEM programs should incorporate strategies such as project-based learning and use appropriate technologies to provide formal and informal learning experiences for students. These instructional components represent a relatively recent focus on student-centeredness within STEM disciplines.

An example from engineering education illustrates changes to instructional approaches over time. As Froyd, Wankat, and Smith (2012) noted, there have been major shifts in the ways engineering students are now educated. The past century has seen the focus move from less theoretical perspectives to ones involving application of engineering and science to design challenges. Moreover, engineering educators today emphasize applying learning sciences research to instructional settings and integrating information, computational, and communications technology into pedagogies and curricula. There has also been a focus on outcomes-based education and accreditation. ABET, Inc., the specialized accreditor for collegiate engineering academic programs and formerly the Accreditation Board for Engineering and Technology, has moved from a quality assurance process based on evaluating program characteristics relative to minimum standards to one based on evaluating and improving the intellectual skills and capabilities of graduates (Prados et al., 2005).

ABET's outcomes-focused approach to accreditation, introduced in the 1990s and known as Engineering Criteria 2000 (EC2000), provides for programs a continuous improvement process based on evaluating the achievement of student outcomes and using evaluation results for program improvement. Because EC2000 focuses on the learning outcomes of graduates, it provides a useful framework for comparing preparation of engineering graduates from diverse educational systems and supports the development of processes for international recognition of engineering educational credentials (Prados et al., 2005).

In STEM contexts, the most valid approaches to assessing the impact of instruction on learning break student outcomes into components (e.g., knowledge content, problem-solving, communication skills) and study the changes in these outcomes separately, rather than presenting a single measure of change in student learning. Assessment procedures should aim to distinguish among the types of learning outcomes measured in a single class (e.g., content knowledge) and the types of outcomes assessed at the program level (e.g., application of knowledge). Each outcome may require a different assessment method. In STEM courses and programs, the usefulness of any assessment approach ultimately depends on its rigor and ease of use. Labor-intensive assessment methods requiring substantial training prior to use are unlikely to find widespread acceptance among STEM faculty (Fairweather, 2008).

Promoting Promising Practices Through Evidence-Based Pedagogy and Changes in STEM Curricula

Tremendous investment over the past few decades has built up a substantial knowledge base about STEM learning. Labov and colleagues (2009) discussed how financial support and commitment from the public and private sectors have resulted in research-based implementation of numerous promising practices for teaching, learning, and assessment in undergraduate STEM education. Such practices range from improvements in teaching in individual classrooms to changes throughout entire departments. They include increased prominence of campus- and national-level centers for STEM-centric teaching excellence and a focus on professional development for STEM faculty. The adoption of these practices has also benefited from large outreach and dissemination efforts.

Virtually all of the new promising practices have focused on student-centered, inquiry-based approaches to teaching and incorporate scenario-based content, instructional activities designed to promote student engagement and faculty interaction, learning outcomes, and varying approaches to assessing student learning, including student feedback gathered in formative assessments (Froyd, 2008). Specific widely adopted examples include peer-led team learning, process-oriented guided inquiry learning, course-based undergraduate research experiences, science writing heuristics, just-in-time teaching, and many others (Auchincloss et al., 2014; Wilson & Varma-Nelson, 2016).

These promising practices tend to be more effective than traditional approaches to STEM teaching, which emphasized lecturing and multiple-choice or short-answer examinations. In one of the largest and most comprehensive meta-analyses of undergraduate STEM education published to date, Freeman and colleagues (2014) found that average examination scores improved by about 6% in active learning sections and that students in classes with traditional lecturing were 1.5 times more likely to *fail* than were students in classes with active learning. The results raise questions about the widespread continued use of traditional lecturing and support for active learning as the preferred, empirically validated teaching practice in STEM classrooms.

STEM faculty members play an important role in creating students' *initial interest* in the discipline by signaling their own accessibility and engagement. Introductory courses in STEM have a strong influence on the number of students who successfully graduate as STEM majors (Henry, 2010). Students who reported feeling comfortable asking questions in class, seeking out tutoring, attending supplemental instruction sessions, and collaborating with other students were also more likely to be engaged. Professors' teaching strategies and attitudes were influential factors of classroom climate that shaped students' academic engagement, while students' behavior, emotions, and cognition were important factors in predicting their engagement (Gasiewski, Eagan, Garcia, Hurtado, & Chang, 2012).

Faculty also play an important role in shaping STEM students' *continued educational experiences.* When professors incorporated active learning pedagogies, employed teaching strategies that offered immediate feedback, ensured that more students had grasped the material, or made the most of new technologies for illustrating concepts, students became more engaged in courses (Gasiewski et al., 2012). Researchers have also linked student engagement in research to robust outcomes in the cognitive domain, including critical thinking and written and oral communication skills. Some evidence suggests that participation in undergraduate research may bolster STEM students' intentions to complete a graduate degree (Strayhorn, 2010).

Several factors influence effective facilitation of students' activities in the STEM classroom or laboratory, including the extent to which STEM educators implement engaging pedagogies, connect classroom and laboratory activities to real-world contexts, and encourage students' active participation in the learning process (Ejiwale, 2012). However, several constraints limit the implementation of evidence-based instructional practices in STEM disciplines. These constraints include expectations of content coverage, lack of instructor time, departmental norms related to valuing teaching, class size and layout, and the time structure of the academic calendar. Each of these constraints can impede faculty members' willingness to incorporate evidence-based instructional practices into STEM curricula (Henderson & Dancy,

2011). Faculty-focused interventions are necessary to improve teaching and learning in the STEM disciplines. Such interventions include promoting student-centered instruction, providing mini-grants and similar rewards for faculty to modify courses with more active learning strategies, and offering sustained professional development opportunities (Derting et al., 2016; Henry, 2010).

Finally, the ways in which changes in STEM educational practices are researched, disseminated, and adopted are functions of the vantage points from which they are investigated. STEM education researchers largely write about change in terms of *disseminating curriculum and pedagogy*, faculty development researchers write about change in terms of *developing reflective instructors*, and higher education researchers write about change in terms of *enacting or changing policy*. Ineffective change strategies include developing and testing so-called best practice curricular materials and then making them available to other faculty, especially through top-down approaches meant to influence instructional practices. Effective change strategies include those that are aligned with or seek to change individuals' beliefs, incorporate long-term interventions, require understanding a college or university as a complex system, and involve designing STEM instructional strategies that are compatible with this system (Henderson, Beach, & Finkelstein, 2011).

Recruiting and Retaining Students by Expanding and Diversifying the STEM Talent Pipeline

The United States's role as a STEM field leader, along with the nation's changing demographics, makes it uniquely qualified to address the challenges of achieving STEM field diversity (NRC, 2011a, 2011b). There are uneven numbers and shortages in specific STEM fields, there are STEM achievement gaps by gender and ethnicity, there is uneven access to STEM resources, and there is in many places a shortage of qualified P–12 STEM teachers. To determine what does and does not work in STEM outreach, instruction, and support efforts for diverse populations, assessment of teaching and learning practices and interventions is needed (Hagedorn & Purnamasari, 2012).

The majority of students who concentrate in STEM make that choice during high school as a result of interest in mathematics and science rather than achievement. Studies of course-taking patterns show that women complete more advanced coursework than men but are less likely to complete the most rigorous courses (Maltese & Tai, 2011). Wang (2013) reported that the choice of a STEM major is influenced by intent to major in STEM, high school math achievement, especially in 12th grade, and initial postsecondary experiences, such as academic interactions and access to financial aid. Intent to major in STEM is also affected by exposure to math and science courses, and math self-efficacy beliefs. Whalen and Shelley (2010) found that predictors of six-year retention and graduation rates for STEM majors included cumulative GPA for the last registered term, number of years living on campus while enrolled, and financial aid received.

Historically minoritized students earn college degrees in STEM fields at lower rates than do their majority peers (Museus & Liverman, 2010). While Black and Latinx students begin college interested in STEM majors at rates equal to or higher than their White peers, they are approximately 24% *less likely* than White students to earn a bachelor's degree in those fields within 6 years. Research similarly indicates that White and Asian students earned the majority of STEM degrees in the United States, but large gains were made in the numbers of women and members of minoritized groups earning degrees over the past 30 years. Gaps between underserved students and their White and Asian counterparts widen at the graduate and professional education levels (Museus & Liverman, 2010).

Evidence suggests that institutions of higher education have the ability to foster success of historically minoritized students in STEM. MacPhee, Farro, and Canetto (2013) conducted a longitudinal study examining academic self-efficacy and performance among STEM majors who are underserved in STEM education and occupations. The authors found increased academic self-efficacy at graduation among women and STEM-minority students (by ethnicity and/or socioeconomic status) who participated in a mentoring program—an indication, perhaps, of the positive impact of mentoring. Broadened diversity in STEM can also be encouraged by targeted faculty development and formal policies built on institutional commitment, engagement, and accountability, including recognizing equity-building initiatives as valid forms of faculty scholarship and as one way to address the educational disparities in STEM fields (Whittaker & Montgomery, 2014).

Other strategies that support increased diversity in STEM fields include summer bridge programs, tutoring, student research experiences, supplemental instruction and learning center support, career counseling and awareness, academic advising, financial support, and curriculum and instructional reform. Each of these requires the support of institutional leadership, engaged faculty, and ongoing assessment of effectiveness in supporting underserved students in STEM (Tsui, 2007). Additional institutional influences include the overall campus culture, holistic and integrated support systems, engagement in educationally purposeful activities, and efforts to foster students' sense of belonging to campus communities (Allen-Ramdial & Campbell,

2014; Museus & Liverman, 2010; Palmer, Davis, & Thompson, 2010; Whittaker & Montgomery, 2012).

Future Trends

Significant interest in STEM education by numerous stakeholders has resulted in ongoing investments in programs, services, interventions, and resources to serve STEM students in various disciplines and institutional contexts. Future trends in STEM education include integrated and interdisciplinary STEM curricula and a continuing focus on rigorous research and assessment practices.

Continuing Integration of STEM Concepts in the Curriculum

Interdisciplinary and *integrated* are two terms that are increasingly being applied to STEM education (Mohr-Schroeder et al., 2015). The National Academy of Engineering (NAE) and the NRC described a model in which goals for STEM students and faculty are clearly defined; outcomes for students and educators are clearly measurable; and the nature and scope of interdisciplinary integration fosters STEM connections, disciplinary expertise, attention to instructional design, and adjustments to the learning environment (NAE & NRC, 2014).

Integrated STEM education is an effort to combine disciplines into one learning context connected to real-world problems. Using relevant technologies, students participate in activities that require learning through integration and application of concepts from mathematics and science. Instructional strategies include cooperative learning, research projects, and challenges that ask students to solve real or simulated problems. These integrated learning approaches are often referred to as problem- or project-based learning (Moore & Smith, 2014).

Kelley and Knowles (2016), for example, proposed a framework for STEM education focusing on an integrated system. *Engineering design* provides the opportunity to locate intersections and build connections among the STEM disciplines. *Scientific inquiry* prepares students to think and act like real scientists, ask questions, hypothesize, and conduct investigations using scientific practices. *Technological literacy* compels educators to provide students opportunities to think about technology's impacts on society. *Mathematical thinking* provides the rationale for students to learn mathematics through connections between what is learned in the classroom and what is required in STEM careers.

Finally, the creative arts are increasingly being incorporated into integrated STEM curricula. Calls for relabeling STEM to STEAM (science, technology, engineering, *arts*, and mathematics) derive from the reported lack of innovative thinking among recent college graduates in the United States. Researchers have argued that progress comes from melding technology with creative thinking through art and design. Higher education will likely see more dual-degree programs and integrated courses drawing on both the creative arts and the STEM disciplines (Connor, Karmokar, & Whittington, 2015; Land, 2013).

Continuing Focus on Rigorous Research and Assessment Practices

Given prior investments, current needs, and anticipated demand for STEM graduates, STEM education must continue to improve. Ongoing improvement will depend and thrive on assessment of the outcomes of various learning interventions. The need for continued assessment has been spurred, in part, by requirements for evaluation of federally funded education grants, coupled with calls by national STEM associations for more widespread adoption of evidence-based pedagogies. Such work has and will continue to involve numerous stakeholders, including instructors, students, teaching assistants, tutors, administrative staff, academic leaders, and educational researchers.

To examine where STEM education needs to progress, Dolan and colleagues (2018) describe the following distinct yet related approaches to generating and using evidence:

- *Scholarly teaching* refers to teaching in ways consistent with research on learning, with little intention of sharing the data beyond the classroom (Angelo & Cross, 1993).
- The *Scholarship of Teaching and Learning* extends scholarly teaching beyond the private environment of the classroom to the public domain through sharing and peer critique, bringing a level of systematic inquiry and professionalism to improving instruction (Shulman, 2001).
- *Educational evaluation* determines the merit, worth, value, or impact of a program or an intervention, with the goal of informing action (Scriven, 2003).
- *Discipline-based educational research* pursues research questions and hypotheses about teaching, learning, and ways of thinking in a discipline that extend beyond single classrooms and programs to yield original and generalizable insights into educational processes and their effects (Dolan et al., 2018).

Each of these approaches shares goals of rigorous inquiry in STEM education, even though they may be employed for different purposes. Moreover, each approach facilitates the evolution of assessment in STEM education by focusing on the use of evidence in designing and improving instructional strategies to attract, educate, and graduate an increasingly diverse population of STEM learners.

Conclusion

STEM education assessment has focused on a long-standing, yet still growing, need to produce college graduates capable of adapting to changes in the increasingly interdisciplinary STEM fields. Assessment has provided significant evidence of how STEM learning occurs, the conditions that foster student success, and the interventions needed to recruit and retain students, especially those historically underserved by STEM. Articulating goals for learning, connecting those goals to evidence-based practices, assessing outcomes, and encouraging widespread adoption of proven practices will help to meet needs for continuing improvement. Integration of STEM content with that of other disciplines, especially the creative arts, will better prepare students for real-world contexts. STEM educators should increasingly value and rely on use of evidence, building on existing knowledge of interventions and practices, to enhance the educational experiences of STEM students and improve the quality of STEM courses, programs, and learning environments. If higher education can address these issues effectively, the STEM disciplines will have the potential to play a leading role in the continued evolution of assessment and improvement in higher education.

Summary of Main Trends

- International competitiveness, demand for STEM labor, and advances in science and technology throughout society demand enhanced goals and effective assessment practices for STEM learning.
- Considerable investment and research have been devoted to STEM education, resulting in numerous promising practices and enhancing our understanding of STEM student learning and success. Adoption of evidence-based pedagogies and changes in STEM curricula is essential for courses and programs to remain relevant.
- To meet needs for a STEM-educated workforce, courses and programs must successfully recruit and retain STEM students. This means

expanding and diversifying the talent pipeline to attract those who have historically been underserved by STEM disciplines.

- Finding innovative solutions to real-world challenges will require integrated, interdisciplinary STEM curricula, including opportunities for students to engage in collaborative, creative, and project-based learning.
- Meaningful improvement in STEM education will continue to rely on rigorous research and assessment practices to inform implementation and scaling of interventions shown to enhance STEM student learning.

Questions for Discussion

- What STEM learning goals should colleges and universities adopt? In what ways can such goals be implemented and assessed?
- How can faculty and staff incorporate evidence-based promising practices into courses, programs, and learning environments? What strategies are useful to encourage adoption across STEM disciplines?
- How can STEM continue to broaden and diversify the pipeline of students drawn to STEM fields? How can STEM disciplines do a better job of attracting, retaining, and educating those who have been historically underserved by STEM programs?
- What kinds of evidence of STEM learning are needed to satisfy the demands of various audiences, purposes, and uses? When, how, and where can such evidence be sought?

We want to hear from you about *Trends in Assessment*:

- Provide reactions or suggestions about trends.
- Share and access resources related to trends.
- Learn about professional development opportunities related to trends.

Visit assessmentinstitute.iupui.edu/trends

References

Allen-Ramdial, S. A., & Campbell, A. G. (2014). Reimagining the pipeline: Advancing STEM diversity, persistence, and success. *BioScience, 64*(7), 612–618.

Angelo, T. A., & Cross, K. P. (1993). *Classroom assessment techniques: A handbook for college teachers.* San Francisco, CA: Jossey-Bass.

Auchincloss, L. C., Laursen, S. L., Branchaw, J. L., Eagan, K., Graham, M., Hanauer, D. I., . . . Dolan, E. L. (2014). Assessment of course-based undergraduate research experiences: A meeting report. *CBE: Life Sciences Education, 13*(1), 29–40.

Borrego, M., & Henderson, C. (2014). Increasing the use of evidence-based teaching in STEM higher education: A comparison of eight change strategies. *Journal of Engineering Education, 103*(2), 220–252.

Bybee, R. W. (2010). Advancing STEM education: A 2020 vision. *Technology and Engineering Teacher, 70*(1), 30.

Connor, A. M., Karmokar, S., & Whittington, C. (2015). From STEM to STEAM: Strategies for enhancing engineering and technology education. *International Journal of Engineering Pedagogy, 5*(2), 37–47.

Derting, T. L., Ebert-May, D., Henkel, T. P., Maher, J. M., Arnold, B., & Passmore, H. A. (2016). Assessing faculty professional development in STEM higher education: Sustainability of outcomes. *Science Advances, 2*(3), e1501422.

Dolan, E. L., Elliott, S. L., Henderson, C., Curran-Everett, D., John, K. S., & Ortiz, P. A. (2018). Evaluating discipline-based education research for promotion and tenure. *Innovative Higher Education, 43*(1), 31–39.

Ejiwale, J. A. (2012). Facilitating teaching and learning across STEM fields. *Journal of STEM Education: Innovations and Research, 13*(3), 87.

Fairweather, J. (2008). *Linking evidence and promising practices in science, technology, engineering, and mathematics (STEM) undergraduate education.* Washington, DC: Board of Science Education, National Research Council, the National Academies.

Freeman, S., Eddy, S. L., McDonough, M., Smith, M. K., Okoroafor, N., Jordt, H., & Wenderoth, M. P. (2014). Active learning increases student performance in science, engineering, and mathematics. *Proceedings of the National Academy of Sciences, 111*(23), 8410–8415.

Froyd, J. E. (2008). *White paper on promising practices in undergraduate STEM education.* Commissioned paper for the Evidence on Promising Practices in Undergraduate Science, Technology, Engineering, and Mathematics (STEM) Education Project, the National Academies Board on Science Education.

Froyd, J. E., Wankat, P. C., & Smith, K. A. (2012). Five major shifts in 100 years of engineering education. *Proceedings of the IEEE, 100*, 1344–1360.

Gasiewski, J. A., Eagan, M. K., Garcia, G. A., Hurtado, S., & Chang, M. J. (2012). From gatekeeping to engagement: A multicontextual, mixed method study of student academic engagement in introductory STEM courses. *Research in Higher Education, 53*(2), 229–261.

Gonzalez, H. B., & Kuenzi, J. J. (2012, August). *Science, technology, engineering, and mathematics (STEM) education: A primer.* Washington, DC: Congressional Research Service, Library of Congress.

Hagedorn, L. S., & Purnamasari, A. V. (2012). A realistic look at STEM and the role of community colleges. *Community College Review, 40*(2), 145–164.

Henderson, C., Beach, A., & Finkelstein, N. (2011). Facilitating change in under-graduate STEM instructional practices: An analytic review of the literature. *Journal of Research in Science Teaching, 48*(8), 952–984.

Henderson, C., & Dancy, M. H. (2011, February). *Increasing the impact and diffusion of STEM education innovations.* Invited paper for the National Academy of Engineering, Center for the Advancement of Engineering Education Forum, Impact and Diffusion of Transformative Engineering Education Innovations. Retrieved from http://www.nae.edu

Henry, R. J. (2010). An assessment of STEM faculty involvement in reform of introductory college courses. *Journal of College Science Teaching, 39*(6), 74–81.

Kelley, T. R., & Knowles, J. G. (2016). A conceptual framework for integrated STEM education. *International Journal of STEM Education, 3*(1), 11.

Kennedy, T. J., & Odell, M. R. L. (2014). Engaging students in STEM education. *Science Education International, 25*(3), 246–258.

Labov, J. B., Singer, S. R., George, M. D., Schweingruber, H. A., & Hilton, M. L. (2009). Effective practices in undergraduate STEM education: Part 1. Examining the evidence. *CBE: Life Sciences Education, 8*(3), 157–161.

Land, M. H. (2013). Full STEAM ahead: The benefits of integrating the arts into STEM. *Procedia Computer Science, 20,* 547–552.

MacPhee, D., Farro, S., & Canetto, S. S. (2013). Academic self-efficacy and performance of underrepresented STEM majors: Gender, ethnic, and social class patterns. *Analyses of Social Issues and Public Policy, 13*(1), 347–369.

Maltese, A. V., & Tai, R. H. (2011). Pipeline persistence: Examining the association of educational experiences with earned degrees in STEM among U.S. students. *Science Education, 95*(5), 877–907.

Mohr-Schroeder, M. J., Cavalcanti, M., & Blyman, K. (2015). STEM education: Understanding the changing landscape. In A. Sahin (Ed.), *A practice-based model of STEM teaching* (pp. 3–14). Rotterdam, the Netherlands: Sense Publishers.

Moore, T. J., & Smith, K. A. (2014). Advancing the state of the art of STEM integration. *Journal of STEM Education: Innovations and Research, 15*(1), 5.

Museus, S. D., & Liverman, D. (2010). High-performing institutions and their implications for studying underrepresented minority students in STEM. *New Directions for Institutional Research, 2010*(148), 17–27.

National Academy of Engineering and National Research Council. (2014). *STEM integration in K–12 education: Status, prospects, and agenda for research.* Washington, DC: National Academies Press.

National Research Council. (2011a). *Expanding underrepresented minority participation: America's science and technology talent at the crossroads.* Washington, DC: National Academies Press.

National Research Council. (2011b). *Successful STEM education: A workshop summary.* Washington, DC: National Academies Press.

Organisation for Economic Co-operation and Development. (2006). *Assessing scientific, reading and mathematical literacy: A framework for PISA 2006.* Paris, France: Author.

Palmer, R. T., Davis, R. J., & Thompson, T. (2010). Theory meets practice: HBCU initiatives that promote academic success among African Americans in STEM. *Journal of College Student Development, 51*(4), 440–443.

Prados, J. W., Peterson, G. D., & Lattuca, L. R. (2005). Quality assurance of engineering education through accreditation: The impact of Engineering Criteria 2000 and its global influence. *Journal of Engineering Education, 94*(1), 165–184.

Project Kaleidoscope. (2017). *Project Kaleidoscope strategic plan*. Washington, DC: Association of American Colleges & Universities.

Scriven, M. (2003). Evaluation theory and metatheory. In T. Kellaghan, D. L. Stufflebeam, & L. A. Wingate (Eds.), *International handbook of educational evaluation* (pp. 15–30). Dordrecht, the Netherlands: Springer.

Seymour, E., & Hewitt, N. (1997). *Talking about leaving: Why undergraduates leave the sciences*. Boulder, CO: Westview Press.

Shulman, L. (2001). From Minsk to Pinsk: Why a Scholarship of Teaching and Learning? *Journal of the Scholarship of Teaching and Learning, 1*(1), 48–53.

Smith, K. A., Douglas, T. C., & Cox, M. F. (2009). Supportive teaching and learning strategies in STEM education. *New Directions for Teaching and Learning, 2009*(117), 19–32.

Strayhorn, T. L. (2010). Undergraduate research participation and STEM graduate degree aspirations among students of color. *New Directions for Institutional Research, 2010*(148), 85–93.

Tsui, L. (2007). Effective strategies to increase diversity in STEM fields: A review of the research literature. *Journal of Negro Education, 76*(4), 555–581.

Wang, X. (2013). Why students choose STEM majors: Motivation, high school learning, and postsecondary context of support. *American Educational Research Journal, 50*(5), 1081–1121.

Whalen, D. F., & Shelley, M. C. (2010). Academic success for STEM and non-STEM majors. *Journal of STEM Education, 11*(1–2), 45.

Whittaker, J. A., & Montgomery, B. L. (2012). Cultivating diversity and competency in STEM: Challenges and remedies for removing virtual barriers to constructing diverse higher education communities of success. *Journal of Undergraduate Neuroscience Education, 11*(1), A44.

Whittaker, J. A., & Montgomery, B. L. (2014). Cultivating institutional transformation and sustainable STEM diversity in higher education through integrative faculty development. *Innovative Higher Education, 39*(4), 263–275.

Wilson, S. B., & Varma-Nelson, P. (2016). Small groups, significant impact: A review of peer-led team learning research with implications for STEM education researchers and faculty. *Journal of Chemical Education, 93*(10), 1686–1702.

ASSESSMENT AT THE
HIGHEST DEGREE(S)

Trends in Graduate and Professional Education

Sarah B. Zahl, Sherry Jimenez, and Max Huffman

Today, outcomes assessment is more widely practiced in graduate and professional programs than it was in the past, with attention focused primarily on competencies and minimum professional standards for graduates. For those graduate and professional disciplines new to assessment, recent adoption results partly from shifting expectations within professional work environments but mostly from evolving accreditation standards. Like undergraduate programs, graduate and professional programs are subject to regional accreditation, but these accreditors have traditionally scrutinized them less closely than their undergraduate counterparts. Instead, disciplinary accrediting bodies have been the primary drivers of assessment and improvement efforts across graduate and professional education. These accreditors' levels of emphasis on outcomes assessment vary, however; some accrediting bodies have required evidence of outcomes assessment for decades, while others have imposed requirements more recently.

Historically, most graduate and professional programs measured outcomes via summative assessments, such as licensure exams, dissertations, or research studies. While those assessment measures still dominate, recent trends emphasize outcomes such as professionalism, collaboration, and ethical decision-making, which are less easily assessed by traditional means. The current landscape thus includes varied summative, formative, and qualitative assessment approaches and frameworks.

In this chapter, we summarize assessment trends across graduate and professional education and highlight developments in specific disciplines.

Historical Background and Literature Review

While the most recent assessment efforts reflect calls for collaborative assessment across graduate and professional education, historical trends in specific disciplines provide the foundation for the practices shaping the current landscape. We begin with a focus on selected individual disciplines that have served as assessment exemplars and then move on to more comprehensive trends later in this section.

Professional programs have traditionally been deeply engaged in outcomes assessment mainly because of prescriptive accreditation standards and strict guidelines related to patient and client safety and responsible practices. While the disciplines we highlight first are professional ones, the best practices and trends we discuss can be implemented across all graduate programs.

Medicine

Dating back to the creation of the Council on Medical Education (CME) in 1904, governing bodies in medicine were among the first to require programs to meet specific standards and benchmarks of quality and effectiveness. These bodies include the Liaison Committee on Medical Education (LCME) and the Commission on Osteopathic College Accreditation (COCA), the accrediting agencies for doctor of medicine (MD) and doctor of osteopathic medicine (DO) schools, respectively, as well as other groups that have driven accountability and standardization across medical education.

Traditional accreditation standards in medicine focused chiefly on career placement and pass rates on licensure examinations as critical assessment outcomes. In 2010, however, *Educating Physicians: A Call for Reform of Medical School and Residency* (Cooke, Irby, & O'Brien, 2010) called for significant reform of the current assessment structures in U.S. medical education. The authors recommended standardizing learning outcomes, assessing critical inquiry and innovation, and focusing on professional identity formation. They emphasized the importance of a cohesive set of professional competencies across all medical programs and encouraged competency assessment across domains rather than viewing competencies as isolated achievements. This report acted as a catalyst for new accreditation standards and evidential support related to interprofessional education, self-directed learning, and practical intelligence and reasoning.

Dentistry

Like medical education, dentistry has early roots in professional accreditation and regulation of educational outcomes. Since 1938, a professional body of dental educators, now the Commission on Dental Accreditation (CODA), has served as the primary driver of program-level assessment and outcomes measurement (Commission on Dental Accreditation, 2018).

Over the past decade, dental education has employed assessment methods consistent with other professional disciplines, including clinical competency exams, lab practicals, multiple-choice assessments, and evaluation of procedural techniques (Albino et al., 2008). Like other health professions programs, graduate programs in dentistry have recently been called on to increase efforts to measure softer skills, such as communication, collaboration, and professional values, to ensure that graduates have "the ability to begin independent, unsupervised dental practice" (American Dental Education Association, 2011, p. 932).

Pharmacy

Pharmacy schools have also been early adopters of assessment of standards and educational outcomes, as required by the Accreditation Council for Pharmacy Education (ACPE; formerly American Council on Pharmaceutical Education), formed in 1932 (ACPE, 2015). Assessment in pharmacy education has focused on formative and summative tools to offer performance-based feedback to students throughout the curriculum.

More recently, pharmacy schools have placed greater emphasis on critical thinking as a key outcome for graduates, as evidenced by the increase of problem-based learning curricula and the exploration and implementation of critical-thinking inventories in many programs (Cisneros, 2008; Gleason et al., 2013; Peeters, Zitko, & Schmude, 2016).

The Center for the Advancement of Pharmacy Education (CAPE) has advocated curricular change across pharmacy education. The most recent CAPE report highlighted the need for increased focus on affective domains of assessment, including measurement of attitudes, skills, and values unique to the pharmacist's role (Medina et al., 2013).

Nursing

Nursing education is unique, with multiple accrediting bodies governing individual programs, increasing the challenges of aligning educational outcomes. Whereas pharmacy, medicine, and dentistry each leads to a single degree and license, nursing encompasses various credentials and curricula, allowing students to take several paths, depending on the level at which they choose to practice.

Because of this structure, multiple studies have emphasized the need for nurses to maximize their education and training through continuous quality improvement and continuity across the various programs and certifications (Benner, Sutphen, Leonard, & Day, 2009; Institute of Medicine, 2010;

Robert Wood Johnson Foundation, 2014). To this end, nursing education has strongly emphasized critical thinking and clinical competence in curricula to ensure that programs are producing high-performing nurses with bachelor's and advanced degrees (Ulfvarson & Oxelmark, 2011; Yanhua & Watson, 2011). As in pharmacy education, problem-based learning has recently been the most prominent method of teaching and assessing these critical thinking competencies (Carvalho et al., 2017).

The Commission on Collegiate Nursing Education emphasizes program quality and educational preparedness at all levels, including bachelor's, master's, and doctoral degrees; postgraduate certifications; and residency. Given the varied paths in nursing education, program effectiveness is measured by an institution's ability to analyze multiple data summaries to inform ongoing programmatic quality improvement (Commision on Collegiate Nursing Education, 2018).

Law

In legal education, the earliest academy-wide discussions of program assessment are frequently traced to a 1921 Carnegie Foundation report, *Training for the Public Profession of the Law* (Reed, 1921). Recent interest in program assessment has coincided with calls for increased training in legal skills. An influential text, *Best Practices for Legal Education: A Vision and a Road Map* (Stuckey, 2007), combined these emphases in a statement of best practices for curricular coverage, pedagogical approaches, and program-level assessment. Law schools have begun to enhance their practices according to three primary principles:

1. Preparing students to practice law effectively
2. Clearly articulating educational goals
3. Regularly evaluating the program of instruction

Like medical and nursing education, legal education was influenced by the *Carnegie Foundation's Preparation for the Professions* book series. *Educating Lawyers: Preparation for the Practice of Law* (Sullivan, Welch, Bond, & Shulman, 2007) called for further development of assessment tools that measure professionalism and practice readiness. The American Bar Association, which accredits law schools, responded with new accreditation standards requiring outcomes assessment. Legal education is moving rapidly toward adoption of outcomes assessment to ensure better teaching aligned with law school missions (Carpenter et al., 2008; Shepard, 2014).

Historical Trends Across Graduate and Professional Education

The nature of professional accrediting bodies and the disciplinary focus of graduate and professional education have been such that most changes to assessment measures and desired learning outcomes have historically occurred at the program level. But we can identify some key trends across programs.

Licensing Examinations as a Critical Measure of Program Outcomes

Most professions require licenses to practice. Because licensing exams are designed to be objective assessments of readiness to begin a career, pass rates on these exams are considered to be evidence of the transferability of a degree to professional practice. Thus, they have historically been used as external assessments of program effectiveness and comparability. Many disciplinary accrediting bodies require institutions to share pass rates as part of their accreditation standards (American Bar Assocation, 2015; American Council for Pharmacy Education, 2015; Commission on Osteopathic College Accreditation, 2017; Liasion Committee on Medical Education, 2018).

Empirical Research as an Outcome of Doctoral Education

Most nonprofessional doctoral programs require a research study or dissertation as the concluding measure of achievement and advancement to graduation. Although the project typically has a disciplinary focus, guidelines and assessment metrics are similar across disciplines. Historically, the dissertation has been understood as a direct indicator of the value of the degree because the research findings are typically shared with the larger disciplinary community.

Public Scrutiny of Debt Outcomes and Return on Investment

While some disciplinary accrediting bodies have only recently required institutions to track student debt outcomes (Commission on Osteopathic College Accreditation, 2017), public scrutiny of the increasing costs of higher education began decades ago. Governmental agencies have increased accountability standards in response to public concerns, particularly in professions with lower salaries such as education, where graduate degrees have historically been required for practice (in some states) or even for small salary increases (National Council on Teacher Quality, 2018).

These historical practices have been catalysts for change and influenced the current landscape and trends across graduate and professional education.

Current Trends

As in undergraduate programs, compliance and improvement continue to be the main drivers for assessment in graduate and professional education (Jankowski, Timmer, Kinzie, & Kuh, 2018). Today, many graduate and professional programs are evaluated by both professional accrediting bodies and their parent institution's regional accrediting group. This dual accountability can be difficult for some programs because they must layer their outcomes assessment to provide evidence for both groups. In addition, the U.S. Department of Education (USDE) has recently increased accountability requirements for professional accrediting bodies as part of a more widespread public scrutiny of higher education. While USDE oversight is not new for professional accrediting bodies (Palomba & Banta, 2001), intensified accountability requirements ultimately trickle down through the professional accreditors to individual programs.

Accountability

While higher education as a whole is increasingly under scrutiny to demonstrate the value of obtaining a degree (Banta, Ewell, & Cogswell, 2016), graduate and professional education is perhaps even more closely monitored because of the additional debt students accrue when they pursue advanced degrees. These general accountability issues, paired with concerns about patient and client safety and practice readiness, have significantly increased expectations for outcomes assessment across graduate and professional education.

In response to the call for greater accountability, programs in the health professions are seeking to measure entrustable professional activities (EPAs). Originally developed in response to concerns about performance gaps between medical school and residency training (and ultimately patient safety), EPAs are tasks that can be entrusted to a trainee once sufficient competence is attained to ensure that the tasks can be carried out in unsupervised settings (ten Cate, 2013). Distinct from competencies, EPAs comprise combinations of competencies (knowledge, skills, and attitudes) that students achieve progressively. Although accrediting bodies in the health professions have not yet mandated the assessment of EPAs, many programs in medicine, pharmacy, and dentistry are in the early phases of mapping the EPAs to curricular outcomes. Assessment of EPAs has been a recent theme at annual conferences such as the Assessment Institute in Indianapolis, the American Association of Colleges of Osteopathic Medicine, and the Association of American Medical Colleges.

Collaboration and Professional Formation

Although interdisciplinary education has been discussed in the health professions literature for more than 40 years (Institute of Medicine, 1972), its conceptualization as *interprofessional education* (IPE) has only recently gained traction. Recent IPE initiatives were created in response to *To Err Is Human: Building a Safer Health System* (Institute of Medicine, 2000), which concluded that 44,000 to 98,000 preventable deaths occurred in hospitals each year because of medical error and communication failures resulting from fragmented delivery of health care.

The report raised awareness across the health professions, and subsequent studies (Institute of Medicine, 2001, 2003; World Health Organization, 2010) focused on the potential benefits of redesigning healthcare training environments to enhance the team approach to patient care. The World Health Organization (2010) further studied the implications of this practice for improvement and made a compelling case for the value of this design across health professions education.

Shortly thereafter, programs in medicine, nursing, pharmacy, and dentistry began implementing new IPE programming and developed assessment mechanisms to measure the impact of this practice. Accrediting bodies began requiring evidence of IPE assessment data in self-study documents and reports (Zorek & Raehl, 2013). Dental schools have been particularly engaged in the implementation of IPE assessment. A recent IPE survey by the American Dental Education Association yielded a response rate of 86% of U.S. and Canadian dental schools (Formicola et al., 2012). Although the level of implementation varies, interest in IPE is clearly very high.

To support the advancement of curricula focused on collaborative practice, six national education associations founded the Interprofessional Education Collaborative (IPEC) in 2009. Representing medicine, dentistry, nursing, pharmacy, public health, and osteopathy, IPEC representatives created core competencies to guide health professions education toward developing graduates who are better equipped to work together to improve patient care outcomes (Berwick, Nolan, & Whittington, 2008). The primary IPEC competency domains include ethics, roles and responsibilities, interprofessional communication, and teamwork (Interprofessional Education Collaborative, 2016). As of 2017, 20 professional organizations were represented in IPEC.

Analogous advances are occurring in graduate programs outside the health professions. For example, in addition to typical outcomes related to knowledge and its application, the Accreditation Board for Engineering and Technology (ABET) now requires evidence of competencies in teamwork, ethics, professionalism, communication, and commitment to lifelong learning (Accreditation Board for Engineering and Technology, 2018). Similarly, the American Bar Association's (2015) publication *Standards: 2018–2019 Standards and Rules of Procedure for Approval of Law Schools* includes communication, professional and ethical responsibilities, and general competence in "other professional skills."

While accreditation standards mandate outcomes assessment, professional schools have the flexibility to conduct assessment in various ways. Emerging literature points to a need for validation of assessment tools (Douglas & Purzer, 2015) and guidance for reporting and facilitating evidence-based changes (Hatfield & Gorman, 2000). Graduate and professional education are also increasingly trending toward assessing professional formation, but the operational strategies and best practices for assessing these outcomes have yet to be determined in many fields.

Proposed Doctoral Framework

The continued trends toward increased accountability and interest in professional formation highlight a need for a cohesive approach to outcomes assessment across graduate and professional education. While the undergraduate world includes various projects and approaches to measuring foundational outcomes across all programs—for example, the Lumina Foundation's Degree Qualifications Profile and Tuning USA Project and the Valid Assessment of Learning in Undergraduate Education (VALUE) rubrics of the Association of American Colleges & Universities (AAC&U)—such organized efforts are slower to emerge in graduate education.

In 2016, the Council for Graduate Schools conducted a research project on the development of doctoral learning outcomes and competency frameworks. *Articulating Learning Outcomes in Doctoral Education* (Denecke, Kent, & McCarthy, 2017) summarizes current trends toward increased scrutiny from accrediting bodies and efforts to enhance accountability and transferability of doctoral degrees. Key recommendations include moving beyond traditional disciplinary focuses into a foundational outcomes framework to measure outcomes across doctoral programs. Like the undergraduate and master's Degree Qualifications Profile (DQP), a doctoral DQP should include doctoral and professional degrees within the same framework to measure transferable skills, such as the following:

- Knowledge
- Intellectual skills

- Collaborative and applied learning
- Civic and global engagement

While there is a great need for an integrative approach to assessment in graduate and professional education, implementing such a framework will be a difficult task. Similar initiatives in other countries have seen varying levels of success. The Ontario Qualifications Framework (Canada) mandated that all universities establish clear expectations for all degree levels, including doctoral programs. The framework has been in operation for nine years and has been broadly successful with minimal resistance (Ontario Ministry, 2009). Conversely, the Bologna Process and the European Qualifications Framework have been challenging, with deployment at the doctoral level suffering from "structural barriers" (Denecke et al., 2017, p. 13). Similarly, the Swedish National Qualifications Framework was originally articulated in 2008, but implementation had not yet reached the doctoral level as of 2016.

Despite the anticipated challenges of an organized assessment framework at the doctoral level, this initiative is likely to gain traction in the near future.

Future Trends

Emerging literature provides several key indicators of potential new assessment trends and supports the continuation of current trends across graduate and professional education.

Accountability

As noted by Denecke and colleagues (2017), graduate and professional programs will continue to face increased scrutiny from the public and accrediting bodies in the future. To address those issues, programs must continue to adopt appropriate assessment structures and produce data that demonstrate the value of pursuing additional education (and accruing additional debt).

Calls for greater educational accountability will become even louder in professions experiencing structural change. For example, the recent increased focus on law school assessment is a direct result of the crisis in enrollment and the recessionary decline in employment outcomes for law school graduates. Legal education is expected to continue to require evidence of achievement of learning outcomes, with an increased focus on such outcomes as professionalism and lifelong learning.

Collaboration and Professional Formation

The continued focus on accountability and return on investment will generate pressure on graduate and professional programs to create authentic forms of assessment to show how students develop transferable skills relevant for practice and professional formation.

In professional programs, accreditation standards will likely be revised to require assessment of the EPAs. Because they measure critical elements of employability (e.g., communication, critical inquiry, and relevant skills for practice), evidence of student attainment of the EPAs speaks to the value and transferability of the degree program in question. Professional accrediting agencies will thus rely on these data to address the increased pressures they are facing from the USDE.

Because the EPAs offer the clearest opportunities for collaborative assessment across graduate and professional disciplines, it is very likely that emerging projects, such as *Articulating Learning Outcomes in Doctoral Education* (Denecke et al., 2017), will include professional formation as an area of focus. This focus will likely lead to additional forms of IPE across various disciplines, an effort that may be extended to include graduate programs in business, law, engineering, education, and even some liberal arts disciplines. All careers require some form of group work and collaboration, so graduate and professional programs will need clearer alignment of assessment outcomes with expectations in the professional settings where graduates will work.

Finally, accreditation standards in professional programs will increasingly require evidence of IPE activities and outcomes. While IPE standards are already required for accreditation in medicine and dentistry, these requirements are just beginning to emerge in other health professions and various graduate disciplines (Zorek & Raehl, 2013). It is also likely that traditional accreditation standards that fall under this umbrella (e.g., group work, collaboration, leadership) will be relabeled as IPE to follow this assessment trend.

Conclusion

Administrators, faculty, and students will be affected by the current and emerging assessment trends across graduate and professional education. Considering the current and future landscape, we are proposing two key recommendations.

Standardize Learning Outcomes

While there have recently been calls for a cohesive set of outcomes across graduate and professional education, programs continue to use varied assessment approaches and frameworks. Undergraduate models typically include general education outcomes, but graduate and professional programs have not embraced this approach. Traditional disciplinary frameworks for outcomes assessment in graduate and professional education run counter to the collaborative and integrative practices that graduates will experience in real-world professional scenarios. These frameworks also maintain assessment siloes and contribute to a lack of communication about the achievement of fundamental competencies required for any profession (e.g., communication, group work, ethics).

Although it may not be possible to completely standardize learning outcomes at the graduate level, it would be quite valuable to develop a set of common minimum outcomes and/or competencies expected of all graduate and professional students by graduation. As suggested by Denecke and colleagues (2017), a doctoral-level DQP would provide a useful framework to assess widely applicable foundational outcomes, such as knowledge, intellectual skills, collaborative learning, and civic and global engagement. Graduate and professional degrees must build on the foundational specialized knowledge accrued in undergraduate programs and require students to develop additional broad, applicable skills for practice.

While developing a doctoral framework would be a daunting task, similar tools have already been used and vetted extensively at the undergraduate and master's level; expanding their scope to the doctoral level would be an appropriate next step. Suggestions are presented in the following sections.

Expanding the DQP

The DQP (Lumina Foundation, 2018) already includes master's-level outcomes in five broadly defined categories. Just as the master's degree outcomes build on the bachelor's degree outcomes, why not use the already defined master's outcomes as the basis for creating doctoral outcomes? This seems to be a logical next step. Expectations at greater levels of depth and achievement would need to be defined and described.

Building on the AAC&U VALUE Rubrics

Although the VALUE rubrics were originally designed for undergraduate assessment, the learning outcomes they address are applicable to graduate and professional programs as well. Outcomes in critical thinking, ethical reasoning, lifelong learning, and civic engagement are particularly relevant to and align with current assessment trends in professional programs. The existing rubrics could be redesigned to require deeper levels of engagement for students in graduate and professional education.

Enhance the Focus on Professional Formation Outcomes

Professional formation outcomes have been increasingly emphasized in graduate and professional education recently, and it is clear that these outcomes will continue as a key focus in the next few years. Increasingly, graduates will be expected to be specialists and generalists at the same time. Professional skills in communication, collaboration, professionalism, and ethics will become even more critical as team-based approaches continue to prevail in workplace environments.

These outcomes should be emphasized and pursued in combination with related initiatives already occurring in professional and interprofessional organizations, such as IPEC. IPEC is already expanding its reach to additional partners in the health professions; this effort is crucial to preparing future health professionals for effective practice. Authentic assessment aims to mimic actual practice scenarios as much as possible; bringing other graduate and professional programs into the fold will help to enhance authenticity.

But while assessment of collaborative practices is increasing across graduate and professional education, "already overcrowded curricula in health professions schools, lack of support from faculty and administration, and financial constraints" (Rafter et al., 2006, p. 417) may create obstacles to further incorporating interprofessional initiatives. Truly interprofessional curricula require specific experiences that can be difficult to simulate in educational settings; designing authentic educational experiences that mimic true practice is thus a significant challenge (Victoroff et al., 2014).

Furthermore, because many professional formation outcomes involve the affective domain, assessment in this area will require approaches different from traditional assessment practices in the cognitive domain. Increased emphasis on these softer skills may present unique challenges for programs in the hard sciences. Training and guidance for faculty and administrators will thus be vitally important. Presenters at the Assessment Institute have begun to tackle this subject, providing concrete examples of assessing these skills in educational settings, but additional specific and practical recommendations are needed.

Resources key to this undertaking are included in the IPEC report and in the National Center for Interprofessional Education's "Nexus" online resources. More institutions should incentivize faculty to take advantage of these resources and engage in the development opportunities they provide. Moreover, while assessment instruments that measure different competencies and subcompetencies surrounding collaborative practice abound, evidence of these instruments' validity and applicability has not yet been provided. Further research is recommended to validate the tools and document best practices.

These recommendations might best be implemented through an interprofessional accreditation advisory group composed of representatives from all recognized accrediting bodies. In terms of participation and goals, such a group would extend the existing Health Professions Accreditors Collaborative (HPAC). This suggestion parallels the recommendation to expand the reach of IPEC. The advisory group would serve as a forum for sharing best practices in accreditation but would target the larger goal of developing harmonized standards. Such harmonization would be most effective in areas of commonality, such as professional formation. It would also facilitate the expansion of IPE across multiple fields.

An interprofessional accreditation advisory group would offer a further benefit: providing a voice for change and improvement in professional education and practice not beholden to any individual profession. It would thus emulate the success of the Carnegie Foundation's contributions to professional education, allowing standards to be updated and improved on a continuous, rather than periodic, basis. By bringing together a variety of peer professions, the advisory group would increase collaboration and engagement in assessment and accreditation practices across the professions.

Summary of Main Trends

- Accreditation standards will persist as the main driver of assessment, accountability, and quality assurance in graduate and professional programs, as they continue to encounter increased scrutiny from the public and accrediting bodies.
- The push for assessment of practical professional knowledge, skills, and dispositions will continue as consumers seek additional indicators of value and transferability.
- Authentic assessment methods to measure professional formation will be increasingly important.
- Leaders of graduate and professional programs are mobilizing to create a foundational set of learning outcomes common to all disciplines, similar to existing undergraduate models.

Questions for Discussion

- What are the major historical factors contributing to heightened monitoring of graduate and professional programs?
- What are the similarities between IPEC competencies and professional formation outcomes prevalent in other graduate and professional programs?
- What are the challenges to integration and assessment of interprofessional competencies and professional formation in graduate and professional programs?
- Based on emerging literature, what future trends are likely to shape assessment of graduate and professional programs?

We want to hear from you about *Trends in Assessment*:

- Provide reactions or suggestions about trends.
- Share and access resources related to trends.
- Learn about professional development opportunities related to trends.

Visit assessmentinstitute.iupui.edu/trends

References

Accreditation Board for Engineering and Technology. (2018). *Criteria for accrediting engineering programs.* Baltimore, MD: Author. Retrieved from https://www .abet.org/accreditation/accreditation-criteria/criteria-for-accrediting-engineering -programs-2018-2019/

Accreditation Council for Pharmacy Education. (2015). *Accreditation standards and key elements for the professional program in pharmacy leading to the doctor of pharmacy degree ("Standards 2016").* Chicago, IL: Author. Retrieved from https:// www.acpe-accredit.org/pdf/Standards2016FINAL.pdf

Albino, J. E., Young, S. K., Neumann, L. M., Kramer, G. A., Andrieu, S. C., Henson, L., . . . Hendricson, W. D. (2008). Assessing dental students' competence: Best practice recommendations in the performance assessment literature and investigation of current practices in predoctoral dental education. *Journal of Dental Education, 1405–1435.*

American Bar Association. (2015). *Standards: 2018–2019 standards and rules of procedure for approval of law schools.* Chicago, IL: Author. Retrieved from https:// www.americanbar.org/groups/legal_education/resources/standards/

American Dental Education Association. (2011). ADEA competencies for the new general dentist. *Journal of Dental Education, 75*(7), 932–935.

Banta, T. W., Ewell, P. T., & Cogswell, C. A. (2016). *Tracing assessment practice as reflected in Assessment Update* (NILOA Occasional Paper No. 28). Urbana, IL: University of Illinois and Indiana University, National Institute for Learning Outcomes Assessment.

Benner, P., Sutphen, M., Leonard, V., & Day, L. (2009). *Educating nurses: A call for radical transformation.* San Francisco, CA: Jossey-Bass.

Berwick, D. M., Nolan, T. W., & Whittington, J. (2008). The triple aim: Care, health, and cost. *Health Affairs (Millwood),* 759–769.

Carpenter, C. C., Davis, M. J., Hafter, J. C., Harbaugh, J. D., Hertz, R., Johnson, C.,...Worthen, K. J. (2008). *Report of the outcomes measures committee.* Chicago, IL: American Bar Association.

Carvalho, D. P. S. R. P., Azevedo, I. C., Cruz, G. K. P., Mafra. G. A. C., Rego, A. L. C., Vitor, A. F., . . . Cogo, A. L. P. (2017). Strategies used for the promotion of critical thinking in nursing undergraduate education: A systematic review. *Nurse Education Today,* 103–109.

Cisneros, R. (2008). Assessment of critical thinking in pharmacy students. *American Journal of Pharmaceutical Education,* 1–7.

Commission on Collegiate Nursing Education. (2018). CCNE standards and professional nursing guidelines. Retrieved from https://www.aacnnursing.org/Portals/42/CCNE/PDF/Procedures.pdf

Commission on Dental Accreditation. (2018). *Accreditation standards for dental education programs.* Chicago, IL: Author. Retrieved from https://www.ada.org/-/media/CODA/Files/pde.pdf?la=en

Commission on Osteopathic College Accreditation. (2017). *Accreditation of Colleges of Osteopathic Medicine: COM Accreditation Standards and Procedures.* Retrieved from https://osteopathic.org/accreditation/standards/

Cooke, M., Irby, D. M., & O'Brien, B. (2010). *Educating physicians: A call for reform of medical school and residency.* San Francisco, CA: Jossey-Bass.

Denecke, D., Kent, J., & McCarthy, M.T. (2017). *Articulating learning outcomes in doctoral education.* Washington, DC: Council of Graduate Schools.

Douglas, K. A., & Purzer, S. (2015). Validity: Meaning and relevancy in assessment for engineering education research. *Journal of Engineering Education, 104* (ISSUE), 108–118.

Formicola, A. J., Andieu, S. C., Buchanan, J. A., Schneider Childs, G., Gibbs, M., Inglehart, M. R., . . . Evans, L. (2012). Interprofessional education in U.S. and Canadian dental schools: An ADEA team study report. *Journal of Dental Education,* 1250–1268.

Gleason, B. L., Gaebelein, C. J., Grice, G. R., Crannage, A. J., Weck, M. A., Hurd, P., . . . Duncan, W. (2013). Assessment of students' critical-thinking and problem solving abilities across a 6-year doctor of pharmacy program. *American Journal of Pharmaceutical Education,* 1–12.

Hatfield, S. R. & Gorman, K. L. (2000). Assessment in education: The past, present, and future. In J. Rucker (Ed.), *Assessment in business education* (pp. 1–10). Reston, VA: National Business Education Association.

Institute of Medicine. (1972). *Educating for the health team.* Washington, DC: National Academy of Sciences.

Institute of Medicine. (2000). *To err is human: Building a safer health system.* Washington, DC: National Academy of Sciences.

Institute of Medicine. (2001). *Crossing the quality chasm: A new health system for the 21st century.* Washington, DC: National Academy Press.

Institute of Medicine. (2003). *Health professions education: A bridge to quality.* Washington, DC: National Academy Press.

Institute of Medicine. (2010). *The future of nursing: Leading change, advancing health.* Washington, DC: National Academy Press.

Interprofessional Education Collaborative. (2016). *Core competencies for interprofessional collaborative practice: 2016 update.* Washington, DC: Author.

Jankowski, N., Timmer, J.D., Kinzie, J., & Kuh, G.D. (2018). *Assessment that matters: Trending toward practices that document authentic student learning.* Urbana, IL: University of Illinois and Indiana University, National Institute for Learning Outcomes Assessment.

Liaison Committee on Medical Education. (2018). Functions and structure of a medical school. Retrieved from http://lcme.org/publications/#Standards

Lumina Foundation (2018). Degree Qualifications Profile. Indianapolis, IN. Retrieved from https://www.luminafoundation.org/files/resources/dqp.pdf

Medina, M. S., Plaza, C. M., Stowe, C. D., Robinson, E. T., DeLander, G., Beck, D. E., . . . Johnston, P. (2013). Center for the Advancement of Pharmacy Education 2013 educational outcomes. *American Journal of Pharmaceutical Education*, 1–10.

National Council on Teacher Quality. (n.d.). Retrieved from https://www.nctq.org/contract-database/home

Ontario Ministry of Advanced Education and Skills Development. (2009). Ontario Qualifications Framework. Retrieved from http://www.tcu.gov.on.ca/pepg/programs/oqf/

Palomba, C. A., & Banta, T. W. (2001). *Assessing student competence in accredited disciplines: Pioneering approaches to assessment in higher education.* Sterling, VA: Stylus Publishing.

Peeters, M. J., Zitko, K. L., & Schmude, K. A. (2016). Development of critical thinking in pharmacy education. *Innovations in Pharmacy*, 1–9.

Rafter, M. E., Dent, B., Pesun, I. J., Heren, M., Linfante, J. C., Mina, M., . . . Casada, J. P. (2006). A preliminary survey of interprofessional education. *Journal of Dental Education*, 417–427.

Reed, A. Z. (1921). *Training for the public profession of law.* New York, NY: Carnegie.

Robert Wood Johnson Foundation. (2014, April 18). Building the case for more highly educated nurses. Retrieved from https://www.rwjf.org/en/library/articles-and-news/2014/04/building-the-case-for-more-highly-educated-nurses.html

Shepard, R. T. (2014). *Report and recommendations: American Bar Association task force on the future of the legal profession.* Retrieved from https://www.americanbar.org/content/dam/aba/administrative/professional_responsibility/report_and_recommendations_of_aba_task_force.authcheckdam.pdf

Stuckey, R. T. (2007). *Best practices for legal education: A vision and a road map.* Columbia, SC: University Publications, University of South Carolina, and Clinical Legal Education Association.

Sullivan, W. M., Colby, A., Welch Wegner, J., Bond, L., & Shulman, L. C. (2007). *Educating lawyers: Preparation for the profession of law.* San Francisco, CA: Jossey-Bass.

ten Cate, O. (2013). Competency-based education, entrustable professional activities, and the power of language. *Journal of Graduate Medical Education*, 6–7.

Ulfvarson, J., & Oxelmark, L. (2011). Developing an assessment tool for intended learning outcomes in clinical practice for nursing students. *Nurse Education Today*, 704–708.

Victoroff, K., Savrin, C., Demko, C., Iannadrea, J., Freudenberger, S., & Mussacchio, C. (2014). Interprofessional clinical experiences in dental education. *Current Oral Health Reports*, *1*(3), 161–166. doi:https://doi.org/10.1007/s40496-014-0021-z

World Health Organization. (2010). *Framework for action on interprofessional education and collaborative practice.* Geneva, Switzerland: WHO Press.

Yanhua, C., & Watson, R. (2011). A review of clinical competence assessment in nursing. *Nurse Education Today*, 832–836.

Zorek, J., & Raehl, C. (2013). Interprofessional education accreditation standards in the USA: A comparative analysis. *Journal of Interprofessional Care*, 123–130.

8

MEASURING FACULTY LEARNING

Trends in the Assessment of Faculty Development

Krista Hoffmann-Longtin, Kyle Fassett, John Zilvinskis, and Megan M. Palmer

From training new course instructors to broadening the pedagogical depth of the institution, faculty development—sometimes referred to as *educational development* or *academic development*—has become a key function within the academy. Faculty developers participate in a wide range of activities, including development of individual faculty members; instructional development of courses, curriculum, and student learning; and organizational development of departments, programs, and units (Diamond, 1988, 2002). Ouellett (2010) provided an overview of the field of faculty development, observing that within the field, scholars have contributed by developing stage models, creating a shared lexicon, and discussing challenges faced by practitioners, such as navigating the complexity of faculty work. Ouellett noted that the charge of faculty developers is to pinpoint and address issues central to faculty work and then understand the extent to which faculty development is improving the academy.

Within the field of assessment, faculty development offices have been frequent partners with assessment and institutional research initiatives. At the Assessment Institute, we have seen faculty developers work with faculty to assess their own teaching (i.e., Martin & Williams, 2018; McDevitt, Garza, & De Oliveira, 2018) and investigate faculty perceptions of assessment and change implementation (Daughtery, 2018). Yet, faculty developers may be just as likely as faculty themselves to practice an "I know it when I see it" standard of measuring learning among the educators they train. Often absent from the work of faculty developers is their own evaluation of the effectiveness of their efforts. Although faculty development

124

professionals are experts in helping educators to assess student learning, further discussion about the best strategies for measuring faculty learning on campus is needed.

As such, the purpose of this chapter is to contribute to the literature by describing trends and outlining areas for growth in the assessment of faculty development programs and interventions. We provide historical examples and discuss current and future trends, offering guidance on how faculty development professionals can monitor achievement of their own programmatic outcomes.

History

Over half a century ago, colleges and universities began offering development programs and reward systems designed to help faculty improve their teaching skills (Centra, 1976; Ouellett, 2010; Skeff et al., 2003; Sutherland, 2018). By promoting excellence in teaching, scholarship, and long-term career development, faculty developers have since come to play essential roles in helping institutions establish rigorous academic cultures (Chism, Holley, & Harris, 2012; Hurney, Brantmeier, Good, Harrison, & Meixner, 2016; Sutherland, 2018). Faculty development offices have been instrumental in helping institutions implement effective educational practices. They have led institutions to adopt standard learner ratings of instruction, implemented collaborative methods for teaching evaluations such as small group instructional diagnosis, and provided training for effective peer review of teaching. Engaging in curriculum review processes, reviewing teaching performance, consulting with individual faculty members on their courses, and hosting course design "boot camps" are common activities for faculty developers (Amundsen & Wilson, 2012). More recently, faculty development offices have been deeply involved in helping faculty gain skills in assessing student learning outcomes and developing and measuring institutional learning outcomes. Faculty development programs focused on the assessment of student learning often occur locally within departments and campuses, as well as at the national level in long-term programs such as those in science, technology, engineering, and mathematics (STEM; Derting et al., 2016).

The process of measuring the impact of faculty development has been frequently stymied, as there are countless factors to consider, such as the length, location, and style of the initiative (Berbano, Browning, Pangaro, & Jackson, 2006; Felten, Kalish, Pingree, & Plank, 2007; Steinert et al., 2016). To date, we have largely relied on participants' satisfaction with programs rather than on behavioral change or return on investment (ROI) to assess the outcomes of our work (Kirkpatrick, 1998). By seeing ourselves primarily as catalysts for student learning (i.e., faculty developers teach faculty who teach students), we as faculty developers may have missed opportunities to measure the impact of our own programs.

As the field has developed, so have research and national conferences focused on faculty development and assessment. The annual Assessment Institute in Indianapolis hosted by Indiana University–Purdue University Indianapolis provides an ideal opportunity to examine how the field is moving toward more comprehensive models of assessing the outcomes, or ROI, of faculty development, while still attending to developing faculty members' assessment expertise.

For example, faculty developers at Wayne State University were concerned about the availability of faculty to participate in development opportunities. To address this issue, developers offered assessment training to educators through several media, such as in-person workshops; small group and individual consultations; and static resources like video tutorials, written instructions, and templates. To measure the effectiveness of this new strategy, Barrette (2015) analyzed the following different data sources: (a) survey results from workshop participants, (b) changes in participation rates, and (c) self-reported quality of assessment plans before and after participation in development opportunities. At the University of Northern Colorado, Sexton and colleagues (2015) offered an assessment leadership institute to improve participants' skills in measuring program-level student learning. In their effort to understand the effectiveness of this intervention, these practitioners developed a pre- and post-institute survey to measure changes in self-reported attitudes, skills, and knowledge.

At Ohio Northern University, Hurtig and Kim (2017) employed more direct measures to assess their new peer mentoring program. Using their annual program assessment reports, the authors rated the quality of submissions in six areas (learning outcome statements, assessment methods, results, adjustments to the program, reflection on assessment practices, and overall) and compared the average annual score between the first year and second year of the program to the year before the program was initiated. Taken together, these examples illustrate important steps toward measuring and improving the effectiveness of faculty development.

As noted previously, there appear to be two distinct ways in which faculty development programs engage with assessment. First, faculty developers write and present about approaches to teaching faculty about assessment or they discuss the extent to which faculty participants respond to novel approaches to engaging them in assessment efforts. Second, and less frequent, are presentations and scholarship on the impact of faculty development programs on key metrics of interest to the institution, such as student learning outcomes, faculty productivity, and faculty vitality.

These two modes of engagement with assessment are apparent each year when proposals are submitted for the faculty development track of the Assessment Institute. The vast majority of proposals, approximately 80%, focus on teaching faculty how to assess rather than on assessing the effectiveness of faculty development. This trend does not carry over to other tracks at the conference. For example, in the student affairs track, the emphasis is not on developing student affairs professionals' assessment skills; rather, the sessions focus on assessing the effectiveness of student affairs programs and services.

We believe this phenomenon is due, in part, to the challenge of measuring faculty development outcomes. Our collective goal needs to be to move the conversation beyond describing faculty development programs toward assessing the outcomes of these programs. By broadening the scope of faculty development outcomes to include measures such as faculty learning, research productivity, and faculty vitality, we are able to more accurately reflect the scope and impact of our work.

Current Trends

As noted, recent years have seen increased efforts to study the effectiveness of faculty development efforts (Hoffmann-Longtin, Merckle, & Palmer, 2018). In their meta-analysis of studies of the impact of faculty development, Chism and colleagues (2012) found that faculty developers often determined whether their efforts were effective across a wide range of domains. These included measures of importance to faculty developers such as faculty members' motivation to seek further development and changes in teaching practices. Other measures, important to both faculty developers and institutions as a whole, studied the impact of faculty development on increased use of interactive teaching strategies, changes in teaching philosophy, gains in the numbers of faculty using instructional technology, and increased student participation in class discussions.

For example, Lawson, Fazey, and Clancy (2006) examined the extent to which engagement in faculty development led to more learning-centered approaches to teaching as well as positive changes in students' approaches to studying. Others have looked at the degree to which grade distributions or student ratings of instruction in courses taught by faculty engaged in faculty development have changed (McShannon & Hynes, 2005; Piccinin & Moore, ·2002). Recently, Condon, Iverson, Manduca, Rutz, and Willett (2016) conducted an extensive study to assess how student learning is affected by faculty participating in teaching development activities.

Other studies of the impact of faculty development attempt to measure the degree to which engagement in communities of practice influences the commitment, teaching skills, and satisfaction of faculty (O'Meara, 2005). Studies of the impact of mentoring have included metrics such as research productivity (Bland, Center, Finstad, Risbey, & Staples, 2005; Miller & Thurston, 2009). Some studies of the effectiveness of faculty development have focused on outcomes such as increased interaction with peers (Bell & Mladenovic, 2008; Morris & Fry, 2006). Within academic medicine, Morzinski and Simpson (2003) studied the results of a two-year faculty development program focused on productivity and retention of faculty. Gjerde, Hla, Kokotailo, and Anderson (2008) reported that their development program for primary care faculty led to improved teaching and clinical skills and gains in self-confidence and interdisciplinary networking and mentoring.

Bilal, Guraya, and Chen (2017) provided a meta-analysis of studies of the impact of faculty development within the health professions. In their initial review of 525 articles, they excluded more than 400 of the articles from the analysis because the articles described faculty development programs but did not address the impact of those efforts. After deeper review of titles and abstracts, the authors excluded an additional 63 articles for the same reasons. Ultimately, only 37 of the 525 articles were found relevant and were included in the analysis. Thus, although more scholarship on faculty development is currently being generated and even the assessment of those efforts is increasing, more rigorous efforts to examine the impact of faculty development work are needed.

Many scholars have called for understanding faculty development as a more evidence-based endeavor (Bamber & Stefani, 2016; Bilal et al., 2017; Bothell & Henderson, 2004; Chism et al., 2012; Chism & Szabó, 1997; Plank & Kalish, 2010). Few programs, however, have actually been able to respond to these calls. As Chism and colleagues (2012) noted, linking engagement in faculty development to student learning outcomes is difficult. Some may argue that establishing such links is the gold standard. Faculty development spans areas broader than teaching, however (Sutherland, 2018). Furthermore, one can and should expect that the impact of faculty development will go beyond the classroom. Bothell and Henderson (2004) recommended following an ROI model where the net program benefits are divided by the costs to create a percentage. Kirkpatrick's (1998) four levels of evaluation provide a framework for faculty developers to understand participants' reactions to interventions, the learning that occurred, any changes in behavior, and new results due to engagement in faculty development.

Given historical and current trends in assessing faculty development, we believe there is an opportunity to focus assessment activities on articulated faculty learning outcomes linked to important institutional metrics.

Future Trends

As discussed, assessing the impact of faculty development is complex. In this section, we present potential reasons for why these calls have yet to be fulfilled and case examples, which use evidence to demonstrate ROI and integrate faculty development and its assessment into an institutional culture of learning.

First, faculty development, as a field, has struggled to develop a coherent theory base for the approaches and models it uses (Steinert et al., 2016; Sutherland, 2018). A few scholars have proposed theories of faculty growth in particular environments and contexts. For example, Chism (2004) offered a model for how faculty learn about incorporating technology into teaching. Her "plan-act-observe-reflect" framework could likely be applied and tested in other contexts. Ramsden (1992) developed a model for understanding how faculty members develop as teachers that has been combined with other adult learning theories and applied to many teaching development programs (Saroyan, Amundsen, & Li, 1997). Bland and colleagues (2005) considered a structure for going beyond individual faculty productivity, offering a theoretical model of faculty and departmental research productivity. Although this model is situated in academic medicine, it offers promising suggestions for faculty development as a field. By moving the faculty development evidence base beyond teaching development into broader faculty success characteristics (promotion and tenure rates, publication rates, satisfaction and vitality scores), we are able to demonstrate the value of the institutional investment in faculty development. More recently, O'Meara, Terosky, and Neumann (2008) offered a more holistic, growth-oriented model, focusing on the organizational practices that encourage faculty members' success in the areas of teaching, research, and work–life balance. These theories represent the wide breadth of faculty developers' work (Austin & Sorcinelli, 2013) and offer opportunities for developing and testing theory-based programs.

Second, creating an organizational culture of learning is not an easy task. Faculty development centers and programs are typically housed in separate units from institutional research or faculty affairs; however, faculty developers are well known for their interest in collaboration (Beach Sorcinelli, Austin, & Rivard, 2016; Chism & Szabó, 1997; Felten et al., 2007). If faculty developers are to demonstrate their ability to move beyond improving one faculty member or program to improving departments, centers, and institutions, we must seek partnerships with institutional research professionals and others across the institution (Sutherland, 2018).

A third problem that faculty developers face when collecting evidence is related to unit of analysis. Because faculty development interventions vary widely in length and structure, it is challenging to compare them to one another and to determine what data to collect and what those data mean (Bamber & Stefani, 2016). Nonetheless, Bamber and Stefani (2016) explained, we can create an argument for a program by "gathering a mix of types of evidence, questioning it, making sense of the evidence . . . and then harnessing the findings to inform future thinking" (p. 245). Faculty development programs often exist in complex institutions, and we must not spend time working in vain to develop the perfect measures of impact.

Fourth, given the breadth of disciplines that make up an institution, faculty developers may find it challenging to identify collaborative outcomes for faculty growth across programs. Hurney and colleagues (2016) developed a framework for addressing this challenge. They collaborated with key institutional constituents to create faculty learning outcomes and mapped these outcomes to the faculty development center's assessment efforts. By collecting multiple types of data, the authors were able to gather information on program quality while simultaneously connecting their work to broader institutional goals. These types of evidence-based approaches are promising because of their ability to demonstrate the impact of faculty development beyond the classroom environment.

Although the challenges are complex, a few other scholars have identified creative ways to move toward more evidence-based practice. One clear future trend in assessment of faculty development is an increased focus on programmatic outcomes that move beyond participant satisfaction. Bamber and Stefani (2016) proposed evaluating programs on three levels: raising awareness, increasing understanding, and changing practice or policy. For example, at the 2017 Assessment Institute, Tarr, Jerolimov, and Rao presented a new learner-centered faculty development program called the "Faculty Teaching Showcase." In addition to collecting satisfaction data, the presenters measured faculty confidence in their teaching abilities and self-efficacy, thus identifying clearer learning outcomes for their program beyond, "Did they like it?"

Recently, Hurney and colleagues (2016) described methods for scaffolding faculty learning outcomes and mapping them to various faculty development programs and services. Building on this work, Hoffmann-Longtin, Morgan, and Palmer (2016) developed common learning outcomes across faculty development programs and then connected program evaluation surveys to broader institutional data such as faculty productivity and promotion rates. Although they could not claim direct causation, the authors argued that these data present a promising case for ROI to higher level administration.

Broadly speaking, to elevate the importance and stature of faculty development, we must commit ourselves to disseminating our assessment work. Calls for accountability in higher education are not decreasing (Austin & Sorcinelli, 2013). Although the challenges to assessing faculty development efforts are numerous, they are not unique to one institution or discipline. By publishing the results of our faculty development efforts, we provide our colleagues with important evidence they need to garner support for their programs. As argued previously, however, this evidence must be theoretically grounded and methodologically sound. Because faculty are often the most expensive line item in an institution's budget, aligning faculty development work with comprehensive outcomes helps illustrate the value of faculty development across the institution.

Conclusion

Historically, faculty development has played a critical role within the academy in improving the quality of education. Developers have extensively studied the advantages and disadvantages of many of the measures of teaching used today in higher education, such as student feedback and peer evaluation; however, they have not done enough to measure the effectiveness of their own efforts. How do we know whether faculty development efforts, themselves, are successful? Other areas within college campuses, such as student affairs, have already put into practice tried-and-true tools of assessment (e.g., theory and measures) to evaluate their own efforts. Just as the field of student affairs has moved to measuring student learning outcomes, faculty developers must measure outcomes as well. What is needed now is thus a shift from *how to teach faculty about assessment* to *how to measure the learning of the faculty we are trying to develop*. Evidence of the influence of faculty development will provide developers with the tools to improve services to faculty and further legitimize their role among campus stakeholders. It is time for faculty developers to move beyond "I know it when I see it."

Summary of Main Trends

- Historically, faculty developers have been involved in assessing teaching and learning and instructing faculty on assessment practices.
- As the field of faculty development has expanded, faculty developers must shift their focus to assessing the impact and outcomes of their own work.
- Although finding and collecting data on the influence of faculty development may be challenging, some practitioners have been successful.
- Further research and dissemination are needed on the evidence and ROI of faculty development.

Questions for Discussion

- How has the relationship between the fields of faculty development and assessment changed over time?
- What are some challenges in teaching faculty how to conduct assessment? How can those challenges be addressed?
- Why is it important to assess the outcomes of faculty development efforts?
- What data sources and/or outcomes beyond those listed in this chapter might be used to assess the effectiveness of faculty development?
- How can proven assessment strategies and concepts be employed to measure the effectiveness of faculty development efforts?

Additional Readings and Resources

- International Consortium for Educational Development (ICED): http://icedonline.net
- Professional and Organizational Development Network in Higher Education (POD): https://podnetwork.org

---

We want to hear from you about *Trends in Assessment*:

- Provide reactions or suggestions about trends.
- Share and access resources related to trends.
- Learn about professional development opportunities related to trends.

Visit assessmentinstitute.iupui.edu/trends

References

Amundsen, C., & Wilson, M. (2012). Are we asking the right questions? A conceptual review of the educational development literature in higher education. *Review of Educational Research, 82*(1), 90–126.

Austin, A. E., & Sorcinelli, M. D. (2013). The future of faculty development: Where are we going? *New Directions for Teaching and Learning, 2013*(133), 85–97.

Bamber, V., & Stefani, L. (2016). Taking up the challenge of evidencing value in educational development: From theory to practice. *International Journal for Academic Development, 21*(3), 242–254. doi:10.1080/1360144X.2015.1100112

Barrette, C. M. (2015, October). *Faculty development in assessment: A multi-faceted approach.* Paper presented at the 2015 Assessment Institute, Indianapolis, IN.

Beach, A. L., Sorcinelli, M. D., Austin, A. E., & Rivard, J. K. (2016). *Faculty development in the age of evidence: Current practices, future imperatives.* Sterling, VA: Stylus.

Bell, A., & Mladenovic, R. (2008). The benefits of peer observation of teaching for tutor development. *Higher Education, 55*(6), 735–752.

Berbano, E. P., Browning, R., Pangaro, L., & Jackson, J. L. (2006). The impact of the Stanford Faculty Development Program on ambulatory teaching behavior. *Journal of General Internal Medicine, 21*(5), 430–434.

Bilal, Guraya, S. Y., & Chen, S. (2017). The impact and effectiveness of faculty development programs in fostering the faculty's knowledge, skills, and professional competence: A systematic review and meta-analysis. *Saudi Journal of Biological Sciences.* Retrieved from https://doi.org/10.1016/j.sjbs.2017.10.024

Bland, C. J., Center, B. A., Finstad, D. A., Risbey, K. R., & Staples, J. G. (2005). A theoretical, practical, predictive model of faculty and department research productivity. *Academic Medicine, 80*(3), 225–237.

Bothell, T. W., & Henderson, T. (2004). Evaluating the return on investment of faculty development. *To Improve the Academy, 22*(1), 52–70.

Centra, J. A. (1976). Faculty development practices in U.S. colleges and universities. In *Institutional research program in higher education.* Princeton, NJ: Educational Testing Service.

Chism, N. V. N. (2004, January 1). Using a framework to engage faculty in instructional technologies. *EDUCAUSE Review.* Retrieved from https://er.educause.edu/articles/2004/1/using-a-framework-to-engage-faculty-in-instructional-technologies

Chism, N. V. N., Holley, M., & Harris, C. J. (2012). Researching the impact of educational development: Basis for informed practice. *To Improve the Academy, 31*(1), 129–145.

Chism, N. V. N., & Szabó, B. (1997). How faculty development programs evaluate their services. *Journal of Staff, Program, and Organization Development, 15*(2), 55–62.

Condon, W., Iverson, E. R., Manduca, C. A., Rutz, C., & Willett, G. (2016). *Faculty development and student learning: Assessing the connections.* Bloomington, IN: Indiana University Press.

Daughtery, K. (2018, October). *What faculty perceptions can tell us about our program's summative assessments.* Paper presented at the 2018 Assessment Institute, Indianapolis, IN.

Derting, T. L., Ebert-May, D., Henkel, T. P., Maher, J. M., Arnold, B., & Passmore, H. A. (2016). Assessing faculty professional development in STEM higher education: Sustainability of outcomes. *Science Advances, 2*(3), e1501422.

Diamond, R. M. (1988). Faculty development, instructional development, and organizational development: Options and choices. In E. C. Wadsworth (Ed.), *Professional and organizational development in higher education: A handbook for new practitioners* (pp. 9–11). Stillwater, OK: New Forums Press.

Diamond, R. M. (2002). Faculty, instructional, and organizational development: Options and choices. In K. H. Gillespie, L. R. Hilsen, & E. C. Wadsworth (Eds.), *A guide to faculty development: Practical advice, examples, and resources* (pp. 2–8). Bolton, MA: Anker.

Felten, P., Kalish, A., Pingree, A., & Plank, K. M. (2007). Toward a scholarship of teaching and learning in educational development. *To Improve the Academy, 25*(1), 93–108.

Gjerde, C. L., Hla, K. M., Kokotailo, P. K., & Anderson, B. (2008). Long-term outcomes of a primary care faculty development program at the University of Wisconsin. *Family Medicine, 40*(8), 579–584.

Hoffmann-Longtin, K., Merckle, R., & Palmer, M. M. (2018). A call for a body of evidence about the impact of faculty development: Assessment Institute insights. *Assessment Update, 30*(5), 6–15. Retrieved from https://doi.org/10.1002/au.30146

Hoffmann-Longtin, K., Morgan, Z. S., & Palmer, M. M. (2016, October). *Where is the evidence? Assessing the impact of faculty development activities.* Paper presented at the 2016 Assessment Institute, Indianapolis, IN.

Hurney, C. A., Brantmeier, E. J., Good, M. R., Harrison, D., & Meixner, C. (2016). The faculty learning outcome assessment framework. *Journal of Faculty Development, 30*(2), 69–77.

Hurtig, J. K., & Kim, E. (2017, October). *Fostering faculty-driven assessment practice: A peer-mentoring program of outcomes assessment in major fields.* Paper presented at the 2017 Assessment Institute, Indianapolis, IN.

Kirkpatrick, D. (1998). *Evaluating training programs: The four levels* (2nd ed.). San Francisco, CA: Berrett-Koehler.

Lawson, R., Fazey, J., & Clancy, D. (2006, October). *The impact of a teaching in higher education scheme on new lecturers personal epistemologies and approaches to teaching.* Paper presented at 14th Improving Student Learning Symposium: Improving Student Learning Through Teaching, Bath, England.

Martin, C. G., & Williams, D. (2018, October). *A model of faculty development for student learning outcomes assessment.* Paper presented at the 2018 Assessment Institute, Indianapolis, IN.

McDevitt, J., Garza, H., & De Oliveira, E. (2018, October). *Engaging faculty in assessment by assignment design.* Paper presented at the 2018 Assessment Institute, Indianapolis, IN.

McShannon, J., & Hynes, P. (2005). Student achievement and retention: Can professional development programs help faculty GRASP it? *Journal of Faculty Development, 20*(2), 87–93.

Miller, T. N., & Thurston, L. (2009). Mentoring junior professors: History and evaluation of a nine-year model. *Journal of Faculty Development, 23*(2), 35–40.

Morris, C., & Fry, H. (2006). Enhancing educational research and development activity through small grant schemes: A case study. *International Journal for Academic Development, 11*(1), 43–56.

Morzinski, J. A., & Simpson, D. E. (2003). Outcomes of a comprehensive faculty development program for local, full-time faculty. *Family Medicine, 35*(6), 434–439.

O'Meara, K. (2005). The courage to be experimental: How one faculty learning community influenced faculty teaching careers, understanding of how students learn, and assessment. *Journal of Faculty Development, 20*(3), 153–160.

O'Meara, K., Terosky, A. L., & Neumann, A. (2008). Faculty careers and work lives: A professional growth perspective. *ASHE Higher Education Report, 34*(3), 1–221.

Ouellett, M. (2010). Overview of faculty development: History and choices. In K. J. Gillespie & D. L. Robertson (Eds.), *A guide to faculty development* (2nd ed., pp. 3–20). San Francisco, CA: Jossey-Bass.

Piccinin, S., & Moore, J. P. (2002). The impact of individual consultation on the teaching of younger versus older faculty. *The International Journal for Academic Development, 7*(2), 123–134.

Plank, K., & Kalish, A. (2010). Program assessment for faculty development. In K. J. Gillespie & D. L. Robertson (Eds.), *A guide to faculty development* (2nd ed., pp. 135–149). San Francisco, CA: Jossey-Bass.

Ramsden, P. (1992). *Learning to teach in higher education.* London, UK: Routledge.

Saroyan, A., Amundsen, C., & Li, C. (1997). Incorporating theories of teacher growth and adult education in a faculty development program. *To Improve the Academy, 16*(1), 93–115.

Sexton, J., Ellis, L., Ku, H., Marston, C., Lightfoot, J., Byrnes, J., & Black, K. (2015, October). *The assessment leadership institute: An evidence-based professional development model to improve faculty skills, knowledge, and attitudes.* Paper presented at the 2015 Assessment Institute, Indianapolis, IN.

Skeff, K. M., Stratos, G. A., Mygdal, W., DeWitt, T. A., Manfred, L., Quirk, M., . . . Bland, C. J. (2003). Faculty development: A resource for clinical teachers. *Journal of General Internal Medicine, 12*(2), 56–63.

Steinert, Y., Mann, K., Anderson, B., Barnett, B. M., Centeno, A., Naismith, L., . . . Ward, H. (2016). A systematic review of faculty development initiatives designed to enhance teaching effectiveness: A 10-year update: BEME Guide No. 40. *Medical Teacher, 38*(8), 769–786.

Sutherland, K. (2018). Holistic academic development: Is it time to think more broadly about the academic development project? *International Journal for Academic Development, 23*(4), 261–273. Retrieved from https://doi.org/10.1080/13 60144X.2018.1524571

Tarr, T., Jerolimov, D., & Rao, A. S. (2017, October). *Designing and assessing learner-centered faculty development programming.* Paper presented at the 2017 Assessment Institute, Indianapolis, IN.

TRANSFORMING ASSESSMENT, ASSESSING TRANSFORMATION

ePortfolio Assessment Trends

Susan Kahn

O ur assessment methods have meaning: They both reflect and construct the kinds of learning we value (Cambridge, 2010; Yancey, 2004). The chapters in this volume collectively describe a growing interest in embedded, authentic assessment strategies, signaling a renewed focus on the role of higher education in students' personal and academic development and a recognition that traditional assessment approaches may not do justice to more complex higher order learning outcomes, noncognitive developmental outcomes, or outcomes that combine cognitive and noncognitive elements like emotional intelligence and self-awareness (Kuh, Gambino, Bresciani Ludvik, & O'Donnell, 2018). Similarly, traditional assessments rarely capture "students' pivotal learning moments" (Yancey, 2019, p. 3), those "aha" experiences that many faculty and staff consider crucial to a meaningful higher education.

The statement frequently made by assessment professionals that learning outcome statements must be *measurable* and *assessable* too often begs the question, "*Measureable* and *assessable* by what means?" Do traditional assessments—tests, essays, even hands-on performances and individual artifacts of authentic learning—provide sufficient information about the learning we care most about? About *how*, as well as *what*, students learn? Are we obliged to be concerned only with learning that can be readily assessed with traditional assessment tools? And what does all this imply for the many institutions, mine included, that aspire to educate "the whole person"?

ePortfolios: An Assessment Approach and a High-Impact Practice

An ePortfolio is a student-created academic website that (ideally) presents a coherent, reflective representation of the student and associated learning, using hyperlinked digital media and narrative as context for a set of authentic performances. As reflective personal academic websites, ePortfolios can tell us much about how students view themselves as learners or emerging professionals; how they are perceiving, connecting, and interpreting their in- and out-of-class learning experiences; and why they may be struggling with particular content or concepts. Longitudinally developed ePortfolios that include a variety of authentic student artifacts, in multiple digital formats, along with reflection (again, possibly in multiple formats), can illuminate trajectories of development and capture the complexity, depth, and breadth of postsecondary learning. As such, they can shed light on aspects of student learning and experience not easily accessible through other assessment methods and provide rich, contextualized information that programs and institutions can use to guide improvement.

ePortfolios are now used on more than half of U.S. college campuses (Dahlstrom, 2015). The possibility of gaining new insights into how and why our students learn accounts for much of ePortfolios' appeal for assessment of higher education outcomes. But ePortfolios are more than an assessment method; they have been recognized as a high-impact practice (HIP) that, when "done well," can improve student learning and promote student success (Kuh, 2017). When integrated into a thoughtful, well-scaffolded learning design, they can strengthen and deepen disciplinary learning; help students make connections among courses, disciplines, and in- and out-of-class learning experiences; and nurture self-awareness and habits of reflective practice. ePortfolios implemented across students' experiences in a program or institution amplify these benefits.

The trends discussed later in this chapter arise from the power of ePortfolios to enhance both learning and assessment.

Why "e"? A Short History of ePortfolios

ePortfolios are direct descendants of reflective print portfolios, which have a long history in college-level writing programs and teacher education programs. These portfolios were meant to cultivate habits of metacognition, reflective practice, and self-critique among students and, in some cases, to demonstrate student achievement of defined learning outcomes. By the late 1980s, other disciplines had become interested in the idea (Batson,

2002; Yancey, 2001), often for assessment purposes, as accreditors, governments, and other stakeholders began to demand evidence of student learning.

The advent of the Internet and other digital tools in the 1990s opened up new avenues of development for portfolios. But the first ePortfolio platforms developed in the early 2000s were often little more than electronic file folders linked to assessment management systems. The advantages of electronic portfolios over paper portfolios were construed in terms of enhanced authenticity, accessibility, and portability. That is, these digital portfolios could include authentic work in a variety of media. A teacher education student could present a video of a lesson she taught. A music student could provide audio of a musical composition or performance. Photographs could help illustrate narrative or reflection on, for example, a laboratory or field experience. ePortfolios were also accessible from any Internet-connected device and portable from course to course or classroom to cocurricular setting (and literally more portable than stacks of paper portfolios).

Later, as ePortfolios came to be understood as web presentations rather than sets of electronic files, practitioners began to see that ePortfolios had additional advantages over paper. The reflections, imagery, framing narrative, and multimodal artifacts typically included in online portfolios offered opportunities for the author to represent learning experiences in context and articulate their significance for development, using examples of authentic work as evidence of skills and capacities. An ePortfolio website presenting a trajectory of academic and personal development or focusing on a student's capabilities at a point in time could be approached by the author and audience as a representation of academic and professional identity, an act of literal self-authorship (Cambridge, 2010; Eynon & Gambino, 2017, 2018; Kahn, 2017, 2019; Yancey, 2004, 2009, 2019).

In 2004, Kathleen Yancey proposed a new definition of *ePortfolio* as "a selected body of plural performances narrated by the writer in a reflective text and located at a particular point in time" (p. 739). In this definition, the ePortfolio is viewed not just as a collection of artifacts but as a composition in its own right, with a reflective text that explains the significance of and connections among the artifacts it contains. Yancey (2004) further argued that the features of an ePortfolio website—the way it structures and demonstrates knowledge and experience through its architecture, visual design, hyperlinks, menus, and navigational paths—provide additional opportunities for students to represent a reflective integrated and integrative learning schema.

In a 2017 keynote address at the Assessment Institute, Yancey extended this argument, positing that a well-guided and well-crafted ePortfolio is not only a "container" of artifacts representing various learning experiences but also, potentially, a learning experience or artifact of a learning experience in its own right (Yancey, 2017). The process of creating an ePortfolio website, including selecting examples of work appropriate for particular audiences and purposes, engaging in various kinds of reflection, choosing or developing visual elements and designs to help convey key ideas, composing a cohesive narrative to contextualize and explicate these elements, and designing an architecture and navigational paths, can, in itself, bring about powerful integrative learning and self-development. She emphasized that we need to think carefully about how we design curricula to support such ePortfolio learning and about what exactly we are assessing when we assess ePortfolios viewed in this way.

Current Trends in ePortfolio Learning and Assessment

Currently, much attention at the Assessment Institute and elsewhere is devoted to ePortfolios as a HIP for teaching and learning and to strategies for effective implementation of ePortfolios as a HIP. ePortfolios thus can be and often are assessed as an intervention intended to boost student learning and success (Eynon & Gambino, 2017, 2018). As an assessment method in themselves, ePortfolios support assessment of the kinds of capacities that they help develop when done well: integrative learning, self-awareness, reflective practice, metacognition, and more. With effective guidance, the reflective components of ePortfolios can illuminate students' perceptions and interpretations of learning experiences, processes, and environments, offering insights into why particular experiences or practices may or may not be effective in bringing about desired learning. ePortfolios thus call for and enable new approaches to assessment that examine complex learning outcomes in nuanced ways and shed light on learning experiences both within and outside the formal curriculum, broadening opportunities for faculty and staff to use assessment to improve learning designs. I return to this idea later in this chapter.

ePortfolios as a HIP

Recent studies and the experience of expert practitioners support Yancey's argument that composing an ePortfolio can promote deeper, more meaningful learning (e.g., Bass, 2014; Cambridge, 2010; Eynon & Gambino, 2017, 2018; Eynon, Gambino, & Torok, 2014; Kahn, 2014, 2018, 2019; Penny Light, Chen, & Ittelson, 2012; Reynolds & Patton, 2014; Yancey, 2004, 2009, 2019). In 2017, George Kuh, author of the 2008 monograph that defined HIPs in higher education, and the Association of American Colleges & Universities (AAC&U) recognized ePortfolios as an 11th HIP, based on findings from a 24-campus national project led by LaGuardia Community College:

> When [ePortfolios are] done well, students who create and continue to add to their ePortfolio as intended benefit in ways similar to students who participate in one or more of the 10 HIPs on the AAC&U list. . . . Compared with their counterparts who did not use ePortfolios, students . . . were generally more engaged in educationally purposeful activities, earned higher grades, and were more likely to complete courses and persist. (Kuh, 2017, p. viii)

But when we say that ePortfolios "done well" are a HIP for teaching and learning, we need to attend to the caveat "done well." As Eynon and Gambino (2017), the 2018 keynoters for the Assessment Institute's ePortfolio track, observed, "key elements of effective ePortfolio practice are often overlooked; as a result, many campus ePortfolio initiatives struggle" (p. 9). Simply adding an ePortfolio requirement to a course or program is not sufficient for high impact. As many programs and campuses have discovered, ePortfolios implemented solely for assessment purposes without appropriate revisions to pedagogy and curriculum may yield some limited information for assessment but they are unlikely to enhance learning or promote student development and success. The defining characteristics of HIPs, as outlined by Kuh in 2008—especially significant effort invested over a period of time, interactions with faculty and peers, meaningful feedback, opportunities to reflect on and integrate learning, and public demonstration of learning—are as important for ePortfolios as for any of the other 10 HIPs, perhaps even more so, for reasons that I hope will become clear.

Both formal studies and practitioner experience have suggested that ePortfolio composition is most effective for learning when it is well guided and scaffolded, approached as an integral component of a cohesively designed curriculum, integrated longitudinally throughout the curriculum, and supported by pedagogies that emphasize the social construction of knowledge, reflection and metacognition, and student agency (e.g., Cambridge, Cambridge, & Yancey, 2009; Eynon & Gambino, 2017, 2018; Kahn, 2014, 2019; Matthews-DeNatale, 2014; Penny Light et al., 2012; Reynolds & Patton, 2014; Yancey, 2019). Well-designed ePortfolio experiences promote an approach to learning that Penny Light and colleagues (2012) called *folio thinking*:

> *Folio thinking* is a reflective practice that situates and guides the effective use of learning portfolios . . . folio thinking aims to encourage students to

integrate discrete learning experiences, enhance their self-understanding, promote taking responsibility for their own learning, and support them in developing an intellectual identity. (pp. 10–11)

Folio thinking, as a pedagogical approach, thus emphasizes reflection and integration of learning—two demonstrated characteristics of HIPs—and development of self-awareness and a sense of agency over one's learning, which research suggests are also characteristics or outcomes of HIPs "done well" (Kuh et al., 2018; Penny Light et al., 2012). Pedagogies and programs designed to support these elements of folio thinking are more likely to result in powerful ePortfolio learning for students and to yield assessment data that provide meaningful insights into what and how students learn. Curricula, for example, need to be scaffolded such that connections between courses and out-of-class experiences are explicit, and intended learning from each component of the curriculum is clearly stated (Eynon & Gambino, 2017, 2018; Matthews-DeNatale, 2014, 2018; Yancey, 2019). Pedagogical strategies need to encourage students to make connections among ideas, courses, disciplines, and in- and out-of-class learning and to monitor and reflect on their thinking and learning. Recent research suggests that intensive professional development, planning, and/or extensive experience are key to ePortfolio practice that is truly high impact (Eynon & Gambino, 2017, 2018).

ePortfolios as a Meta-HIP

Susan Scott and I have suggested that ePortfolios might be approached and assessed as a "meta"-HIP (Kahn, 2014; Kahn & Scott, 2013). ePortfolios can function as a meta-HIP in two ways. First, a well-designed ePortfolio experience can amplify the impact of another HIP by intensifying and combining the elements that make a HIP high impact, such as reflection; feedback; integration of learning; and, especially, public demonstration of learning in the form of the ePortfolio itself—a multimedia website that captures, demonstrates, interprets, and integrates the student's experience of and learning from the HIP. Second, such an ePortfolio website can offer a window into aspects of students' experiences and interpretations of HIP learning that might otherwise remain invisible. The use of digital media in ePortfolios, in particular, can support a multifaceted representation of students' HIP experience and encourage the reflective use of visual imagery, video, and even spoken narrative to depict and articulate impact and learning. Thus, just as metadata provide information about other data or as metafiction comments on the nature and conventions of fiction, so ePortfolios, one HIP, offer us insight into what and how students learn from other HIPs and from the ePortfolio development process itself.

Beyond HIPs, ePortfolios can bring a "meta" dimension into all of our educational practices—our course and curriculum designs, pedagogies, learning environments, cocurricular experiences, and more. Several faculty members on my own campus have remarked that students' ePortfolios, and especially their reflections, offered insights into not only what and how students were learning but also how students were experiencing their academic programs, illuminating program identity in addition to student identity. Gail Matthews-DeNatale of Northeastern University has written about how a review of students' ePortfolios showed faculty that students were not experiencing or interpreting the curriculum of a master's-level education program as faculty had planned, spurring a major curriculum overhaul (Matthews-DeNatale, 2014). The ePortfolio literature supports the idea that ePortfolios can tell us a great deal about students' perceptions of program and institutional processes and practices (Cambridge, 2010; Matthews-DeNatale, 2014; Yancey, 2019), yielding valuable information for assessment and improvement. I will return to this idea shortly.

ePortfolio Assessment: From Artifacts and Competencies to ePortfolios, Integration, and the Ineffable

The early days of ePortfolio assessment were typified by a focus on single artifacts associated with specific outcomes or competencies. ePortfolios were (and quite often still are) seen as collections of pieces of evidence, and ePortfolio assessment was seen as an enhanced form of traditional authentic assessment. Often, a given assignment, submitted in digital form, was connected to one or more desired outcomes and assessed across students and perhaps course sections, using appropriate rubrics, to determine overall achievement of the outcome at particular points in students' educational experiences. This approach had all of the advantages of established authentic assessment methods, with the added benefits to authenticity conferred by digital media: Artifacts assessed could include videos of class presentations in a speech course or simulated clinical interactions in a health profession field or musical performances in a music curriculum, all easily accessible online from anywhere at any time. ePortfolio software platforms were often structured to support such an artifact-by-artifact assessment approach, and disciplinary accreditors responded positively to it, as several programs at my institution found; accrediting team members could use the ePortfolio software to drill down from a learning outcome to artifacts demonstrating the outcome and could see how faculty had graded or assessed artifacts at different levels of proficiency.

This artifact-by-artifact approach also had advantages for curriculum and assignment development. At Indiana University–Purdue University Indianapolis (IUPUI), we found that programs adopting ePortfolios for assessment and accreditation began rethinking their curricula, mapping courses and assignments to desired learning outcomes or competencies, and striving to ensure that students had sufficient experience with skills as they progressed through the curriculum to achieve intended outcomes. Such approaches in the best cases created more intentionally and explicitly integrated and cumulative curricula that were a significant benefit of ePortfolio adoption—a first step toward high-impact ePortfolio pedagogy and curriculum and, often, toward more holistic assessment models.

Meanwhile, as we have seen, ePortfolio research and practice were increasingly demonstrating that with careful guidance and supportive learning designs, ePortfolios could advance students' integrative learning capacities, sense of agency, identity development, and other abilities related to folio thinking. In other words, the processes of composing and constructing the ePortfolio, explaining the relationships of artifacts to one another and to the whole ePortfolio, reflecting on parts of or the whole ePortfolio, and arranging its elements to create an integrated multimodal narrative supported significant intellectual and personal development. With the idea that ePortfolio composition was itself a powerful learning experience, some researchers and practitioners (e.g., Cambridge, 2010; Yancey, 2004) argued early on that we should be not only assessing individual artifacts but also examining entire ePortfolios holistically for evidence of such learning and development as well as for learning of other higher order skills.

More recently, other voices have added to calls for holistic ePortfolio assessment. At the 2017 Assessment Institute, for example, Kuh, Gambino, Bresciani Ludvik, and O'Donnell presented a workshop, "Using ePortfolio to Document and Enhance the Dispositional Learning Impact of HIPs," in which they argued that, done well, ePortfolios could both cultivate and document what they termed *dispositional learning*—skills such as cognitive flexibility, openness to new perspectives, fluid intelligence, self-awareness and self-regulation, and emotional intelligence. These kinds of outcomes include noncognitive, as well as cognitive, components and are often described as *ineffable* or not susceptible to assessment. In the workshop and in a later Occasional Paper for the National Institute for Learning Outcomes Assessment, the authors argued that a reflective ePortfolio, seen as "an evolving multimedia collection of artifacts, reflections, and experiences that form a digital narrative of a student's academic journey" (Kuh et al., 2018, p. 16), could indeed make such learning visible and available for assessment. Here, they noted, "the role of reflection in ePortfolios is essential, because the reflective component helps to make the implicit 'beneath the surface' learning explicit" (Kuh et al., 2018, p. 17). Spanning "the entire student learning experience" (p. 17), an ePortfolio thus

> makes authentic learning and personal development visible, comprehensible, and meaningful, induces students to draw connections between various learning and personal development experiences inside and outside of class on and off the campus, fosters integrative learning, and deepens dispositional attributes. (p. 17)

These scholars did not argue explicitly for whole ePortfolio assessment; rather, their focus on hard-to-assess, ineffable developmental outcomes; integrative learning; and coherent learning narratives presumed that the whole ePortfolio was the unit of analysis. Indeed, Eynon and Gambino (2018) noted elsewhere that they "see signs of a shift in focus from individual student artifacts to holistic ePortfolio assessment" (p. 296). Such a shift is necessary, they added, if we are to "move beyond measuring discrete learning outcomes to assessing integrative learning and identity development" (p. 297) and if we are to take full advantage of what we can learn from students' ePortfolios. A number of rubrics for holistic ePortfolio assessment can be found on the Internet, and several are included in the suggested additional resources at the end of this chapter.

Holistic approaches also yield benefits for assessing higher order learning outcomes that are more traditional focuses of assessment, such as writing and critical thinking. As Darren Cambridge (2010) persuasively argued, whole ePortfolios provide us with a more detailed and complete portrait of students' achievement of these abilities than individual artifacts do. Whole ePortfolio assessment thus creates opportunities for us to reconsider and reformulate outcomes statements in ways that do greater justice to the complexity of the learning we want students to achieve. Cambridge (2010) offered this example from a hypothetical written communication rubric for the dimension "context and/or purpose for writing" (p. 104):

> The portfolio has a sophisticated and nuanced definition of purpose that is used to focus all elements. The portfolio is responsive to the assigned task and demonstrates initiative in defining task and audience. The portfolio makes clear how samples of writing within the portfolio each demonstrate their own definition of purpose and are responsive to their defined task, and the portfolio explains differences in the level of sophistication of purpose and initiative across the collection of writings, demonstrating growth over time and/or the ability to respond to a variety of rhetorical situations. (p. 104)

One could not assess this outcome as stated by examining only one piece of writing in an ePortfolio. Assessing for this rubric dimension would require "consideration of the whole [ePortfolio], the parts, and how they are related" (Cambridge, 2010, p. 105), as well as evidence of effective use of the digital medium, including navigation and narrative explaining what each writing artifact demonstrates and how the various writing artifacts are related to one another. The opportunity to reframe learning outcomes in nuanced terms more appropriate to learning in higher education may prove attractive to some faculty who have resisted what they see as over-simplification of learning, even in authentic assessment approaches (e.g., Goodwin, 2011).

Furthermore, at their best, ePortfolios can capture those elusive "aha" moments, what Laura Wenk (2019) called "pivotal experiences, . . . the experiences or moments when a student's conceptions or interests shifted drastically because of new insights" (p. 74). At Wenk's institution, Hampshire College, faculty found that while students often wrote about such moments in the paper portfolios used previously, the switch to ePortfolios brought a change; students were more likely to document their pivotal experiences with artifacts, images, pages, and other contextual materials, enabling readers to discern more easily how, why, and under what circumstances a particular moment of insight occurred. Wenk observed that the activity of organizing and arranging ePortfolios—and the accompanying reflection into how best to convey relationships among experiences, concepts, and other learning—can sometimes bring about these "aha" moments. In my own experience of teaching with ePortfolios, I have found that well-designed reflection prompts, embedded in a supportive pedagogical and curricular design, can stimulate these insights. I have written elsewhere about how a reflection assignment that asked students to write multiple versions of their life or educational stories, and to reflect on the relationships between the stories, helped senior English majors understand that identity and self are cognitive constructions, not objective realities. For some students, this metacognitive understanding of identity was empowering, even transformational (Kahn, 2019).

This discussion brings us back to the "meta" aspects of ePortfolios. Well-guided ePortfolios can offer us new insights into students' learning experiences and perceptions of these experiences, showing us how our pedagogical, curricular, and cocurricular practices and processes shape students' learning experiences and contribute to achievement of intended outcomes. We can glean much understanding of student learning by studying groups of ePortfolios, seeking and finding patterns that tell us what practices are working well or not, and gaining more actionable information for improvement than is typically offered by other assessment methods. Higher education has not yet taken full advantage of the potential of ePortfolios to offer information about needed improvements.

Finally, focusing more directly on learning processes, experiences, and environments—how and why our students learn best—can help us put learning, rather than assessment, at the center of our thinking, as Keston Fulcher proposes in chapter 11. For example, something as simple as a written reflection on or visual depiction of what mental steps a student took to solve a mathematics problem or revise a piece of writing can aid in identifying stumbling blocks or content and concepts that students find particularly difficult or easy to master. Such artifacts can reveal how students are interpreting class materials or even comments we make about their individual work. Periodically asking students to reflect on and document how their thinking has changed, what experiences or realizations led to those changes, and what connections they see among learning experiences can provide unexpected insights into how students perceive and understand the learning experiences and environments we design.

Future Trends

The trends outlined previously are likely to continue to develop, particularly the relatively new focuses on ePortfolios as a HIP and meta-HIP, on ways in which they can both advance and demonstrate higher order outcomes such as dispositional and integrative learning, and on holistic ePortfolio assessment as a means to capture complex learning and understand *how* as well as *what* students learn. In the near future, I foresee a focus on ePortfolio literacy and "ePortfolio-making," shifts in our use of ePortfolios and related technologies, and issues of faculty rewards for ePortfolio work.

Digital Literacy and ePortfolio Literacy

Yancey (2019) argued that the most successful ePortfolio experiences are undergirded by a curriculum that teaches students the skills they need to develop effective ePortfolios: not only reflection, metacognition, and integrative learning but also *ePortfolio-making*—the ability to exploit the affordances of digital media to curate, structure, and design an ePortfolio website to create a compelling multimodal learning narrative for a particular audience or audiences (Yancey, 2019). In turn, ePortfolio-making both involves and represents reflection, metacognition, integrative learning, and other abilities we want ePortfolios to advance. This conversation is in its early stages, and its relationship to ongoing discussions of ePortfolio pedagogy and aligned curricula has yet to be fully articulated. As ePortfolio research and practice continue to grow more sophisticated and mature, the role of ePortfolio-making and its relationship to the construction of knowledge and self is likely to continue as a focus of discussion.

ePortfolio Technology

I have said little about technology up to this point because the ePortfolio field is currently focused primarily on pedagogy and curriculum, not technology. But ePortfolios clearly do require technology, and our technology choices often make the difference between successful and unsuccessful ePortfolio implementation. In my own experience, students have preferred Web development platforms like Weebly, Wix, and WordPress to ePortfolio platforms, not only in part because they often regard ePortfolio platforms as "owned" by the institution but also in part because ePortfolio software, in general, offers less flexibility, user-friendliness, and ability to personalize the look and feel of an ePortfolio website. However, ePortfolio vendors are aware that they are competing not only with one another but also with a variety of Web development tools, and we are already seeing some improvements to the Web development capabilities of commercial platforms. Some institutions are choosing to forgo ePortfolio platforms in favor of Web development software; others are offering some combination of solutions whereby faculty, staff, and students are allowed to choose their preferred tools. It will be interesting to watch as the markets for commercial ePortfolio platforms and campus practices continue to evolve.

ePortfolios and Faculty Roles

Deploying ePortfolios for maximum benefit to students and maximum usefulness for assessment demands considerable commitment, whether individually or collectively, in cases where ePortfolios are adopted by programs or institutions. At many institutions, particularly large state universities and private research campuses, faculty may not expect this investment of time and effort to be rewarded in terms of tenure, promotion, and salary. Differences in institutional priorities and reward systems may explain why some of the best known, most successful ePortfolio initiatives have been at community colleges and small, primarily undergraduate, institutions.

Creative solutions to this dilemma certainly exist. Many faculty and staff have turned their ePortfolio practice into opportunities for the Scholarship of Teaching and Learning. Some programs and institutions allocate resources for internal grants to support ePortfolio work or compensate faculty and staff for time spent on ePortfolio assessment. Others have found innovative strategies for embedding ePortfolio professional development, practice, and assessment into work that faculty and staff are already doing (see Eynon and Gambino's 2018 volume *Catalyst in Action: Case Studies of High-Impact ePortfolio Practice* for several examples). This issue is unlikely to go away, and as more programs and institutions adopt ePortfolios, I expect that they will continue to consider how best to navigate the tension between the time high-impact ePortfolios demand and the other responsibilities of faculty and staff.

Conclusion

As I suggested in the introduction to this chapter, ePortfolios bring together many of the assessment and educational trends that recur throughout this volume: authentic assessment; attention to the personal, academic, and professional development of students in addition to traditional focuses on individual outcomes and competencies achieved; and a strengthened focus on learning processes, practices, and designs as we continue moving toward learning-centered paradigms. For these reasons, I believe that ePortfolio use will continue to increase and that the knowledge base on effective ePortfolio teaching, learning, and assessment practice, already quite robust, will continue to grow.

A truism in the assessment community is that the best assessment methods also produce meaningful learning. ePortfolios, done well, exemplify this principle, supporting students, faculty, and staff in creating more powerful in- and out-of-class learning experiences and offering unique insights into how and why these experiences occur. It is for these reasons that I believe ePortfolios can enable us to both transform assessment and assess transformation.

As I write this conclusion, a small group of ePortfolio researchers and practitioners at IUPUI is developing a taxonomy delineating the characteristics of high-, higher-, and highest impact ePortfolio practice. Once we have a satisfactory draft of this taxonomy, we expect to disseminate it widely and solicit comments from others in the field. We also plan to post the draft taxonomy to the website for this volume. I invite readers of this chapter to contribute to this work in progress, which we hope will become an important resource supporting faculty, staff, programs, institutions, and—most of all—students in deriving the maximum benefit from their ePortfolio efforts.

Summary of Main Trends

- ePortfolios are both a HIP for teaching and learning and an assessment approach that recognizes the complexity of postsecondary learning.
- ePortfolios flourish in and support development of cohesive, integrated curricula and thoughtful learning designs that encourage folio thinking and identity development.
- ePortfolios, done well, can cultivate and document dispositional learning linked to personal, academic, and professional development.
- Assessment of whole ePortfolios offers us insights into learning that other assessment approaches do not, including insights into *how* as well as *what* students learn and into so-called ineffable learning outcomes.

Questions for Discussion

- What are the most important differences between paper portfolios and ePortfolios?
- What educational values do ePortfolios reflect?
- How can ePortfolios most benefit educational programs? How can they most benefit students?
- How would you recommend that a program or institution begin an ePortfolio initiative?

Suggested Additional Resources

A number of ePortfolio galleries and rubrics for holistic ePortfolio assessment can be found on the Internet. Following are just a few of many examples.

ePortfolio Galleries

- St. Olaf College Archived Web Portfolios: https://wp.stolaf.edu/cis/web-portfolios-archive/
- LaGuardia Community College ePortfolio Gallery: https://eportfolio.laguardia.edu/student_work.htm

Rubrics for Holistic Assessment of ePortfolios

- Auburn University ePortfolio Project Rubrics: http://wp.auburn.edu/writing/eportfolio-project/faculty-support/rubrics/

- iRubric: ePortfolio Evaluation Rubric: www.rcampus.com/
  rubricshowc.cfm?sp=yes&code=R48XX4&

We want to hear from you about *Trends in Assessment*:

- Provide reactions or suggestions about trends.
- Share and access resources related to trends.
- Learn about professional development opportunities
  related to trends.

Visit assessmentinstitute.iupui.edu/trends

References

Bass, R. (2014). The next whole thing in higher education. *Peer Review, 16*(1), 35.

Batson, T. (2002, November 26). The electronic portfolio boom: What's it all about? *Campus Technology.* Retrieved from http://campustechnology.com/articles/2002/11/the-electronic-portfolio-boom-whats-it-all-about.aspx

Cambridge, D. (2010). *ePortfolios for lifelong learning and assessment.* San Francisco, CA: Jossey-Bass.

Cambridge, D., Cambridge, B. L., & Yancey, K. B. (Eds.). (2009). *Electronic portfolios 2.0: Emergent research on implementation and action.* Sterling, VA: Stylus.

Dahlstrom, E. (with Christopher Brooks, D., Grajek, S., & Reeves, J.). (2015, December). *ECAR study of undergraduate students and information technology, 2015* (Research Report). Louisville, CO: EDUCAUSE Center for Analysis and Research. Retrieved from https://library.educause.edu/~/media/files/library/2015/8/ers1510ss.pdf?la=en

Eynon, B., & Gambino, L. M. (2017). *High-impact ePortfolio practice.* Sterling, VA: Stylus.

Eynon, B., & Gambino, L. M. (Eds.). (2018). *Catalyst in action: Case studies of high-impact ePortfolio practice.* Sterling, VA: Stylus.

Eynon, B., Gambino, L. M., & Torok, J. (2014). Completion, quality, and change: The difference e-portfolios make. *Peer Review, 16*(1), 8–13.

Goodwin, S. W. (2011). Fearful symmetries: Rubrics and assessment. In D. Heiland & L. J. Rosenthal (Eds.), *Literary study, measurement, and the sublime: Disciplinary assessment* (pp. 133–151). New York, NY: Teagle Foundation.

Kahn, S. (2014). E-portfolios: A look at where we've been, where we are now, and where we're (possibly) going. *Peer Review, 16*(1), 4–7.

Kahn, S. (2018). New learning about learning: An introduction to ePortfolio assessment. In C. Secolsky & D. B. Denison (Eds.), *Handbook on measurement, assessment, and evaluation in higher education* (2nd ed., pp. 560–572). New York, NY: Routledge.

Kahn, S. (2019). Identity development as curriculum: A metacognitive approach. In K. B. Yancey (Ed.), *ePortfolio as curriculum: Models and practices for developing students' ePortfolio literacy* (pp. 89–105). Sterling, VA: Stylus.

Kahn, S., & Scott, S. B. (2013). Scaling up ePortfolios at a complex urban research university: The IUPUI story. Retrieved from http://iupui.mcnrc.org/scaling-story/

Kuh, G. D. (2017). Foreword: And now there are 11. In B. Eynon & L. M. Gambino, *High-impact ePortfolio practice* (pp. vii–xi). Sterling, VA: Stylus.

Kuh, G. D., Gambino, L. M., Bresciani Ludvik, M., & O'Donnell, K. (2017, October). *Using ePortfolio to document and enhance the dispositional learning impact of HIPs.* Workshop presented at the 2017 Assessment Institute, Indianapolis, IN.

Kuh, G. D., Gambino, L. M., Bresciani Ludvik, M., & O'Donnell, K. (2018). *Using ePortfolio to document and deepen the impact of HIPs on learning dispositions* (Occasional Paper No. 32). Urbana, IL: National Institute for Learning Outcomes Assessment.

Matthews-DeNatale, G. (2014). Are we who we think we are? ePortfolios as a tool for curriculum redesign. *Journal of Asynchronous Learning Networks, 17*(4), 41–55.

Matthews-DeNatale, G. (2018). Self as story: Meaning-making and identity integration in capstone ePortfolios. In B. Eynon & L. M. Gambino (Eds.), *Catalyst in action: Case studies of high-impact ePortfolio practice* (pp. 1–14). Sterling, VA: Stylus.

Penny Light, T., Chen, H. L., & Ittelson, J. C. (2012). *Documenting learning with ePortfolios: A guide for college instructors.* San Francisco, CA: Jossey-Bass.

Reynolds, C., & Patton, J. (2014). *Leveraging the ePortfolio for integrative learning: A faculty guide for transforming student learning.* Sterling, VA: Stylus.

Wenk, L. (2019). Hampshire College ePortfolios: A curriculum on reflection to support individualized educational pathways. In K. B. Yancey (Ed.), *ePortfolio as curriculum: Models and practices for developing students' ePortfolio literacy* (pp. 107–122). Sterling, VA: Stylus.

Yancey, K. B. (2001). Introduction: Digitized student portfolios. In B. L. Cambridge, S. Kahn, D. P. Tompkins, & K. B. Yancey (Eds.), *Electronic portfolios: Emerging practices in student, faculty, and institutional learning* (pp. 15–30). Washington, DC: American Association for Higher Education.

Yancey, K. B. (2004). Postmodernism, palimpsest, and portfolios: Theoretical issues in the representation of student work. *College Composition and Communication, 55*(4), 738–762.

Yancey, K. B. (2009). Reflection and electronic portfolios: Inventing the self and reinventing the university. In D. Cambridge, B. Cambridge, & K. B. Yancey (Eds.), *Electronic portfolios 2.0: Emergent research on implementation and impact* (pp. 5–16). Sterling, VA: Stylus.

Yancey, K. B. (2017, October). *ePortfolios, assessment, and curriculum: Putting our assessment criteria and our ePortfolio curriculum in dialogue.* Paper presented at the 2017 Assessment Institute, Indianapolis, IN.

Yancey, K. B. (2019). Introduction. In K. B. Yancey (Ed.), *ePortfolio as curriculum: Models and practices for developing students' ePortfolio literacy* (pp. 1–11). Sterling, VA: Stylus.

PART TWO

LOOKING TO THE FUTURE

LOTS OF ASSESSMENT, LITTLE IMPROVEMENT?

How to Fix the Broken System

Keston H. Fulcher and Caroline O. Prendergast

Improvement features prominently in the National Institute for Learning Outcomes Assessment's (NILOA's) *Assessment That Matters: Trending Toward Practices That Document Authentic Student Learning.* Jankowski, Timmer, Kinzie, and Kuh (2018) argue that improvement is a major driver of assessment. Changes to curriculum, pedagogy, policy, professional development, advising, and resources are cited as examples of assessment-influenced modifications intended to improve student learning. Nevertheless, Jankowski and colleagues (2018) also highlight academe's shortcomings with respect to improvement:

> While use of assessment results is increasing, documenting improvements in student learning and the quality of teaching falls short of what the enterprise needs. Provosts provided numerous examples of expansive changes at their institutions drawing on assessment data, but too few had examples of whether the changes had the intended effects. (p. 26)

The paper's conclusion—that we have scant evidence of assessment-evidenced improvement—is consistent with the observations of assessment critics (e.g., Banta & Blaich, 2011; Gilbert, 2015; Worthen, 2018). Furthermore, assessment insiders have similarly acknowledged this lack of improvement (e.g., Blaich & Wise, 2011; Eubanks, 2018; Fulcher, Good, Coleman, & Smith, 2014).

To focus readers on the lingering gap between assessment and improvement, Jankowski and colleagues (2018) raise important questions:

Did the policy change or alteration of the assessment process actually have the intended impact? Did the assignment modifications lead to better demonstrations of student learning? Can we really connect . . . learning . . . at the course-level to institution-level learning outcome statements and understand student learning as a campus? (p. 26)

These and related questions are the focus of the newly formed learning improvement and innovation track at the Assessment Institute. Because the track is new, as of 2018, there are no previous presentations or documents from which to draw.

Instead, we share emerging thoughts about the topic from recent national gatherings, articles, research, and our work at the Center for Assessment and Research Studies at James Madison University (JMU). Particularly influential for this chapter are conversations, presentations, and articles stemming from the Learning Improvement Summits (Horst & Ames, 2018).

Purpose

The purpose of the learning improvement and innovation track is to help higher education conduct and assess learning improvement efforts, particularly at the program and institutional levels. We define *improvement* as making informed curricular and pedagogical modifications and then reassessing to confirm that the changes improved student learning outcomes. This "simple model" design also requires a baseline (Fulcher et al., 2014). We need to compare knowledge, skills, or abilities before and after an intervention has taken place. If any one of these macro steps is missing—assess, intervene effectively, reassess—by definition, learning improvement cannot be evidenced.

Strategy 1: Adopt a Learning Improvement Heuristic

An obstacle to improvement is that assessment practitioners foreground assessment and background learning improvement (Stitt-Bergh, Kinzie, & Fulcher, 2018). Indeed, most assessment cycles begin with writing student learning outcomes, take several steps related to methodology and reporting, and end with using results for improvement (see Figure 10.1). This representation implies that learning improvement is merely a logical by-product of an assessment process.

To use a business analogy, we say the thinking behind this model is as absurd as hoping that good accounting processes will lead to higher profits.

Figure 10.1. Example of an assessment cycle.

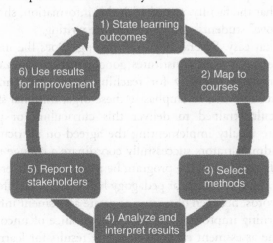

Good accounting processes should accurately capture better profits; however, better profits do *not* result from good accounting processes. Likewise, good assessment processes should capture learning improvement, but better assessment processes do *not* result in learning improvement. In sum, to conceptualize learning improvement as a mere step in the assessment process is to wildly overvalue assessment's role in learning improvement.

Even in the simple model—assess, intervene, reassess—*assess* is two thirds of the formula. The frequency of words, however, does not proportionally represent the time and energy required for the assessments and the intervention. A more proportional representation based on the amount of resources necessary might look like this:

assess, INTERVENE, reassess

The assessment and reassessment are no doubt necessary, but they are bit players. At its best, assessment can accurately indicate where student learning achievement is high and where it is low. Nevertheless, even if diagnostic, most assessments shed little light on what interventions would effectively move the learning needle. Similarly, the assessment process does not change the teaching patterns already in place.

For example, imagine that an institution assesses writing. The assessment team uses a well-developed rubric to evaluate representative writing samples. The process accurately determines that students struggle with organizing ideas into paragraphs and sentences. Traditional models of the assessment cycle suggest that the faculty, armed with this information, should next take steps to "improve" students' ability to organize writing.

It is not that easy. Several steps are missing. Does the institution have agreed-on criteria for what constitutes good writing organization? Is there a common university strategy for teaching writing organization? If so, what classes are supposed to emphasize these organizational skills? To what degree are faculty trained to deliver this curriculum or pedagogy? To what degree are faculty implementing the agreed-on curriculum or pedagogy? Could administrators successfully coordinate a change that affects all students? Furthermore, will the program be reassessed to determine whether the changes to the curriculum or pedagogy had the desired effect?

In other words, between obtaining accurate assessment information and evidencing learning improvement lies a vast distance of unconnected dots. One step in the assessment cycle labeled "use results for learning improvement" does not bridge this distance.

Given the paucity of learning improvement examples, it is safe to say that the traditional assessment model has *not* successfully guided practitioners to the promised land of learning improvement. As Stitt-Bergh and colleagues (2018) observed about typical assessment, "practitioners . . . fail to see the action and improvement forest from the methodological trees" (p. 28).

Subsuming assessment processes under learning improvement is the first of three major strategies we endorse to accelerate learning improvement in higher education. The second strategy, related to innovation, is to develop and disseminate technical practices that enhance improvement efforts. The third strategy is to attend to social dynamics of program-level and institution-level improvement.

Contrasting the Traditional Assessment Model With a Learning Improvement Model

To elucidate the difference between foregrounding assessment and foregrounding improvement, we share two examples of reports adapted from Fulcher's presentation at Auburn's Learning Improvement Summit 2. The featured program is the fictitious bachelor's degree in 1980s pop culture (POPC). For simplicity's sake, each report focuses on only one student learning outcome, ethical reasoning. Pay attention to how the second report foregrounds improvement. It emphasizes the change in intervention from one year to the next, and it illuminates how the assessment methodology is specifically designed to show the impact of the intervention (pre-intervention assessment versus post-intervention assessment). From the outset, the second report helps readers decide whether improvement resulted from program changes. In the traditional assessment report, the learning improvement story is muffled and incomplete.

Traditional Assessment-Focused Report (Foregrounds Assessment Process)

1. Program learning outcome: Students will analyze an ethical situation related to 1980s pop culture and provide a recommendation for action, including rationale.
2. Courses/experiences in the degree plan that address this outcome:
   a. POPC 3022: Ethics introduced in this Introduction to the 1980s course.
   b. POPC 3356: In this Icons of the 1980s class, students analyze the case of Michael Jackson outbidding his friend Paul McCartney on the Beatles catalogue.
   c. POPC 4450: The final assignment in this Lessons of the 1980s course allows students to choose from several ethical situations. They choose a situation and write a 10-page paper.
3. Assessment method: The POPC 4450 final assignment is evaluated via a behaviorally anchored rubric designed to assess ethical reasoning skills. The rubric comprises criteria broken out into five levels of proficiency: *insufficient* (0), *marginal* (1), *good* (2), *excellent* (3), and *extraordinary* (4). Related to this student learning outcome (SLO), the two most pertinent rubric criteria are "Strength of Analysis" and "Quality of Recommendation." All students take POPC 4450 as seniors.
4. Target for achievement: A student average of *good* (2) on the "Analysis" and "Recommendation" criteria.
5. Results:
   a. This year's average score for "Analysis" was 2.5 (midway between *good* and *excellent*).
   b. This year's average score for "Recommendation" was 1.5 (midway between *marginal* and *good*).
6. Target met? The results were mixed. We surpassed our target for "Analysis" but missed the mark for "Recommendation."
7. Action plan for improvement of student learning:
   a. We followed through with last year's plan, which entailed collecting baseline data on ethical reasoning before making any changes to POPC 4450. We implemented the final project in POPC 4450 and

followed through with collecting the data. This year, we have data to interpret our students' performances.

b. We are satisfied with students' ability to analyze ethical situations. We therefore will keep our instruction and curriculum the same for this area. Our faculty agree, however, that students are ineffective at providing a high-quality recommendation. Diving into the results, we discovered that students rarely referred back to their ethical analyses when providing a recommendation. In essence, their analyses and recommendations were disjointed. Next year, we will provide opportunities for students to practice tying the analyses and recommendations together.

Learning Improvement–Focused Report (Foregrounds Improvement)

1. Area targeted for learning improvement: One of our student learning outcomes (SLOs) is "Students will analyze an ethical situation related to 1980s pop culture and provide a recommendation for action, including rationale." It is the second part of this SLO—**students offering a recommendation for action, including rationale**—that we are targeting for improvement. We chose this area for improvement based on the previous year's students' poor performance. Furthermore, with respect to the SLO, what good is effective ethical analysis if it isn't tied to good decision-making?

2. Improvement scope (e.g., section, course, program, institutional): Program level. All graduating students (approximately 100) in the bachelor for 1980s pop culture program will experience the curriculum changes.

3. Changes in curriculum and pedagogy meant to result in learning improvement appear in **bold**. *[Note to reader: The bolded components distinguish this report from the traditional assessment report; these new interventions are introduced here, and their impact is tested later in the report.]*

   a. POPC 3022: Ethics introduced in this Introduction to the 1980s course.

   b. POPC 3356: In this Icons of the 1980s class, students analyze the case of Michael Jackson outbidding his friend Paul McCartney on the Beatles catalog. **The instructor models tying in analyses with recommendations for what Michael Jackson should have done and contrasts that with examples where analyses and recommendations are unlinked.**

   c. POPC 4450: The final assignment in this Lessons of the 1980s course allows students to choose from several ethical situations. Each student selects an ethical situation to analyze in a 10-page paper. **Students are given the rubric for the paper. The teacher emphasizes to the class the difficulties past cohorts have had with linking analyses and recommendations. She then provides strategies to address these struggles. Students practice this skill via two graded homework assignments prior to completing the final paper.**

4. Type of measure: **Direct.** The final assignment from POPC 4450 is evaluated via a behaviorally anchored rubric designed to assess ethical reasoning skills. The rubric is composed of criteria broken out into five levels of proficiency: *insufficient* (0), *marginal* (1), *good* (2), *excellent* (3), and *extraordinary* (4). For this SLO, the two pertinent rubric criteria are "Strength of Analysis" and "Quality of Recommendation." Note that POPC 4450 is a requirement for all students and is taken right before graduation. All students are tested at the end of this class via the aforementioned writing assignment. Given that all students take POPC 4450, the results support **program-level** inferences.

5. Baseline data: With respect to ethical recommendation, last year's students scored a **1.5**—midway between *marginal* and *good.*

6. Reassessment data: This year's cohort scored a **2.5** or midway between *good* and *excellent.*

7. Improvement interpretation: We attribute the 1-point gain in providing ethical recommendations—from *marginal–good* to *good–excellent*—to the changes outlined in step 3. We infer that program-level learning improvement was achieved.

Compare the Two Focused Reports

The learning-improvement–focused report starts by targeting an area for improvement, and the subsequent steps tell the improvement story. Furthermore, the learning-improvement–focused report focuses on changes in the learning environment expected to bring about improvement. In contrast, the assessment report emphasizes chronological steps and then asks—at the end—what actions will be taken for improvement. In other words, the learning improvement report is designed to tell a story about improvement. In contrast, an assessment report speaks to an assessment process and, well, tells an assessment story. The assessment story might, but probably will not, branch off into a change story intended to bring about an improvement. Nevertheless, Kuh noted in his foreword to Blaich and Wise's (2011) article that instances of change are rare; showing that the changes had a positive effect on student learning (i.e., improvement) is even rarer.

Even if higher education were to prioritize improvement (assess, effectively intervene, reassess), naysayers would continue launching critiques. They might rightfully argue that the wished-for interpretation—that changes in learning environment caused observed learning improvement—cannot be supported by the loose methodologies often practiced in higher education. This likely criticism brings us to the next strategy. In addition to adopting a better heuristic, higher education must also embrace technical methods; these methods can help us support causal claims with respect to how changes in the learning environment relate to improved learning.

Strategy 2: Develop and Disseminate Technical Practices That Enhance Improvement Efforts

Learning systems in higher education are complex. Academic programs typically involve multiple faculty members working across multiple courses with dozens or hundreds of students. Understandably, zooming out to analyze learning improvement at the program level can be difficult. For this reason, higher education needs to adopt a series of technical, but practical, approaches to shining light on often-invisible program mechanics. The following sections will explain the benefits of three such techniques—program theory, implementation fidelity, and sound measurement—within the context of learning improvement initiatives.

Program Theory

To improve a program, we must understand how the program works. We need to know which components of the program are expected to help students achieve specific SLOs, as well as how and why the components will be useful. Program theories document the expected relationship between program components and their intended outcomes. Ideally, program theories provide empirical support for pedagogical and curricular choices, explaining why the intended outcomes should result from the program. In simpler language, good program theory entails tight alignment among SLOs, teaching and curriculum, and theory.

In typical practice, though, clear rationales are rarely provided to justify programmatic decisions. "Floating" activities untethered to specific SLOs are an example of poor program theory. Slightly better, but still poor, are SLOs that are linked to activities but without a rationale for why the activity should result in achievement of the SLO. Brief examples of each of these levels of quality, as well as an example of good program theory, are outlined in Table 10.1. Only the third example (based on Sanchez, Fulcher, Smith, Ames, &

TABLE 10.1
Examples of Program Theory

	Student Learning Outcome (SLO)	*Intervention*	*Rationale*
1. Very poor	Absent.	Students will read about the importance of ethical reasoning.	Absent.
2. Poor	For a specific ethical situation or dilemma, students will evaluate courses of action by applying ethical reasoning considerations.	Faculty will be provided with reference materials addressing the importance of ethical reasoning.	Faculty will be more likely to teach about ethical reasoning if they understand its importance. Therefore, their students will become more proficient in ethical reasoning.
3. Good	For a specific ethical situation or dilemma, students will evaluate courses of action by applying ethical reasoning considerations.	During orientation, all first-year students will participate in a 75-minute small group discussion about ethical reasoning. Each group will watch a video about an ethical dilemma, which group members will then discuss with a trained facilitator. Students will be provided with information about key ethical reasoning questions to guide their discussion.	Behavioral economics research (e.g., Ariely, 2013) suggests that intuitive responses can be slowed by prompting recall of ethical conduct codes. The discussion activity is expected to lead to achievement of the SLO by (a) providing students with an opportunity to apply ethical reasoning considerations to a specific ethical dilemma and (b) encouraging students to engage in critical thinking (rather than intuitive responses) by discussing key ethical reasoning questions for evaluating ethical dilemmas.

Hawk, 2017) provides theoretically informed links between program features and intended outcomes (Bickman, 1987).

Implementation Fidelity

Even the best-designed programs may struggle to evidence improvement if they are not implemented as planned. Although it may seem obvious that we want the programs we design to match the programs that students experience, the alignment between intentions and reality is often overlooked in educational research. Implementation fidelity is a tool that can be used to determine if, and how, the program that students experience (the *implemented* program) differs from the program that was designed (the *intended* program). This process is aided by the program theories described previously, which identify key components of the program that must be experienced for improvement to occur. To claim that learning improvement resulted from an intervention, we must document that the intervention actually occurred.

Studies of implementation fidelity require observation of a program to see what actually happens when the program takes place. Then, observational data are used to examine the level of adherence to the planned program. Adherence data may include whether key program components actually occurred, how well (and for how long) the components were implemented, and whether program participants were responsive (Smith, Finney, & Fulcher, 2017).

For example, consider the intervention described in Table 10.1. The "good" example identified two important components of the intended program: practice applying ethical reasoning considerations and discuss key ethical reasoning questions. An implementation fidelity study might be used to answer the following questions about the program:

- Did students practice applying ethical reasoning considerations to the ethical dilemma?
- Did students actually discuss the key ethical reasoning questions?
- Were students actively engaged with all components of the program?

In addition, the intervention was specified to last 75 minutes and include a conversation facilitated by a trained faculty or staff member. These specifications suggest additional questions, such as the following:

- Did the program last the full 75 minutes?
- Did the faculty or staff leader adequately facilitate the conversation?

Imagine we find that students do not achieve the SLO and the program was implemented with low fidelity. In this scenario, we have implementation failure (Rogers, 2000). Because the *intended* program did not occur, we do not know it is effective. All we know is that the *implemented* program did not work. Conversely, if we find the program was implemented with high fidelity and students still do not meet the SLO, it is possible that theory failure—a problem with the theory or design underlying the program—is to blame (Rogers, 2000). Clearly, this information would affect the decisions we make next about the program: Should we invest in rebuilding the program, or should we focus instead on developing our facilitators?

Although implementation fidelity research also appears in the fields of program evaluation, behavioral psychology, education, and health research (Capin, Walker, Vaughn, & Wanzek, 2018; Swanson, Wanzek, Haring, Ciullo, & McCulley, 2011), it has received only limited attention in higher education research (Smith, Finney, & Fulcher, 2017). More widespread use of implementation fidelity research could be an important step in encouraging learning improvement initiatives: If programs can gather information about how their intentions relate to their realities, decisions about program efficacy can be made with more clarity and evidence.

Measurement

Clear program theory and strong implementation fidelity are useful, but not sufficient, for evidencing learning improvement. We must also consider a foundational concept in assessment: sound measurement. High-quality measures allow us to see whether improvement has occurred.

A primary consideration here is the alignment between the measure and the SLO. Quite simply, it is impossible to gather information about an SLO with a measure designed to assess something entirely different. For example, attempting to assess students' application of ethical reasoning considerations with a measure of factual knowledge about ethical reasoning will not yield useful information. Students' scores might capture their content knowledge but fail to represent their ability to apply that knowledge. Without that information, we are unable to make accurate inferences about achievement of the SLO.

Misalignment between the SLO and the selected measures reduces our ability to draw useful inferences from our data (American Educational Research Association, American Psychological Association, & National Council on Measurement in Education, 2014). Measures and SLOs can be misaligned in two ways (Messick, 1989). First, scores may be systematically influenced by something other than the SLO. This "noise" may obscure true changes in student ability. Second, the measure may not include key components of the SLO. If so, real increases in students' abilities may not be captured because the test does not enable students to fully demonstrate those abilities. In other words, the "signal" is incomplete. These two alignment threats significantly weaken our ability to make claims about improvement. Even if the intervention has truly been successful, we cannot provide evidence for improvement if our measurement tools cannot detect a change.

The higher education literature has unfortunately confounded measurement with instrument type, insinuating that multiple-choice tests are most associated with the "measurement model" (Ewell, 2009). As a result, "measurement" is often seen as an overly standardized, surface-level approach to understanding student learning. That is an unfortunate framing. Measurement and the brief treatment here apply to data from any type of instrument. Whether collecting data using multiple-choice tests, essays scored by rubrics, or portfolios, we endeavor to increase the learning "signal" in the data and reduce the noise.

Strategy 3: Attend to Social Dynamics

Without commitment of faculty who deliver the interventions, even the best laid plans do not translate into better student learning. Thinking back to our earlier discussion, for example, there is no "fidelity" in implementation fidelity without faculty collaboration.

Especially when we consider program-level and institution-level improvement, eliciting and coordinating commitment from faculty is complex. For example, imagine that an improvement initiative required coordinated interventions across two sequential courses and that three faculty taught each course (six faculty total). That would mean that each set of three faculty would have to coordinate with each other (horizontal alignment) and also with the faculty teaching courses before or after their own (vertical alignment), as illustrated by Figure 10.2.

Such coordination has proven extremely challenging. As Bok (2009) noted, higher education is not structured to support learning. Graduate students who eventually become professors often receive little training in teaching. Faculty typically receive few incentives or rewards for good teaching relative to research and grant-writing. Furthermore, tenure and promotion are almost always based on individual achievement as opposed to group achievement.

To create a pathway for program-level learning improvement as suggested by Figure 10.2, the educational development and assessment offices at

JMU codeveloped a program-level learning improvement request for proposals (RFP). The RFP requires faculty to make a case for selecting a particular learning area to improve. The main elements of the RFP document are as follows:

- Program overview
- Area targeted for improvement
- Faculty team and their commitment to improvement
- Investigate current efforts with respect to area targeted for improvement
- Propose tentative learning modifications
- Propose improvement timetable

We launched our learning improvement pilots using the RFP approach. Since then, three programs have been selected. The first, Computer Information Systems, has successfully completed the cycle with great success; this program was able to evidence learning improvement in the form of increased student skills in requirements elicitation (Lending, Fulcher, Ezell, May, & Dillon, 2018).

While the RFP process has been successful at JMU, much work has yet to be done to elicit faculty commitment. Compared to the other strategies laid out in this chapter, attending to social dynamics is the least well explored and understood in the higher education literature. Collectively, we need

Figure 10.2. Horizontal and vertical alignment.

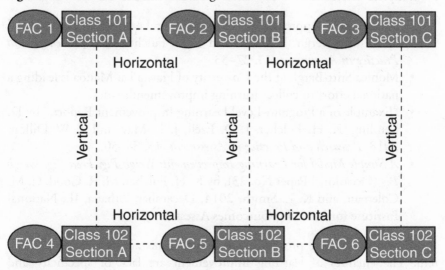

to identify and develop strategies to answer questions such as the following: How can institutions facilitate and reward faculty working together to improve student learning? How can institutions provide professional development opportunities that give faculty the skills, time, and space to strategize together? All else considered, learning improvement does not happen without faculty inspiration and collaboration.

Summary

This chapter opened by highlighting NILOA's call for better use of assessment for student learning improvement. Similar calls have been made over the past four decades. Nevertheless, the world has few examples to show, especially if we are seeking program-level or institution-level evidence of assess, effectively intervene, reassess.

In this chapter, we suggest attacking improvement scarcity through three strategies. We summarize each and provide suggestions for further reading.

Adopt a Learning Improvement Heuristic

Consider reframing how assessment interfaces with improvement. Improvement stories start with identifying an area to be improved, not by writing SLOs and then engaging in perfunctory methodology and reporting. Let's bring assessment into improvement processes. The other way—bringing learning improvement into assessment processes—has, in large part, been a failure. Suggested further readings and resources (see the references section for complete information about these resources) include the following:

- "Refining an Approach to Assessment for Learning Improvement," by M. Stitt-Bergh, J. Kinzie, and K. H. Fulcher, 2018, *Research and Practice in Assessment, 13*, 27–33.
- Monica Stitt-Bergh at the University of Hawai'i at Manoa is leading a national effort to collect learning improvement stories.
- "Example of a Program-Level Learning Improvement Report," by D. Lending, K. H. Fulcher, J. D. Ezell, J. L. May, and T. W. Dillon, 2018, *Research and Practice in Assessment, 13*, 34–50.
- *A Simple Model for Learning Improvement: Weigh Pig, Feed Pig, Weigh Pig* (Occasional Paper No. 23), by K. H. Fulcher, M. R. Good, C. M. Coleman, and K. L. Smith, 2014, December, Urbana, IL: National Institute for Learning Outcomes Assessment.

Incorporate innovative processes that tighten links across the learning system. The enemies of learning improvement are lack of specificity and misalignment—in other words, insufficient clarity about the area targeted for improvement and loose relationships among SLOs, interventions, evidence-based theory, implementation, and methodology. Tools more commonly found in health care, PK–12 education, and social psychology research could be brought to bear on this common problem. For example, program theory, implementation fidelity, and validity frameworks can connect and tighten learning improvement components. The following resources may be useful for further information about these tools:

- "Connecting Assessment Practices With Curricula and Pedagogy Via Implementation Fidelity Data," by K. L. Smith, S. J. Finney, and K. H. Fulcher, 2018, *Assessment and Evaluation in Higher Education.*
- "The Functions of Program Theory," by L. Bickman, 1987, *New Directions for Program Evaluation, 33,* 5–18.
- *The Concept of Validity: Revisions, New Directions, and Applications,* by R. W. Lissitz (Ed.), 2009, Charlotte, NC: Information Age Publishing.

Facilitate and reward faculty for working together to improve student learning. Program- and institution-level improvement requires coordination among faculty members. We provided an RFP process as an example. Suggested further readings and resources include the following:

- "The Quality Improvement Toolkit," by K. Schoepp and S. Benson, 2017, *The Online Journal of Quality in Higher Education, 4*(3), 24.
- JMU Learning Improvement: Request for Proposals, n.d., www .jmu.edu/learningimprovement/learning-improvement-by-design/ learning-improvement-rfp.shtml
- Learning Improvement Initiative, n.d., www.jmu.edu/assessment/ sass/learning-improvement-initiative.shtml

Conclusion

Ask yourself the following questions:

- When speaking about assessment, do you highlight the importance of improvement?
- Do you have plentiful examples of improvement (a reassessment that shows increased learning due to an intervention) at the program and institutional levels?

If you answered yes to the first question and no to the second, then you're a member of the assessment dissonance club, a group that speaks to assessment's power to aid improvement but can offer few examples to back the claim. Perhaps it is time to join a new club, one that values learning improvement, engages in practices that lead to improvement, and uses assessment to evidence such improvement. In this chapter, we have offered a few strategies to help you transfer from one club to the other.

Questions for Discussion

1. Why is it important to focus on improvement as part of assessment processes? What challenges do individuals and programs face in doing so?
2. What strategies are useful for moving to a more learning-focused improvement paradigm? In what ways can these strategies guide improvement efforts?
3. What is meant by the phrase, "Let's bring assessment into improvement processes"? How does this approach differ from more traditional models that view improvement as a final step in assessment processes?

We want to hear from you about *Trends in Assessment*:

- Provide reactions or suggestions about trends.
- Share and access resources related to trends.
- Learn about professional development opportunities related to trends.

Visit assessmentinstitute.iupui.edu/trends

References

American Educational Research Association, American Psychological Association, & National Council on Measurement in Education. (2014). *Standards for educational and psychological testing.* Washington, DC: American Educational Research Association.

Ariely, D. (2013). *The honest truth about dishonesty: How we lie to everyone—especially ourselves.* New York, NY: HarperCollins.

Banta, T. W., & Blaich, C. (2011). Closing the assessment loop. *Change: The Magazine of Higher Learning, 43*(1), 22–27.

Bickman, L. (1987). The functions of program theory. *New Directions for Program Evaluation, 33,* 5–18.

Blaich, C., & Wise, K. (2011). *From gathering to using assessment results: Lessons from the Wabash national study.* (NILOA Occasional Paper No. 8). Urbana, IL: University of Illinois and Indiana University, National Institute for Learning Outcomes Assessment.

Bok, D. (2009). *Our underachieving colleges: A candid look at how much students learn and why they should be learning more—New edition* (Vol. 50). Princeton, NJ: Princeton University Press.

Capin, P., Walker, M. A., Vaughn, S., & Wanzek, J. (2018). Examining how treatment fidelity is supported, measured, and reported in K–3 reading intervention research. *Educational Psychology Review, 30*(3), 885–919.

Eubanks, D. (2018, Fall). A guide for the perplexed. *Intersection.* Retrieved from https://www.aalhe.org/

Ewell, P. T. (2009, November). *Assessment, accountability, and improvement: Revisiting the tension.* (NILOA Occasional Paper No. 1). Urbana, IL: University of Illinois and Indiana University, National Institute for Learning Outcomes Assessment.

Fulcher, K. H., Good, M. R., Coleman, C. M., & Smith, K. L. (2014, December). *A simple model for learning improvement: Weigh pig, feed pig, weigh pig.* (Occasional Paper No. 23). Urbana, IL: University of Illinois and Indiana University, National Institute for Learning Outcomes Assessment.

Gilbert, E. (2015, August 14). Does assessment make colleges better? Who knows? *The Chronicle of Higher Education.* Retrieved from https://www.chronicle.com/

Horst, S. J., & Ames, A. J. (2018). Bringing together assessment and learning improvement: Dreaming big for an inaugural summit. *Research and Practice in Assessment, 13,* 6–10.

Jankowski, N. A., Timmer, J. D., Kinzie, J., & Kuh, G. D. (2018). *Assessment that matters: Trending toward practices that document authentic student learning.* Urbana, IL: University of Illinois and Indiana University, National Institute for Learning Outcomes Assessment.

JMU learning improvement: Request for proposals. (n.d.). Retrieved from http://www.jmu.edu/learningimprovement/learning-improvement-by-design/learning-improvement-rfp.shtml

Learning improvement initiative. (n.d.). Retrieved from https://www.jmu.edu/assessment/sass/learning-improvement-initiative.shtml

Lending, D., Fulcher, K. H., Ezell, J. D., May, J. L., & Dillon, T. W. (2018). Example of a program-level learning improvement report. *Research and Practice in Assessment, 13,* 34–50.

Lissitz, R. W. (Ed.). (2009). *The concept of validity: Revisions, new directions, and applications.* Charlotte, NC: Information Age Publishing.

Messick, S. (1989). Validity. In R. L. Linn (Ed.), *Educational measurement* (3rd ed., pp. 13–104). New York, NY: American Council on Education and Macmillan.

Rogers, P. J. (2000). Program theory: Not whether programs work but how they work. In D. L. Stufflebeam, G. F. Madaus, & T. Kellaghan (Eds.), *Evaluation models: Viewpoints on educational and human services evaluation* (2nd ed., pp. 209–233). Dordrecht, the Netherlands: Springer.

Sanchez, E. R. H., Fulcher, K. H., Smith, K. L., Ames, A., & Hawk, W. J. (2017). Defining, teaching, and assessing ethical reasoning in action. *Change: The Magazine of Higher Learning, 49*(2), 30–36.

Schoepp, K., & Benson, S. (2017). The quality improvement toolkit. *The Online Journal of Quality in Higher Education, 4*(3), 24.

Smith, K. L., Finney, S. J., & Fulcher, K. H. (2017). Actionable steps for engaging assessment practitioners and faculty in implementation fidelity research. *Research and Practice in Assessment, 12,* 71–86.

Smith, K. L., Finney, S. J., & Fulcher, K. H. (2018). Connecting assessment practices with curricula and pedagogy via implementation fidelity data. *Assessment and Evaluation in Higher Education.* doi:10.1080/02602938.2018.1496321

Stitt-Bergh, M., Kinzie, J., & Fulcher, K. H. (2018). Refining an approach to assessment for learning improvement. *Research and Practice in Assessment, 13,* 27–33.

Swanson, E., Wanzek, J., Haring, C., Ciullo, S., & McCulley, L. (2011). Intervention fidelity in special and general education research journals. *Journal of Special Education, 47*(1), 3–13.

Worthen, M. W. (2018, February 23). The misguided drive to measure "learning outcomes." *The New York Times.* Retrieved from https://www.nytimes.com/2018/02/23/opinion/sunday/colleges-measure-learning-outcomes.html?searchResultPosition=1

USING ASSESSMENT
TRENDS IN PLANNING,
DECISION-MAKING,
AND IMPROVEMENT

Michele J. Hansen

E
nvisioning the future role of higher education in serving the needs of the next generation of learners will require a dramatic shift in our assessment and improvement models. We will need to rethink what we assess, how we assess, and how we leverage assessment results. This chapter focuses on how to use the assessment trends discussed in this volume for planning, decision-making, and improvement. We also highlight the roles of policymakers, campus leaders, faculty members, assessment practitioners, and scholars in applying new thinking about assessment to guide their assessment planning moving forward. Overall, our assessment planning should take a holistic, developmental view of students; focus on students' ability to integrate and apply learning to complex problems that transcend disciplinary boundaries; emphasize authentic, embedded assessment evidence; and ensure that assessment approaches are culturally responsive and promote student equity.

For example, an approach that investigates student equity employs methods that examine whether all students have learning opportunities that are responsive to their diverse learning needs. It must also, at a minimum, disaggregate outcomes by student groups (first-generation, gender, historically marginalized groups, underresourced, nontraditional, transfer, and more). To ensure that these conditions are met in courses, programs, and interventions, institutions must focus on assessing the quality of experiences in addition to the outcomes of those experiences. Good assessment planning will thus include considering how students perceive, interpret, and engage in learning experiences (process or formative assessment) as a necessary complement to outcomes assessment.

New assessment and improvement approaches will further require that institutions leverage multiple types and levels of assessment data. Although assessment of cognitive learning outcomes like critical thinking, writing, and quantitative reasoning will remain important, other types of assessment data may also be needed to provide a holistic view of student gains. These data might include retention and degree completion rates, as well as students' interpersonal and intrapersonal growth, self-awareness, social intelligence, civic and life skills, professionalism, and commitment to lifelong learning. Moreover, as institutions focus on using assessment for internal improvement and external accountability, assessment data will need to be collected at multiple levels (course, program, institution) to meet the decision-making needs of internal and external stakeholders, including policymakers.

This volume comes at a pivotal time. Rather than viewing it as a perfunctory collection of chapters espousing the value of implementing effective assessment methods and using the findings to improve students' learning outcomes, we hope that readers can use it to support their institutions in preparing students to be reflective, actively engaged citizens who make meaningful contributions in a rapidly changing and complex society. Ideally, the assessment trends advocated throughout this volume will also help institutions respond to the shifting needs of students as they face unprecedented changes fueled by technological innovations that are changing the nature of work, industry, and society as a whole. We will thus need to integrate data from student and academic affairs to achieve a holistic picture of student learning, development, and success. Thoughtful assessment in the current higher education landscape will necessitate varied assessment approaches, understanding of student development theories, and other new frameworks. We hope that this chapter will be a useful guide to putting these trends into practice while considering unique institutional contexts.

Putting Assessment Trends Into Practice: What to Assess

As we have noted, contributors throughout this volume emphasize that meeting the needs of today's students and society requires rethinking what, exactly, we should assess. New focuses take a more holistic view of the impact of higher education on students and include the nature and quality of student learning experiences; student developmental gains; and noncognitive, as well as cognitive, outcomes. We must also assess how well our curricula and cocurricula are successfully preparing students for careers and citizenship in a complex, globalizing, and increasingly technological world.

Assessing Students Holistically

Contributors throughout this volume advocate in various ways for a broader view of the student experience that goes beyond traditional cognitive learning outcomes. To ensure that institutions are continuously using assessment results to improve outcomes for all students, assessment planners and practitioners should seek to assess students holistically and collect critical data at multiple points during students' academic life cycles. Such approaches should result in an improved understanding of the needs of today's learners and a focus on issues of equity, learner agency, and institutional types and missions (Higher Learning Commission, 2018).

Kinzie and Kuh (2016) argued that a broad view of student success and development should consider student–institutional fit, integration, social and human capital, career readiness, labor outcomes, well-being, and institutional factors such as access and affordability. Ideally, then, our assessment efforts should identify proven curricular and cocurricular practices that enable students to experience more effective learning environments, stronger academic preparation, improved persistence to graduation, more confidence in their communication and critical thinking skills, and enhanced ability to enter the workforce or enroll in graduate programs with the knowledge, skills, and abilities necessary to continue their education, begin professional careers, and act as engaged citizens. As such, assessing the whole student entails collecting data on students' cognitive levels (critical thinking, writing, oral communication, quantitative reasoning) and on their social, affective, and behavioral levels (i.e., self-efficacy, growth mind-set, self-awareness, leadership, and social intelligence).

This broader view of assessment also considers the full range of outcomes that our institutions are designed to promote. Higher education institutions often have missions to develop students who are poised to engage in lifelong learning and make meaningful contributions to society. Students who are lifelong learners and active citizens must possess a repertoire of skills, dispositions, and habits of mind, including self-awareness and confidence as students and future professionals, effective study habits, understanding of when to seek help, selection of degrees and careers aligned with interests and strengths, and ability to apply knowledge to solve complex problems. Validly assessing this broader range of cognitive motivational and learning mind-sets requires that assessment planners draw on disciplines such as behavioral economics, anthropology, sociology, and psychology. Such assessment will also demand understanding of a broad range of theories and concepts shown to affect student learning and success: *growth mind-set* (Dweck, 2006), *academic hope* (Rand, 2009; Snyder, Shorey, & Rand, 2008; Snyder et al., 2002), *self-efficacy* (Bandura, 1986, 1997; Zajacova, Lynch, & Espenshade, 2005), *sense of belonging* (Walton, 2014; Walton & Cohen, 2011; Yeager & Walton, 2011), *grit and resilience* (Connor & Davidson, 2003; Duckworth, Peterson, Matthews, & Kelly, 2007), and *self-leadership* (Houghton & Neck, 2002).

Most interventions, courses, and pedagogies in higher education are designed to influence numerous student outcomes at different points during students' journeys to degree completion. For example, student affairs interventions and high-impact practices (HIPs; e.g., learning communities, service-learning, internships, and undergraduate research) often have goals to not only improve students' cognitive gains but also change students' attitudes, behaviors, and affective states, and boost their GPAs and persistence rates. Kilgo, Ezell Sheets, and Pascarella (2015) found that HIPs allow students to engage in active and collaborative learning that has far-reaching positive effects across multiple liberal learning outcomes, including critical thinking and intercultural effectiveness. As we have seen in chapter 2 of this volume, HIPs provide pathways to student success. According to Kuh (2008), HIPs can focus student time and energy in ways that "channel student effort toward productive activities and deeper learning" (p. 7). Investigations of HIPs and other educational interventions suggest that assessment should consider other important outcomes such as engagement in learning and deep learning.

Preparing Students to Persist to Degree Completion and Function Effectively in a Complex, Globalizing World

Attempting to ease students' transitions during college and ensure that they are making progress to degree completion requires that educators consider the types of data available throughout students' varied journeys. During the early stages of students' learning careers, a variety of indicators of student success and progress can be obtained, including academic performance in general education courses, progress on course learning objectives, indicators of intrapersonal and interpersonal competence, one-year retention rates, credit hours gained, and more. During later stages, indicators of progress may include on-time graduation rates, credit hours earned, academic performance in the major, attainment of degree program learning outcomes, commitment to career goals, leadership ability, intercultural competence, and ability to engage with diverse others.

It has become increasingly important to assess graduating students' career and employment outcomes. According to the National Association of Colleges and Employers (NACE), employers consider new college graduates' capacities for leadership, teamwork, and effective communication when evaluating them for job openings (Snyder, Shorey, & Rand, 2006). NACE contends that twenty-first-century skills include leadership, ability to work in a team, communication skills (written and oral), problem-solving skills, strong work ethic, analytical and quantitative skills, technical skills, initiative, computer skills, flexibility and adaptability, and creativity.

If our higher education institutions value promoting students' holistic development, our assessment practices should reflect this focus, defining the knowledge, skills, attitudes, and values that students need to develop in order to cultivate identities and commitments, be civically engaged, understand the diversity of cultures, develop informed perspectives on social issues, and participate actively in public problem-solving. For students to become productive citizens in a world in which lower skilled labor is being replaced by computers and robots, Aoun (2017), author of *Robot-Proof: Higher Education in the Age of Artificial Intelligence*, argued that an educational shift is necessary. We need to rebalance our curricula to develop graduates with "creative mindsets and the mental elasticity to invent, discover, or create something valuable to society" (p. xvii) rather than concerning ourselves solely with "topping up students' minds with high-octane facts" (p. xvii). New student literacies such as *data literacy*, *technological literacy*, and *human literacy* will be necessary. Graduates will need data literacy to manage the flow of big data; technological literacy to understand how their machines work; and human literacy, from the humanities, communication, and design, to function as members of society in a world populated with artificial intelligence powered by advanced technologies (Aoun, 2017). Graduates must also be equipped with lifelong learning skills that enable them to adapt to change. Developing students with these capacities will require higher education to focus on integrative learning that crosses disciplinary boundaries. Assessment approaches will need to determine the extent to which students are able to apply learning from multiple disciplines and in- and out-of-class experiences to address complex social issues.

Putting Assessment Trends Into Practice: How to Assess

The trends discussed in this volume suggest that assessment approaches must strive to be effective within increasingly complex educational settings, aim to prepare diverse students for a rapidly changing, globalizing world, and serve a widening array of stakeholders. To meet these needs, we must look beyond traditional assessment strategies, systematically using multiple methods to gather multiple types of data, in order to discern the impact of higher education on student development and identify needed improvements. Formative and authentic, embedded assessment methods are becoming more important as we seek to improve student learning experiences, help students make meaningful connections among these experiences, and implement interventions with greater fidelity. Multiple and authentic methods that seek to understand student experiences can also help us carry out our responsibility to ensure that we are responding to the learning needs of a diversifying student body and providing all students with equitable access to learning opportunities.

Using Multiple Types of Assessment Data to Assess the Quality of Learning Experiences Throughout Students' Transitions

As we have noted, our assessment activities should aim to provide information for decision-making at multiple levels of analysis: courses, single interventions and programs like HIPs and student affairs offerings, degree-granting programs, and institution-wide. Assessment approaches should be designed to work within complex educational settings and take into account stakeholders' needs, priorities, resources, and time lines. *Assessment* is often viewed as Suskie (2009) defined it:

> [a] continuous cycle of improvement . . . comprised of a number of features: establishing clear, measurable expected outcomes of student learning; ensuring that students have sufficient opportunities to achieve those outcomes; systematically gathering, analyzing, and interpreting evidence to determine how well student learning matches expectations; and using the resulting information to understand and improve student learning. (p. 4)

Suskie (2009) further observed that, "While assessment focuses on how well student learning goals are achieved, evaluation addresses how well the major goals of a program are achieved" (p. 12). The assessment trends in this book, however, support more expansive approaches that go beyond traditional assessment and program evaluation. These trends individually and collectively focus on systematic investigations that explore the effects of our interventions, programs, and institutions on students' identity development, learning outcomes, and transferable skills. These lines of inquiry call for multiple methods of assessment to gather various types of assessment data, both direct and indirect.

To determine whether our institutions are helping students attain their academic learning and personal growth goals, we need to define specific assessable outcomes and incorporate direct and indirect measures of student learning and change. As we have seen, the capacities and skills necessary for engagement in a diverse and global society will require the cognitive skills and abilities to communicate effectively, explore complex issues, and engage with diverse peers. Indirect measures can supplement direct measures of learning by providing information about how and why learning is occurring (Suskie, 2009). Educators may use a variety of methods to assess learning outcomes indirectly, including self-assessment, peer feedback, end-of-course evaluations, questionnaires, focus groups, and exit interviews. Locally developed and national surveys such as the National Survey of Student Engagement may be useful in assessing student learning indirectly by providing information on the amount of time and effort students put into educationally purposeful activities and programs and the extent to which learning experiences enhance their self-reported learning and personal development outcomes.

Another assessment trend focuses on assessing the nature and quality of learning experiences (process assessment). Process assessment can ensure that learning experiences and educational interventions are implemented as planned, reach intended student populations, and are executed with fidelity—that is, include the essential elements and practices to ensure that intended outcomes are attained. For example, according to Kuh (2008), creating opportunities for students to participate in at least two HIPs during their undergraduate programs, one in the first year and one taken later within the major field, is an effective way to enhance students' academic success and engagement. But Kuh also noted, "To engage students at high levels, these practices must be done well" (p. 20). If HIPs have varying outcomes, we need to understand how impact varies not only across different practices but also among instances of the same practice. Research has shown that there are "conditions that matter" (Kuh, Kinzie, Schuh, Whitt, & Associates, 2010) when implementing HIPs, including expectations set at appropriately high levels, significant investment of time and effort, interactions with faculty and peers, experiences with diversity, frequent and constructive feedback, periodic and structured opportunities for reflection, relevance through real-world applications, and public demonstration of competence (Kuh, 2008; Kuh et al., 2010; Kuh, O'Donnell, & Reed, 2013).

Influenced by research on the conditions that matter, institutions such as Indiana University–Purdue University Indianapolis and The California State University have developed taxonomies that allow users to assess the extent to which they are incorporating these conditions into their HIP practices. Although there is a solid body of evidence on HIP learning outcomes, we lack a good understanding of how variables related to implementation fidelity influence these outcomes (Thorington Springer & Hatcher, 2017). The taxonomy approach provides additional clarification of process variables that may contribute to differences in student learning. Thorington Springer, Powell, Graunke, Hahn, and Hatcher (chapter 2, this volume) discuss several institutions that have developed taxonomies to ensure that HIPs are implemented with fidelity and incorporate the "conditions that matter." The taxonomies serve as valuable resources for instructors; they can assist in improving course design and sustaining the effectiveness of HIP experiences for student learning and growth. Instructors can also use such taxonomies to document course revision and improvements, where appropriate.

Using the assessment trends also requires applying a combination of qualitative and quantitative assessment and of formative and summative assessment approaches to assess students' varied experiences as they navigate the college environment in pursuit of their personal learning goals. Given the heightened importance of data to inform decision-making and resource allocation, continued investment in HIPs, student affairs interventions, and pedagogical innovations will be highly dependent on systematic assessment. Collecting formative assessment data will be critical in providing feedback to program directors and instructors so that they can make continuous adjustments based on students' early experiences. Such early feedback can inform decision-making so that intended outcomes are attained.

Even in graduate education, recent trends suggest a shift toward additional formative and qualitative measures that allow faculty to understand the degree to which students are developing into professionals, collaborators, and ethical decision-makers (Zahl, Jimenez, & Huffman, chapter 7 of this volume). Qualitative research approaches such as interviews, focus groups, and surveys of students and instructors can be helpful in understanding how learning activities are implemented and experienced. The use of mixed-method evaluation designs (Creswell, 2009; Frechtling, 2002; Greene, Caracelli, & Graham, 1989) allows assessment planners to obtain qualitative and quantitative evidence that demonstrates how well educational experiences promote student success and learning. In a mixed-method expansion context, the purpose is to employ qualitative methods to assess learning processes (measures of how students are experiencing and engaging in learning taken during experiences) and quantitative methods to assess outcomes (measures of achievement of intended learning outcomes, persistence rates, and academic performance taken at the end of experiences).

Focusing on Authentic Embedded Assessment

One trend that clearly emerges from the preceding chapters is an increased focus on authentic, embedded assessment strategies. Many undergraduate and graduate programs seek to develop students as lifelong learners by enhancing their communication, critical thinking, and problem-solving abilities. Authentic, embedded assessments ask students to demonstrate in meaningful ways what they know and are able to do. *Authentic assessment* tasks are often multidimensional and require sophisticated levels of cognitive skills like problem-solving and critical thinking. *Embedded assessment* is defined by Wilson and Sloane (2000) as "opportunities to assess student progress and performance [that] are integrated into the instructional materials and are virtually indistinguishable from the day-to-day classroom activities" (p. 182). Authentic, embedded assessments often focus on direct measures that require students to demonstrate their knowledge and skills.

The Valid Assessment of Learning in Undergraduate Education (VALUE) rubrics developed by AAC&U (Rhodes, 2010) may be useful for systematically measuring students' learning gains. Rubrics can be especially helpful for evaluating artifacts like writing samples, reflections, oral presentations, and other projects that students include in paper or electronic portfolios. Embedded assessments have the advantage of being part of the existing work of instructors and students, rather than "add-on" activities. Sound assessment programs routinely involve the collection of embedded, authentic measures of learning.

ePortfolios and signature assignments are two examples of authentic, embedded methods that support holistic assessment of student learning, provide opportunities for students to apply their learning experiences inside and outside the classroom and across disciplinary boundaries, and allow them to reflect on self and integrate diverse learning experiences. Kahn presented ePortfolios as an effective method for understanding "how students view themselves as learners or emerging professionals; how they are perceiving, connecting, and interpreting their in- and out-of-class learning experiences; and why they may be struggling with particular content or concepts" (p. 138, this volume). Kahn argued that ePortfolios offer a view into students' reflective representation of themselves conveyed through authentic work, reflections, and hyperlinked digital media and narrative. Moreover, ePortfolios are both an assessment method and a recognized HIP that can deepen disciplinary learning, self-awareness, and integrative thinking. Buyarski and colleagues (2015) contended that ePortfolios can help students engage purposefully in four domains that collectively enable us to view student learning holistically: increasing awareness of self and others, setting self-concordant goals, developing hope, and shaping educational and career plans.

Signature assignments similarly require that students reflect and engage in deeper learning. Moreover, they can be used as pedagogical tools as well as an authentic assessment method. Institutions can adapt and apply signature assignments to fit their institutional context. According to AAC&U, "signature assignments require students to demonstrate and apply their proficiency in one or more key learning outcomes. This often means synthesizing, analyzing, and applying cumulative knowledge and skills through problem- or inquiry-based assignments or projects" (Association of American Colleges & Universities, n.d.) Signature assignments should be well aligned with course-level learning objectives and focus on emulating real-world applications of course knowledge. They often require students to reflect on their work and may be collaboratively designed by faculty who teach different sections of a given course (Ewell, 2014). As such, ePortfolios and signature assignments, which can be used together, enable institutions to engage in meaningful dialogue about student learning and can yield assessment information that reflects students' most meaningful learning experiences.

Incorporating Culturally Responsive Assessment Approaches That Account for Student Diversity and Ensure Equity

Equitable assessment approaches that account for student diversity and ensure that all students have access to the learning opportunities they need are an important emerging trend. To determine whether all of our students are benefiting equally from their education, we need to assess the extent to which our institutions are serving the diverse needs of our students and providing all of them with opportunities to engage in powerful learning experiences. As colleges educate a more diverse and global student population, the need to make sure that all students— regardless of race, ethnicity, gender identity, socioeconomic status, sexual orientation, age, ability, and other characteristics—succeed is more pressing than ever (Montenegro & Jankowski, 2017). Montenegro and Jankowski urged assessment planners and practitioners to take equity and social justice issues into account as they design assessments. In this way, we can seek to avoid assessment approaches that sustain privilege, validate certain types of learning and evidence over others, and reinforce some students' sense that they do not belong in higher education.

Culturally responsive assessment takes into account institutional contexts and considers the student populations the institution serves, uses language that is appropriate for all students when developing learning outcomes, acknowledging students' differences in the planning phases of an assessment effort, developing and/or using assessment tools that are appropriate for different students, and being intentional in using assessment results to improve learning for all students. (Montenegro & Jankowski, 2017, p. 10)

Finley and McNair (2013) contended that improving underserved students' learning and success and ensuring that HIPs and other opportunities are structured to optimize learning gains for all students require long-term commitment and continuous inquiry and self-examination among campus leaders. They further noted,

Designing and sustaining an educational environment that results in high-quality learning experiences and equity in student achievement requires a genuine commitment of time and effort, an exploration of the student experience, institutional assessment and data analysis, and the ability and courage to implement change. (Finley & McNair, p. 34)

Equitable assessment methods rely on multiple and varied sources of data. They not only include qualitative data on students' experiences but also combine this evidence with data from direct, authentic, embedded assessments—students' actual work (Finley & McNair, 2013). In order for us to fully understand the impacts of our educational practices on student learning and success, equitable assessments disaggregate findings and examine the differential effects of programs on both underserved and traditionally advantaged student groups. To this end, assessment practitioners should disaggregate data by student income, ethnicity, gender, first-generation status, age, transfer status, and other nontraditional student characteristics.

Inclusive assessment practices further require moving beyond data disaggregation to using these data to advance more equitable outcomes for all students. Our assessment practices should also include examination of representational equity, or what Hurtado and Halualani (2014) referred to as *compositional diversity*, which focuses on numbers of men and women and numbers of students from historically underserved groups who are participating in various learning experiences. A sufficient understanding of how diverse groups of students are experiencing our institutions, however, will also require examination of other dimensions of institutional diversity, such as the psychological and behavioral aspects of campus climate. Moreover, a focus on culturally responsive assessment reminds campus leaders to assess institutional performance using disaggregated data and to initiate action plans in response to assessment findings. If we are to realize the vision of culturally responsive assessment, we must understand how our pedagogical designs and learning contexts affect student circumstances, interests, goals, motivation, self-efficacy, and ability to persist to degree completion.

Putting Assessment Trends Into Practice: How to Use Assessment for Decision-Making and Improvement

As demands for assessment information increase, researchers are beginning to question received wisdom about who is responsible for generating and using assessment data to improve student outcomes. While faculty involvement is crucial to enacting improvement, responsibility for assessment and improvement should be shared widely, with faculty, teaching and learning centers, institutional research (IR) offices, and assessment offices all playing a role in creating data-informed improvement cultures that support student success and progress toward strategic priorities. Assessment and improvement activities should further be aligned with institutional missions and strategic priorities in order to help leaders make data-driven strategic decisions. We must also develop more effective strategies for integrating and communicating assessment findings to internal and external stakeholders in ways that enable them to use these findings to adjust practices or make policy decisions, depending on their roles. In the face of public skepticism about the value of higher education, institutions must seek more effective means of using assessment results to communicate student achievement to external audiences.

Creating an Improvement Culture

The demand for robust assessment data to inform decisions about improving student outcomes has grown exponentially in recent years. Assessment practitioners and scholars, institutional researchers, and campus leaders are often charged with determining which approaches are the most effective in improving student learning, engagement, academic performance, retention, and degree completion. In addition, campus administrators and policymakers may be responsible for making decisions about which instructional strategies to implement, continue, or expand to ensure attainment of desired student learning outcomes and institutional strategic metrics.

Traditional approaches have held that assessment should be faculty-driven, with faculty carrying out the work of assessment and improvement (Banta & Palomba, 2015; Palomba & Banta, 1999). Emerging research, however, focuses on wider stakeholder involvement and on supporting faculty use of assessment findings to effect improvement. Jankowski, Timmer, Kinzie, and Kuh (2018) argued that assessment professionals and institutional researchers should work collaboratively to assist faculty and staff in developing the understandings and tools needed to produce meaningful assessment results and ensure that they understand how to use these results to improve student learning.

Furthermore, although many college campuses offer support for assessment activities, policies on promotion and tenure lag behind. For this reason, Jankowski and colleagues (2018) recommended that institutional research and assessment offices, along with faculty-led assessment committees, support institution-wide assessment activities rather than overrelying on faculty to shoulder an increasingly heavy assessment workload. Such shared responsibility and commitment to using assessment results for internal improvement efforts, like program review, enhancement of cocurricular programs, resource allocation, trustee and governing board deliberations, and equity goals, are more likely to result in a culture of improvement.

Facilitating conversations among faculty and staff can also help to support the use of assessment to improve student learning. Stanny (2018) pointed out that centers for teaching and learning play a critical role here, serving as sources of expertise, guiding faculty discussions about curriculum and pedagogy, and leading efforts to help faculty implement effective active learning strategies, assignments, and curricular change. In addition, according to Stanny, improvement cultures make progress more visible, enabling all stakeholders to better understand the purposes and meanings of incremental changes made by faculty.

Ensuring that improvements are visible and discernible is particularly important given recent trends. In chapter 10, Fulcher and Prendergast defined *improvement* as "making informed curricular and pedagogical modifications and then reassessing to confirm that the changes improved student learning outcomes" (p. 158, this volume). Jankowski and colleagues (2018) argued that improvement, along with compliance, continues to be a major driver of assessment. If done well, our assessment efforts will result in changes to curriculum, pedagogy, policies, professional development, advising, peer mentoring, and allocation of resources that lead to improved student learning. But many assessment scholars have highlighted the difficulties educators have encountered in attempting to use assessment results for improvement and documenting meaningful effects on student learning outcomes or teaching quality (Banta & Blaich, 2010; Jankowski et al., 2018). The need to do a better job of improving learning based on assessment findings has spurred development of a new Assessment Institute track on learning improvement and innovation.

In an effort to help ensure that the diverse array of assessment data we collect is used to measurably improve student success and learning across higher education institutions, the Association for Institutional Research released a *Statement of Aspirational Practice for Institutional Research* to guide assessment and data use practices (Swing & Ross, 2016). The statement includes as major themes: (a) an expanded definition of *decision makers*, (b) a student-focused paradigm, (c) student-focused structures and leadership for IR, and (d) leadership for the IR function. The central premise of the statement is that IR and assessment leaders need to leverage multiple sources of data and create data-informed decision cultures so that our students are successful.

The creation of data-informed decision cultures requires integrating data from diverse sources, ensuring assessment data quality, promoting data literacy, building relationships with decision makers, and striving to engage students in decisions about their learning experiences. It is also crucial to engage decision makers within multiple spheres of influence throughout the institution, including those in student-facing roles such as advisers, faculty members, and peer mentors, in addition to students themselves. No longer is it sufficient to provide data to meet the needs of external policymakers and top campus leadership for accountability purposes; student learning and success will improve only if actionable data are available to decision makers at all levels. Accordingly, assessment leaders may need to provide data at different levels of analysis (student level, course level, program level, institution level, state level, and national level) to meet decision makers' needs.

Using Assessment Results to Improve and Demonstrate Student Learning and Success

Battles debating the demonstrated value of higher education have been waged on several fronts. The *Strada–Gallup 2017 College Student Survey* (Strada Education Network & Gallup, 2017) suggested that "only a third of students believe they will graduate with the skills and knowledge to be successful in the job market (34%) and in the workplace (36%)." Other polls have suggested that many people believe that higher education is not contributing to American society, although the facts suggest that higher education contributes substantially (Cole, 2018). As college costs have continued to increase, students as well as family members and policymakers are questioning the worth of a college degree. As such, it is critical that higher education institutions use assessment findings to continuously improve students' learning experiences and to demonstrate the value of these experiences to policymakers, funders, and families. Assessment planners and practitioners must also take into account the diverse needs of various decision makers and their domains of influence.

Within institutions, programs and learning experiences may not be valued or sustained if they are not viewed as critical to institutional goals and strategic metrics. As such, assessment strategies should take into account institutional missions and the data needed to assess progress toward strategic planning priorities and goals. Assessment data should align with strategic planning goals for improving student learning, academic performance, engagement levels, and persistence rates. While comprehensive outcomes assessment is crucial, assessment practitioners must also enact feedback mechanisms that provide accurate, timely information to support data-driven strategic decisions at the institutional level and to communicate to external stakeholders.

Assessment must also respond to the expectations of diverse stakeholders for information on access, completion, quality, and efficiency. With the advent of several national initiatives aimed at ensuring that college students attain degrees in a timely manner, including the Completion Agenda, policymakers and education leaders are paying close attention to which practices contribute to student degree attainment. Institutional leaders and policymakers must be intentional about implementing initiatives to strategically improve student learning. The focus on students' accumulation of credits, retention, and graduation rates should not, however, cause us to ignore student learning outcomes. Assessment data should demonstrate how high-quality experiences help to ensure that students not only earn degrees but also gain the critical knowledge, skills, abilities, and attitudes necessary to keep pace with societal change and engage in innovative and complex problem-solving. It is our hope that the assessment trends described in this volume will equip students, families, policymakers, and institutional decision makers with the assessment information they need to communicate about the true value of higher education in improving individual lives and society as a whole.

Conclusion

Ideally, the assessment trends discussed in this volume will allow institutions to meet the needs of the next generation of learners. But this will require a dramatic shift in the way we approach assessment planning and practice and facilitate the use of results to improve. We will need to reconsider what we assess, how we assess, and how we leverage assessment results. This chapter focuses on applying emerging assessment trends to planning, decision-making, and improvement. In addition, we highlight how policymakers, campus leaders, faculty members, assessment practitioners, and scholars can use the assessment trends to create a culture of improvement. Assessment planning and practice should focus on responding to the needs of our increasingly diverse learners, preparing them for a rapidly changing and complex society, and supporting their holistic learning and development. In the best-case scenarios, assessment and institutional research leaders work collaboratively with faculty members and campus leadership to ensure that assessment results are used to continuously improve students' learning experiences and outcomes so that they develop into enlightened, engaged citizens who work to promote a well-functioning democracy.

We want to hear from you about *Trends in Assessment*:

- Provide reactions or suggestions about trends.
- Share and access resources related to trends.
- Learn about professional development opportunities related to trends.

Visit assessmentinstitute.iupui.edu/trends

References

Aoun, J. E. (2017). *Robot-proof: Higher education in the age of artificial intelligence.* Cambridge, MA: MIT Press.

Association of American Colleges & Universities. (n.d.). *Integrating signature assignments into the curriculum and inspiring design.* Washington, DC: Author. Retrieved from https://www.aacu.org/sites/default/files/Signature-Assignment-Tool.pdf

Bandura, A. (1986). *Social foundations of thought and action: A social cognitive theory.* Englewood Cliffs, NJ: Prentice Hall.

Bandura, A. (1997). *Self-efficacy: The exercise of control.* New York, NY: W. H. Freeman.

Banta, T. W., & Blaich, C. (2010). Closing the assessment loop. *Change: The Magazine of Higher Learning, 43*(1), 22–27. doi:10.1080/00091383.2011.538642

Banta, T. W., & Palomba, C. A. (2015). *Assessment essentials: Planning, implementing, and improving assessment in higher education* (2nd ed.). San Francisco, CA: Jossey-Bass.

Buyarski, C. A., Aaron, R. W., Hansen, M. J., Hollingsworth, C. D., Johnson, C. A., Kahn, S., . . . Powell, A. (2015). Purpose and pedagogy: A conceptual model for an ePortfolio. *Theory Into Practice, 54(4)*, 283–291. doi:10.1080/00405841. 2015.1076691

Cole, J. (2018, April 11). What's the value of higher education? *Yale Insights.* Retrieved from https://insights.som.yale.edu/insights/what-s-the-value-of-higher-education

Connor, K. M., & Davidson, J. R. T. (2003). Development of a new resilience scale: The Connor-Davidson Resilience Scale (CD-RISC). *Depression and Anxiety, 18*(2), 76–82. doi:10.1002/da.10113

Creswell, J. W. (2009). *Research design: Qualitative, quantitative, and mixed method approaches* (3rd ed.). Thousand Oaks, CA: Sage.

Duckworth, A. L., Peterson, C., Matthews, M. D., & Kelly, D. R. (2007). Grit: Perseverance and passion for long-term goals. *Journal of Personality and Social Psychology, 92*(6), 1087–1101. Retrieved from http://dx.doi.org/10.1037/0022-3514.92.6

Dweck, C. S. (2006). *Mind-set: The new psychology of success.* New York, NY: Random House.

Ewell, P. T. (2014, March). *Developing effective signature assignments: Lessons from the DQP.* Paper presented at Indiana Signature Assignment Workshop, Indianapolis, IN.

Finley, A., & McNair, T. (2013). *Assessing underserved students' engagement in high-impact practices.* Washington, DC: Association of American Colleges & Universities.

Frechtling, J. (2002). *The 2002 user-friendly handbook for project evaluation.* Arlington, VA: National Science Foundation.

Greene, J. C., Caracelli, V. J., & Graham, W. F. (1989). Toward a conceptual framework for mixed-method evaluation designs. *Educational Evaluation and Policy Analysis, 11*, 255–274.

Higher Learning Commission. (2018, December). Defining student success data: Recommendations for changing the conversation. Retrieved from http://download.hlcommission.org/initiatives/StudentSuccessConversation.pdf

Houghton, J. D., & Neck, C. P. (2002). The revised self-leadership questionnaire: Testing a hierarchical factor structure for self-leadership. *Journal of Managerial Psychology, 17*(7), 672–691. Retrieved from http://ulib.iupui.edu/cgi-bin/proxy .pl?url=/docview/215868182?accountid=7398

Hurtado, S., & Halualani, R. T. (2014). Diversity assessment, accountability, and action: Going beyond the numbers. *Diversity and Democracy, 17*(4).

Jankowski, N. A., Timmer, J. D., Kinzie, J., & Kuh, G. D. (2018). *Assessment that matters: Trending toward practices that document authentic student learning.* Urbana, IL: University of Illinois and Indiana University, National Institute for Learning Outcomes Assessment.

Kilgo, C. A., Ezell Sheets, J. K., & Pascarella, E. T. (2015). The link between high-impact practices and student learning: Some longitudinal evidence. *Journal of Higher Education and Educational Planning, 69*(4), 509–525.

Kinzie, J., & Kuh, G. (2016, November). *Report prepared for the Lumina Foundation: Review of student success frameworks to mobilize higher education.* Bloomington, IN: Indiana University, Center for Postsecondary Research.

Kuh, G. D. (2008). *High-impact educational practices: What they are, who has access to them, and why they matter.* Washington, DC: Association of American Colleges & Universities.

Kuh, G. D., Kinzie, J., Schuh, J. H., Whitt, E. J., & Associates. (2010). *Student success in college: Creating conditions that matter.* San Francisco, CA: Jossey-Bass.

Kuh, G. D., O'Donnell, K., & Reed, S. (2013). *Ensuring quality and taking high-impact practices to scale.* Washington, DC: Association of American Colleges & Universities.

Montenegro, E., & Jankowski, N. A. (2017, January). *Equity and assessment: Moving towards culturally responsive assessment* (Occasional Paper No. 29). Urbana, IL: University of Illinois and Indiana University, National Institute for Learning Outcomes Assessment.

Palomba, C. A., & Banta, T. W. (1999). *Assessment essentials: Planning, implementing, and improving assessment in higher education.* San Francisco, CA: Jossey-Bass.

Rand, K. L. (2009). Hope and optimism: Latent structures and influences on grade expectancy and academic performance. *Journal of Personality, 77*(1), 231–260.

Rhodes, T. (2010). *Assessing outcomes and improving achievement: Tips and tools for using rubrics.* Washington, DC: Association of American Colleges & Universities.

Snyder, C. R., Shorey, H., Cheavens, J., Pulvers, K. M., Adams, V., III, & Wikilund, C. (2002). Hope and academic success in college. *Journal of Educational Psychology, 94*, 820–826.

Snyder, C. R., Shorey, H. S., & Rand, K. L. (2006). Using hope theory to teach and mentor academically at-risk students. In W. Bukist & S. F. Davis (Eds.), *Handbook of the teaching of psychology* (pp. 170–174). Malden, MA: Blackwell.

Stanny, C. J. (2018, July). Promoting an improvement culture [Viewpoints discussion board]. National Institute for Learning Outcomes Assessment. Retrieved from https://blogs.illinois.edu/view/915/670671

Strada Education Network & Gallup. (2017). *Strada–Gallup 2017 college student survey: Crisis of confidence: Current college students do not feel prepared for the workforce.* Retrieved from https://news.gallup.com/reports/225161/2017-strada-gallup-college-student-survey.aspx

Suskie, L. (2009). *Assessing student learning: A common sense guide* (2nd ed.). San Francisco, CA: Jossey-Bass.

Swing, R. L., and Ross, L. E. (2016). *Statement of aspirational practice for institutional research.* Association for Institutional Research. Retrieved from http://www.airweb.org/aspirationalstatement

Thorington Springer, J., & Hatcher, J. A. (2017). Assessing high-impact educational practices: Quality, diversity, and inclusive excellence. *Assessment Update, 29*(5), 6–12. Retrieved from https://doi.org/10.1002/au.30108

Walton, G. M. (2014). The new science of wise psychological interventions. *Current Directions in Psychological Science, 23,* 73–82.

Walton, G. M., & Cohen, G. L. (2011). A brief social-belonging intervention improves academic and health outcomes of minority students. *Science, 331,* 1447–1451.

Wilson, M., & Sloane, K. (2000). From principles to practice: An embedded assessment system. *Applied Measurement in Education, 13,* 181–208.

Yeager, D. S., & Walton, G. M. (2011). Social-psychological interventions in education: They're not magic. *Review of Educational Research, 81,* 267–301.

Zajacova, A., Lynch, S. M., & Espenshade, T. J. (2005). Self-efficacy, stress, and academic success in college. *Research in Higher Education, 46*(6), 677–706.

META-TRENDS IN ASSESSMENT

Perspectives, Analyses, and Future Directions

Stephen P. Hundley, Susan Kahn, Jeffery Barbee,
and Partners of the Assessment Institute

T he Assessment Institute in Indianapolis is now the nation's oldest and largest event of its type, as many readers of this volume know. Over the years, we have developed partnerships with professional associations and research organizations devoted to the study, practice, and advancement of learning, assessment, and improvement in higher education. Each year, the Assessment Institute's program is enriched by the intellectual contributions made by these valued partners, some of which appear in earlier chapters of this volume—the National Institute for Learning Outcomes Assessment (NILOA) in chapter 1, Campus Compact in chapter 4, and the Center for Assessment & Research Studies (CARS) in chapter 10. For this closing chapter, we asked leaders from our Assessment Institute partners to summarize the major trends in assessment they foresee in the next three to five years and to discuss how their organizations are preparing to address these trends. It concludes with our synthesis of the larger meta-trends that recur throughout this volume, as well as in other current assessment scholarship.

A Future for Assessment: Teams, Inquiry, and Support
Association for the Assessment of Learning in Higher Education (AALHE)

Monica Stitt-Bergh, Jane Marie Souza, and Jeremy D. Penn

AALHE provides resources and a forum to support assessment practitioners' professional development. Since 2009, the AALHE and its members have learned about and shared ways to benefit students, programs, and higher education institutions using the tools and processes of learning outcomes assessment. The seeds we see planted now, and that we expect will grow in the next several years, include a team approach to assessment, a culture of inquiry (research) for program- and institution-level learning outcomes assessment, and a stronger connection between assessment and student success in learning.

It Takes a Village

Past assessment literature emphasized the importance of institution leaders' commitment to assessment. Now we are beginning to recognize that assessment requires teamwork to engender student learning improvement and transform institutions into learning organizations. At a minimum, assessment teams need faculty and others with expertise in learning assessment, educational development, and instructional design. Also important to teams are students, faculty and staff in cocurricular programs, institutional researchers, and advisers, along with institutional leaders. To support team approaches, AALHE and its members have increased efforts to connect with other professional organizations in higher education, such as AAC&U, NILOA, AIR, the POD Network, and others. In addition, technology providers can and should be more than business partners; as team members, we can collaborate with them on effective and efficient ways to capture learning evidence and present information.

Inquiry (Research) on Learning Outcomes Assessment

Initially, outcomes assessment efforts focused on implementation in programs and institutions. Now that the field has developed, inquiry about assessment is growing. Researchers are testing theoretical approaches and analyzing what works for whom, for example. The platforms for distributing knowledge about learning outcomes assessment will both continue to increase and allow for a variety of approaches to generating knowledge about assessment. AALHE, along with other organizations, will continue to promote and support sharing scholarly inquiry through conferences and publications. It is through vibrant scholarly research that learning outcomes assessment will thrive.

Assessment as Support for Student Learning Success

Accountability requirements have too often limited the definition of *student success* to retention, graduation, and employment rates. A growing number of faculty, assessment practitioners, educational developers, and others believe that learning quality should be part of the student success equation, and we are starting to see examples of assessment processes that advance learning quality for all groups of students. External stakeholders have the greatest potential to promote this trend and transform how student success is defined. We view accreditors as critical partners and are reaching out to both regional and specialized accreditors to join the conversation.

AALHE sees these emerging trends as positive because of their great potential to enhance learning. We therefore look forward to collaborating with others to nurture strong partnerships, promote rigorous assessment scholarship, and pursue success for all students.

Visit aalhe.org for more information about AALHE.

Meaningful, Authentic, and Actionable: ePortfolios and Trends in Assessment Now and for the Future
Association for Authentic, Experiential, and Evidence-Based Learning (AAEEBL)

Tracy Penny Light, Helen L. Chen, and C. Edward Watson

AAEEBL, the professional association for ePortfolio practitioners and researchers in the United States and abroad, has been deeply involved in advancing the informed implementation of ePortfolios since its founding in 2009. As such, it has been a forum for discussion of the role that ePortfolios play in assessment—discussion that began well before AAEEBL's inception.

Historically, assessment was a starting point for ePortfolio implementation, as institutions and accreditors sought authentic evidence of student achievement of desired learning outcomes. Over time, though, ePortfolios caught the attention of different stakeholders who identified varied assessment needs and interests, as well as different understandings and definitions of *assessment* itself. A search for research on ePortfolios and assessment on the AAC&U "PEARL" database (eportfolio.aacu.org) yields a wide range of studies that explore everything from traditional examples of evidence of learning outcomes or competencies visible in an ePortfolio to assessment of the effectiveness of new pedagogical and curricular designs and to the ability of ePortfolios to demonstrate student identity development. These variations are attributable to shifts in the wider interests of higher educators over the past decade and to the ways in which ePortfolio practices have enabled a much broader group of stakeholders to leverage these practices to address their own assessment needs and interests. Three aspects of assessment continue to influence the work of stakeholders interested in both curricular and cocurricular learning.

Meaningful

One feature of ePortfolio assessment that has permeated the literature is the ability of ePortfolios to enable students to document the many ways in which they make meaning of content and concepts presented in various curricular and cocurricular learning contexts. Assessment of learning that moves beyond demonstrating that an outcome has been achieved allows assessors to gain more insight into *why* and *how* meaning-making occurs. This capacity expands opportunities for quality assurance, as faculty and others can better understand which assignments and activities worked well and the ways in which learners connect learning across learning contexts.

Authentic

By offering learners opportunities to document their learning within and among learning contexts, we enable them to engage in more authentic learning and enable stakeholders to engage in more authentic assessment. As Susan Kahn noted (chapter 9, this volume), ePortfolios provide opportunities to assess a wide range of learning outcomes and activities, including integrative learning, self-awareness, reflective practice, metacognition, and others. By designing assessment strategies that leverage this flexibility, stakeholders can gain more insight into not only how learners engage with curricular and cocurricular learning opportunities but also how learning shapes individual identity development across the learning career.

Actionable

By attending to how learners engage authentically with the curriculum and cocurriculum across their learning careers, we can also find ways to make evidence gleaned from ePortfolios actionable, whether by undertaking curricular redesign and development, incorporating new learning activities to foster folio thinking, or creating new learning opportunities that are more meaningful and authentic for *all* learners regardless of their backgrounds or experiences.

Future Opportunities

As Susan Kahn (chapter 9, this volume) noted, higher education has not yet fully taken advantage of all of the data that ePortfolios can provide on not only learning outcomes but also the practices and processes, whether curricular or cocurricular, that determine the impact and effectiveness of learning experiences. We agree with this insight. By designing assessment strategies that leverage ePortfolios to provide meaningful, authentic, and actionable evidence of learning, stakeholders across our institutions can foster opportunities for learners to develop skills and abilities that they can transfer across contexts. At AAEEBL, we are working to enable sharing of the practices, pedagogies, research, and technologies that support meaningful, authentic, and actionable assessment across institutions and disciplinary communities.

Visit aaeebl.org for more information on AAEEBL.

Preparing for the Future of Assessment in General Education
Association for General and Liberal Studies (AGLS)

John G. Frederick and Stephen Biscotte

AGLS is a community of practitioner-scholars that provides strategic, effective, and innovative support for peers engaged in the day-to-day work of general and liberal learning in twenty-first-century higher education. The AGLS mission statement is a guidepost for our practitioner-scholars, who focus on "all things Gen Ed" and liberal learning, including, among others, teaching and learning; assessment of program, course, and cocurricular learning outcomes; administration of general education programs; and general education program designs and models.

The most common assessment practices and needs continue to emphasize students' demonstration of discrete learning outcomes or knowledge evidenced in student artifacts created for program assessment and/or accreditation purposes. AGLS has noted, however, that some institutions have intentionally integrated their general education curricula with cocurricular experiences, such as service-learning, civic engagement, signature assignments, and experiential learning. Cocurricular transcripts to capture these experiences are gaining ground in value or in some cases blending with traditional academic transcripts. We are also seeing widespread introduction of new fields of knowledge to general education curricula. These fields include design thinking; computational reasoning; entrepreneurship; leadership; data analysis; and inter-, multi-, and transdisciplinary and integrative learning opportunities. Assessment in these fields and of these forms of experiential learning depends on constant formative feedback and tools nimble enough for simultaneous use by collaborators from diverse disciplinary backgrounds.

As assessment demands grow and become more complex, AGLS members are further considering the extent to which computers can support assessment via adaptive learning modules, formative and summative assessment with tools embedded in the learning management system (LMS; e.g., Canvas or Blackboard), collection of digital artifacts such as videos and images as part of an ePortfolio, and ways in which technology might contribute to (or hinder) the pursuit of equitable assessment practices.

AGLS responds to changing trends in general education assessment by providing tools and resources directly to those in need and by bringing members together, both in person and virtually, to share best practices and lessons learned. Each September, the association hosts a "Constitute," which is structured around the best components of conferences and institutes, with a standing track dedicated to assessment issues. This track regularly accounts for over one quarter of the program, with sessions consistently well attended. Over the past two years, tracks on civic engagement and digital learning have been introduced to invite dialogue focused specifically on these trends.

In addition, AGLS is committed to remaining in constant contact with members and connecting them with each other through electronic mailing lists, Google Groups, and Twitter. AGLS has also published *Improving Learning in General Education: An AGLS Guide to Assessment and Program Review* (2007), which takes a systems thinking approach to continuous quality improvement and invites institutions to review their commitment to the principles of a student-centered, outcomes-and-assessment approach to general and liberal education. In conjunction with the guide, AGLS provides consultations to individual campuses that seek assistance with general education revision, assessment, and/or innovation.

Visit agls.org for more information on AGLS.

A Data-Informed Future: Trends in Assessment
Association for Institutional Research (AIR)

Leah Ewing Ross and Stephan C. Cooley

Data-informed decision cultures (cultures of evidence) are essential components of institutions' efforts to improve student success. As such, the AIR is committed to facilitating and supporting colleges and universities in their quest to realize and sustain such cultures.

The foundation of a data-informed decision culture is acknowledgment of all aspects of an institution's approach to data use and data capacity, both formal and informal. Data are collected, stored, and analyzed in myriad units across the institution, including and beyond dedicated offices of assessment, institutional research (IR), and/or institutional effectiveness (IE). These practices mirror the trend toward growth of data use evident in nearly every industry and sector of the world economy and almost every aspect of our personal lives. More data are available every day, the methods of gathering data are getting easier, the costs of storing data are decreasing, and advancements in analytical tools are expanding the number of people who can perform analyses. This trend will continue in the coming years, and the assessment field must be poised to address and exploit it.

Assessment, IR, and IE have always championed evidence-based cultures; use of data for decision-making leads to better decisions and better outcomes. But while all stakeholders want access to information to make decisions, the proliferation of data and analytic tools does not automatically translate to access to the right information at the right time. To ensure that stakeholders·have what they need when they need it, a delicate balance must be achieved—and constantly facilitated—among attention to the question or problem at hand, access to data, provision of information, and follow-through. AIR provides the training, education, and resources designed to help assessment, IR, and IE professionals navigate this space in terms of skill development, scholarship, and professional growth.

Strong data-informed decision cultures acknowledge all data use and capacity, including expanded sets of decision makers beyond traditional clients (e.g., presidents and provosts), and all data producers, including assessment professionals. Yet realization of a data-informed decision culture is not a destination. Rather, it is a journey that requires commitment to the use of data in decision-making and higher education professionals who think and strategize about data and their use across the institution, school, or program.

AIR supports institutions in this work by facilitating the evolution of the field, broadly defined to include data professionals in a wide variety of roles, ranging from assessment, IR, and IE to business intelligence and more. The association's contributions in this arena include assessing what currently exists (e.g., the National Survey of Institutional Research Offices); envisioning the future, including, among other changes, development of new models for data production and data use in the *Statement of Aspirational Practice for Institutional Research* (Swing & Ross, 2016a) and "A New Vision for Institutional Research" (Swing & Ross, 2016b); and providing education and training opportunities in such forms as webinars, IPEDS training, workshops, conference presentations for professionals in a variety of roles, and more.

Visit airweb.org for more information on AIR.

The Value of Liberal Education and America's Promise: Trends and Tensions
Association of American Colleges & Universities (AAC&U)

Terrel L. Rhodes

Given the adage that the more things change, the more they stay the same, expecting big changes in assessment would not be a good bet. Coupling the adage with the frequent observation that higher education does not demonstrate a history of rapid change, one might expect modest, if any, change occurring in the next three to five years. Trends in higher education would normally require a longer time horizon—yet some shifts have already begun and accelerated, and they are likely to influence and challenge higher education more immediately.

In brief, technology will continue its dance with higher education as its proponents try to make it a solution to improving efficiency and access, support in terms of public perceptions and financial resources will continue to decline or will remain constant, and tensions and shifting demands for answers will persist. So, what can we expect that is also new?

Integration and Bundling

Technology, combined with needed broadening of access to college education for all people, will put pressure on higher education *not* to settle for easy, simplistic, disintegrative, and reductionist focus and content. We now have the means to deliver what we do more conveniently and efficiently. We do not need more one-off, take-a-course approaches. Instead, we need to put more emphasis on nurturing students' development of higher order skills and abilities to think, inquire, and act to bring diverse learning experiences together. Our mission is *higher education*, not *lite education*. More integrative, higher order learning experiences and outcomes are pressing necessities. AAC&U continues to develop frameworks for assessments and pedagogies that integrate learning: Valid Assessment of Learning in Undergraduate Education (VALUE) rubrics and the VALUE Institute, purposeful pathways for faculty, road maps for community college leadership, and general education maps and markers (GEMs).

Cost Allocation and Quality

There was a time when popular perceptions equated quality with higher cost or price, but the public is beginning to recognize that an education credential does not equate to high-quality learning regardless of the cost. In the next few years, we need to shift the discourse from win–lose to win–win. Research overwhelmingly supports the importance for all students of essential, cross-cutting, higher order skills and abilities that can be practiced in multiple settings. Assessment *for* learning is on a rising trajectory. AAC&U continues to support these priorities through its summer workshops, focused conferences on best practices, four journals on theory and implementation, and cross-sector opportunities for discussion and collaboration among higher education institutions.

Public Good and Equity, and Extrinsic and Intrinsic Worth

Higher education remains a key to individual flourishing, intrinsic worth, self-concept, and personal agency, as well as to the public good, societal equity, social capital, and global survival. If higher education confines itself to cognitive and formal education without integrating affective and intro-spective and reflective practice, we will fail in our mission to improve the future of humanity. AAC&U thus continues to engage with Teaching to Increase Diversity and Equity (an AAC&U initiative), agency through stu-dent ePortfolios, signature work, and high-impact practices. We have the knowledge and tools to achieve desired change. We now need the resolve to act.

Visit aacu.org for more information on AAC&U.

Perspective on Assessment and Tensions and the National Survey of Student Engagement
Center for Postsecondary Research (CPR) and National Survey of Student Engagement (NSSE)

Jillian Kinzie

Twenty years ago, when the NSSE was created, the designers had two core objectives in mind: to refocus the national discourse about college quality on teaching and learning and to provide colleges and universities with diag-nostic, actionable information to inform efforts to improve undergraduate education. These goals are still relevant in higher education's current cli-mate of assessment and accountability, yet most institutions are now better equipped with evidence of the quality of the undergraduate experience, and many have incorporated student engagement results into their institu-tional improvement efforts. The availability of valid, reliable, and compa-rable data about students' exposure to practices that matter for learning has enhanced assessment initiatives and seems to have advanced educational quality.

In the next three to five years, I expect that higher education's focus on accountability for improving completion rates and reducing equity gaps among students will persist. We will see an even stronger emphasis on ensur-ing learning outcomes achievement for *all* students, along with a continuing emphasis on experiences that prepare students for the twenty-first-century workplace. With these goals in mind, assessment trends will likely include the following:

- Reliance on a wider range of data about quality and equity in undergraduate education and, in particular, student learning
- Tighter connections between assessment and teaching and learning
- Increased assessment and documentation of the value of experiential learning within and outside the classroom.

Data on Quality and Outcomes

The need for a wider array of data on the quality of undergraduate education is certain to be an assessment trend. Student learning outcomes will continue to be consequential and will require evidence from a broader range of assessment methods, including measures of authentic student learning, such as classroom-based performance assessments, rubrics, and capstones. To fully portray the complexity of college student learning, assessment regimes will need to blend evidence from national surveys, authentic measures, real-time analytics, and homegrown assessment tools. Documenting the achievements of new majority students and ensuring equity in outcomes will take on even greater significance.

Connections Between Assessment and Teaching and Learning

Current efforts to use assessments to inform improvements in instructional practice and learning support and ultimately improve student outcomes are likely to intensify. Strengthening connections between assessment and teaching and learning will allow institutions to be accountable for not only gathering evidence of student learning but also responding to these findings in ways that demonstrably improve teaching, learning, and student success.

As the pressure to demonstrate the value of higher education for preparing students for employment and productive citizenship grows, assessment efforts must define the experiences that contribute to essential skills, employability, and citizenship outcomes and evidence institutional and program quality with respect to graduates' skills in these areas. Employment six months after graduation is an important metric, but it falls short of demonstrating quality and identifying the in- and out-of-class experiences that contribute to student gains. Institutions and students need to know where and how well these skills develop.

Finally, assessing students' experiences with empirically confirmed educational practices will be as important in the near term as it was at the NSSE's inception. Seeking feedback from students about their experiences is an important way to honor students as accurate, credible reporters of their activities and the ways they have benefited from college. It is both reasonable and appropriate that we pay attention to what college students say about their undergraduate educations and then use this information to improve.

Visit cpr.indiana.edu for more information on CPR.

Visit nsse.inidiana.edu for more information on NSSE.

Building Connections: Future Trends in Assessment
Higher Education Data Sharing Consortium (HEDS)

Charles Blaich and Kathleen Wise

HEDS has been bringing private colleges and universities together to share both data and best practices for nearly 40 years. Early on, these efforts focused on sharing operational data, such as admissions, salary, and work-load information. In the past decade, however, the consortium's work has shifted toward assessment. In 2016, HEDS recognized this shift by revising its mission, directly on its homepage, from a focus on institutional data to "sharing data, knowledge, and expertise to advance undergraduate liberal arts education, inclusive excellence, and student success at member institutions."

We believe that the most important issue for the future of assessment is not the extent to which institutions are developing assessment programs but the extent to which the assessment programs that institutions have developed are paying off in improvements to student learning and faculty and staff teaching skills.

Accreditation requirements have been a critical factor in promoting the expansion of assessment in higher education (Jankowski, Timmer, Kinzie, & Kuh, 2018). It is not surprising, therefore, that the way institutions do assessment is shaped by the accreditation-based forces that continue to propel its growth. As Peter Ewell (1987, 2009) noted, assessment motivated by external requirements tends to be structured in fundamentally different ways than assessment that emerges from organic improvement efforts within an institution. In our experience, this means that assessment conducted primarily to meet accreditation standards is more likely to be rote, quantitatively heavy, and meaning-lite. It's also more likely to be experienced by faculty and staff as disconnected from their efforts to improve student learning.

Going forward, HEDS will focus on increasing the return on investment of assessment efforts at institutions. In our view, a key step toward doing this is to acknowledge and build connections among three important, but different, forms of assessment.

Assessment to Monitor Learning

Assessing to monitor learning means collecting evidence designed to keep an eye on learning outcomes or experiences (Blaich & Wise, 2018). This form of assessment is akin to creating a dashboard warning light. The complexity of the data collection is sufficient to let you know the extent to which students are meeting learning goals but insufficient to respond effectively and improve areas where student learning falls short. The action that this form of assessment prompts is further investigation into what's happening.

Assessment to Improve Learning

Here, we refer to collecting evidence to understand whether students are meeting or missing learning goals, along with evidence on the curricular, experiential, and pedagogical factors that may be contributing to these different levels of learning. This kind of assessment requires evidence of sufficient quality to ensure that interventions have an impact on student learning (Fulcher, Good, Coleman, & Smith, 2014).

Assessment for Improving Teaching Skills

Many assessment programs are based on the belief that presenting faculty and staff with assessment data will, on its own, lead to improved learning. Improving the quality of teaching requires deeper conceptual changes, however, than those that emerge when confronting discomforting data (Henderson, Beach, & Finkelstein, 2011). To promote improvement in teaching, assessment evidence needs to be linked with research-based understandings of how to support wider adoption of effective teaching practices (Bryk, 2015).

Going forward, HEDS will focus on developing and integrating these different forms of assessment for institutions.

Visit hedsconsortium.org for more information on HEDS.

Meta-Trends in Assessment: A Summary of Ideas, Opportunities, and Issues for Higher Education

As we conclude this volume on trends in assessment, we acknowledge with gratitude the many scholars who contributed their ideas about assessment's enduring principles and future directions. Together and individually, they provided thoughtful discussions, resources, references, and examples of how assessment trends are unfolding in courses and programs, across campuses and in our communities, and in international contexts, and they showed us how assessment can do more to engage students in educationally purposeful and meaningful activities. Following are 10 meta-trends in assessment that appear as recurrent themes throughout this volume and in work disseminated elsewhere by assessment leaders, researchers, and practitioners.

Meta-Trend 1: Assessment Continues to Make Important Contributions to Understanding and Improving Student Learning and Success

Systematic approaches to assessment can both demonstrate and ensure that institutional stakeholders take student learning and success seriously and that results of assessment are communicated transparently to various internal and external audiences. Such approaches can help to cultivate a culture of evidence-based decision-making throughout the institution (Ewell, 2008). Assessment efforts have offered faculty and staff opportunities to better understand their particular students' strengths and difficulties across courses, programs, cocurricular activities, and entire campuses. But too few institutions are collecting truly actionable data or integrating and using their data as effectively as possible (Parnell, Jones, Wesaw, & Brooks, 2018).

How can we ensure that our assessment data are both *useful* and *used* to inform educational planning, decision-making, and resource allocation at our institutions?

Meta-Trend 2: The Need to Navigate Tensions Between Accountability and Improvement in Higher Education Remains a Key Issue

Access to and participation in higher education are expanding at a time of heightened public scrutiny of the aims, purposes, and return on investment of a college education. Concurrently, pressures to retain and support students to timely degree completion compel institutions to perform efficiently in moving students through their educational pathways while still designing and implementing meaningful learning experiences for those students. One initial impetus for assessment was to provide accountability to external stakeholders for the teaching and learning undertaken in colleges and universities. But if we have learned anything from the past 30 years of experience, it is that assessment for accountability alone will not improve student learning or higher education institutions; compliance-oriented approaches to assessment too often lead to mechanistic, top-down assessment processes that alienate the very faculty and staff charged with carrying them out, as periodic critiques of assessment in the press attest (e.g., Worthen, 2018). Instead, faculty and staff need to take the lead in designing processes whereby they can carry out meaningful assessments, examine findings, determine whether and what changes are needed, implement those changes, and investigate subsequent results, all in the context of striving for consequential improvement. Our focus should be on improvement, as Fulcher and Prendergast (chapter 10, this volume) suggest; by focusing thus, we will also generate evidence that addresses accountability needs (Dowd & Tong, 2007; Ewell, 2009).

Meta-Trend 3: Sound Assessment Programs Continue to Require Leadership and Broadened Stakeholder Engagement

How do institutions communicate commitment to student learning and to the assessment and improvement efforts that undergird this commitment? It begins with senior leaders—presidents, provosts, and institutional govern-ance leaders—who set the "tone at the top" through their words and actions. As we have noted, faculty leadership is also essential to ensuring a collective focus on student learning and widespread adoption of thoughtful assessment and improvement practices at all levels of the institution (Hundley, 2019). The range of stakeholders involved in assessment also includes those who work in areas such as community engagement, global learning, and student affairs, among others, as we have seen in this volume. As Banta and Blaich (2010) pointed out, high turnover rates in faculty and administrative leader-ship for assessment often make it both a challenge and a priority to sustain assessment and improvement efforts.

Meta-Trend 4: Assessment Strategies and Approaches Are Becoming More Inclusive, Equity-Oriented, and Reflective of the Diverse Students Our Institutions Serve

Ensuring that students have equitable access to learning experiences and resources and are able to benefit from them must be a priority for higher education. Inclusive assessment strategies seek to determine who has oppor-tunities to engage in particular learning experiences, disaggregate assessment findings to determine which groups of students are more or less successful, and develop interventions to close equity gaps. Learning experiences should be designed to acknowledge and include diverse perspectives and ideas, and we must empower students to bring their own voices and lived experiences to the learning environment and to have them valued. As McNair, Albertine, Cooper, McDonald, and Major (2016) suggested, "a student-ready college is one that strategically and holistically advances student success, and works tirelessly to educate *all* students for civic and economic participation in a global, interconnected society" (p. 5, emphasis in original).

Meta-Trend 5: Assessment Is Broadening Its Perspective on Outcomes to Include Students' Personal, Academic, and Professional Development

A recurrent theme in this volume and other recent higher education litera-ture is that colleges and universities are responsible for supporting students' holistic development (e.g., Bok, 2006; Cronon, 1998; Nussbaum, 2016). Higher education institutions shape the citizens, professionals, scholars, and leaders of the future. Indeed, Zahl, Jimenez, and Huffman (chapter 7, this volume) remind us that this is true at graduate and professional levels, as well as at the undergraduate level. Today, especially, the new majority students who fill our classrooms must learn to see themselves as capable of academic and professional success and develop the self-awareness and other habits of mind that will support their success in and beyond their higher education experiences (Ben-Avie, Kuna, & Rhodes, 2018; Kahn, 2019). This means that learning environments and experiences must be designed to promote both disciplinary knowledge and the development of what Kuh, Gambino, Bresciani Ludvik, and O'Donnell (2018) termed *neurocognitive* and *dispo-sitional* skills. Yet, too often, assessment has treated students as packages of discrete competencies—a stance that both disregards the larger values, atti-tudes, and dispositions we cultivate in students, whether intentionally or not, and alienates faculty who understand a higher education as something more than sets of competencies acquired. We must develop and adopt assessment strategies and methods that enable us to better understand these sometimes ineffable, but powerful, aspects of student learning in our institutions.

Meta-Trend 6: Authentic Measures of Student Learning, From a Range of Experiences and Contexts, Are Increasingly Necessary and Valued

One of the strongest arguments for authentic assessment is that students themselves can offer the most direct and richest information about what they are learning and what they are struggling with. The best authentic measures offer actionable insights into *how* and *why* students learn, in addition to *what* they learn. Innovations and interventions that generate more meaning-ful authentic evidence and improve assessment of this evidence are needed. This volume discusses several promising practices: *assignment charrettes*, which center assessment on intentionally designed authentic assignments aligned with outcomes; *high-impact practices*, which, when done well, include thoughtful design and well-guided reflection; *ePortfolios*, which support inte-grative learning and identity development and give us insights into student perceptions of learning experience; and *VALUE rubrics*, which are designed for assessment of authentic student work. Comprehensive learner records represent another emerging concept that supports authentic assessment. These records encourage student engagement in a wider range of learning activities, incorporate what students learn in both classroom and cocurricular spaces, and help students integrate and evaluate their learning through documentation valued by students, employers, and others (Green & Parnell, 2018). Practices like these can offer us the kinds of actionable information that are most useful for determining needs and strategies for improvement.

Meta-Trend 7: Assessment Is Expanding Its Focus to Include the Learning Processes *and Practices That Support Achievement of* Outcomes

Many assessment leaders call for a focus on learning outcomes in assessment (Banta & Palomba, 2014; Suskie, 2018). Indeed, we often refer to assessment as *outcomes assessment*. But, as we noted previously, authentic measures, such as reflective ePortfolios, can also help us understand the experiences, practices, and environments that encourage learning and development to occur. A focus on the learning processes that generated (or did not generate) desired learning and developmental outcomes can move us toward more truly learner- and learning-centered assessment and improvement practices, as called for by Fulcher and Prendergast (chapter 10, this volume). The Transparency in Learning and Teaching (TILT) initiative is one new approach that engages students and faculty in discussing learning goals and processes. As Winkelmes (2013) described it, TILT makes assignments "transparent, requiring explicit conversation among teachers and students about the processes of learning and the rationale for required learning activities" (p. 48). A focus on learning processes, practices, and experiences provides more actionable information for improvement than outcomes alone can offer. Indeed, teaching and learning practices and experiences have long been at the center of the Scholarship of Teaching and Learning.

Meta-Trend 8: Ongoing High-Quality Professional Development Remains Essential to Sustained, Systematic, and Well-Designed Assessment Practices

Institutions committed to effective assessment practices strive to develop capacity for this work across the campus. Professional development opportunities can be offered through teaching and learning centers, campus and unit assessment bodies, and other venues. Capacity-building for assessment often engages assessment and institutional research professionals in providing internal consulting and assistance in developing interventions and measures and interpreting findings. As Banta and Palomba (2015) suggested, "Development opportunities are essential during the entire assessment cycle—from the outset as plans are developed, through the implementation phase, to interpretation of results, and use of results to make improvements" (p. 27). Leveraging the capabilities of institutional systems and processes that support assessment, including learning management systems, institutional accreditation and program review processes, and the work of campus-wide councils and committees, is another important capacity-building strategy.

Meta-Trend 9: Assessment Work Must Be Valued and Recognized to Result in Sustained Improvement

Too often, the time, energy, and effort needed to effectively engage in assessment work is not sufficiently valued by administrators and colleagues. This must change. Rewarding, recognizing, and promoting assessment work involves incorporating assessment into ongoing institutional practices and processes. These include annual merit increases; incentives that target strategic institutional priorities; and promotion, tenure, and advancement opportunities. This approach is consistent with long-standing calls to reconsider faculty roles, rewards, and recognition in a manner that is more holistic and consistent with institutional missions (Boyer, 1990; Dolan et al., 2007; Glassick, Huber, & Maeroff, 1997). For assessment to sustain improvement and engage faculty and staff, reward and recognition systems for assessment must be embedded in the institution's culture, reflecting a larger set of values derived from institutions' teaching and learning missions. These systems must further transcend individual leaders' priorities and be reviewed and updated periodically to ensure that they continue to meet their intended purposes. Today, external recognitions such as the Excellence in Assessment Designation are available to institutions that demonstrate exemplary integration of assessment across the institution (Kinzie et al., 2017); individuals and programs that contribute to a culture of effective, evidence-based teaching and learning practices should be similarly recognized internally.

Meta-Trend 10: Assessment Remains a Work in Progress

Despite numerous examples of assessment methods, practices, and outcomes demonstrating credible evidence of progress, experts agree that assessment still has a long way to go to realize its full potential. Now is the time to reconsider what and how we assess and, most important, how assessment results can best be used to foster genuine improvements in student achievement, especially as our student body becomes ever more diverse. Kuh and colleagues (2015) identified strategies for supporting more meaningful and consequential assessment. These included aligning assessment with relevant issues facing students and their learning today, engaging key end users of assessment results by treating them as partners in learning, and focusing on the anticipated use of assessment results by making them relevant and actionable. We would further recommend that assessment more intentionally incorporate scientific understandings of learning developed in the past few decades and be tied more closely to the Scholarship of Teaching and Learning, which has historically sought to design more effective teaching and learning practices. Assessment is more complex than some of its proponents have recognized, and learning is even more complex. While much has been discussed, written, and debated about assessment in higher education in the past 35 years, it nonetheless remains a work in progress.

Conclusion

The Assessment Institute in Indianapolis, along with its partner associations and research organizations, remains committed to its role as a principal venue for showcasing assessment work. We invite you to join us by contributing your own important issues, ideas, and opportunities for higher education to the annual program. Please visit assessmentinstitute.iupui.edu to learn more about ways to become involved.

We want to hear from you about *Trends in Assessment*:

- Provide reactions or suggestions about trends.
- Share and access resources related to trends.
- Learn about professional development opportunities related to trends.

Visit assessmentinstitute.iupui.edu/trends

References

Association for General & Liberal Studies. (2007). *Improving learning in general education: An AGLS guide to assessment and program review.* Retrieved from https://www.agls.org/wp-content/uploads/2019/04/AGLS-Guide-to-Program-Review-Electronic.pdf

Banta, T. W., & Blaich, C. (2010). Closing the assessment loop. *Change: The Magazine of Higher Learning, 43*(1), 22–27.

Banta, T. W., & Palomba, C. A. (2015). *Assessment essentials: Planning, implementing, and improving assessment in higher education* (2nd ed.). San Francisco, CA: Jossey-Bass.

Ben-Avie, M., Kuna, K., & Rhodes, T. (2018). Assessment as a strategy, not a stand-alone activity. *Peer Review, 20*(4), 4–6.

Blaich, C., & Wise, K. (2018). The more things change, the more they stay the same: New challenges to using evidence to improve student learning. *Research and Practice in Assessment, 13*, 11–14.

Bok, D. (2006). *Our underachieving colleges: A candid look at how much students learn and why they should be learning more.* Princeton, NJ: Princeton University Press.

Boyer, E. (1990). *Scholarship reconsidered: Priorities of the professoriate.* San Francisco, CA: Jossey-Bass.

Bryk, A. S. (2015). Accelerating how we learn to improve. *Educational Researcher, 44*, 467–477.

Cronon, W. (1998). "Only connect . . ." The goals of a liberal education. *The American Scholar, 67*(4), 73–80.

Dolan, E. L., Elliott, S. L., Henderson, C., Curran-Everett, D., John, K. S., & Ortiz, P. A. (2018). Evaluating discipline-based education research for promotion and tenure. *Innovative Higher Education, 43*(1), 31–39.

Dowd, A. C., & Tong, V. P. (2007). Accountability, assessment, and the scholarship of "best practice." In J. C. Smart (Ed.), *Higher education: Handbook of theory and research* (pp. 57–119). Dordrecht, the Netherlands: Springer.

Ewell, P. T. (1987). *Assessment, accountability and improvement: Managing the contradiction.* Washington, DC: American Association for Higher Education.

Ewell, P. T. (2008). Assessment and accountability in America today: Background and context. *New Directions for Institutional Research, 2008*(S1), 7–17.

Ewell, P. T. (2009, November). *Assessment, accountability, and improvement: Revisiting the tension* (Occasional Paper No. 1). Urbana, IL: University of Illinois and Indiana University, National Institute for Learning Outcomes Assessment.

Fulcher, K. H., Good, M. R., Coleman, C. M., & Smith, K. L. (2014, December). *A simple model for learning improvement: Weigh pig, feed pig, weigh pig* (Occasional Paper No. 23). Urbana, IL: University of Illinois and Indiana University, National Institute for Learning Outcomes Assessment.

Glassick, C. E., Huber, M. T., & Maeroff, G. I. (1997). *Scholarship assessed: Evaluation of the professoriate.* San Francisco, CA: Jossey-Bass.

Green, T., & Parnell, A. (2018). Collaborative assessment of learning: Lessons learned from the development of comprehensive learner records. *Assessment Update, 30*(5), 10–13.

Henderson, C., Beach, A., & Finkelstein, N. (2011). Facilitating change in undergraduate STEM instructional practices: An analytic review of the literature. *Journal of Research in Science Teaching, 48*, 952–984.

Hundley, S. P. (2019). Editor's notes. *Assessment Update, 31*(1), 3.

Jankowski, N. A., Timmer, J. D., Kinzie, J., & Kuh, G. D. (2018, January). *Assessment that matters: Trending toward practices that document authentic student learning*. Urbana, IL: University of Illinois and Indiana University, National Institute for Learning Outcomes Assessment.

Kahn, S. (2019). Identity development as curriculum: A metacognitive approach. In K. Yancey (Ed.), *ePortfolio as curriculum: Models and practices for developing students' ePortfolio literacy* (pp. 89–105). Sterling, VA: Stylus.

Kinzie, J., Hinds, T. L., Jankowski, N. A., & Rhodes, T. L. (2017). Recognizing excellence in assessment. *Assessment Update, 29*(1), 1–16.

Kuh, G. D., Gambino, L. M., Bresciani Ludvik, M., & O'Donnell, K. (2018). Accentuating dispositional learning from HIPs using ePortfolio. *Assessment Update, 30*(3), 8–9.

Kuh, G. D., Ikenberry, S. O., Jankowski, N., Cain, T. R., Ewell, P. T., Hutchings, P., & Kinzie, J. (2015). *Using evidence of student learning to improve higher education.* San Francisco, CA: Jossey-Bass.

McNair, T. B., Albertine, S., Cooper, M. A., McDonald, N., & Major, T., Jr. (2016). *Becoming a student-ready college: A new culture of leadership for student success.* San Francisco, CA: Jossey-Bass.

Nussbaum, M. C. (2016). *Not for profit: Why democracy needs the humanities* (rev. ed.). Princeton, NJ: Princeton University Press.

Parnell, A., Jones, D., Wesaw, A., & Brooks, D. C. (2018). *Institutions' use of data and analytics for student success: Results from a national landscape analysis.* Washington, DC: NASPA: Student Affairs Administrators in Higher Education, the Association for Institutional Research, and EDUCAUSE.

Suskie, L. (2018). *Assessing student learning: A common sense guide.* Hoboken, NJ:John Wiley & Sons.

Swing, R. L., & Ross, L. E. (2016a). *Statement of aspirational practice for institutional research.* Association for Institutional Research, Tallahassee, Florida. Retrieved from http://www.airweb.org/aspirationalstatement

Swing, R. L., & Ross, L. E. (2016b). A new vision for institutional research. *Change: The Magazine of Higher Learning, 48*(2), 6–13.

Winkelmes, M. A. (2013). Transparency in teaching: Faculty share data and improve students' learning. *Liberal Education, 99*(2), 48–55.

Worthen, N. (2018, February 23). The misguided drive to measure "learning outcomes." *The New York Times.* Retrieved from https://www.nytimes.com/search?query=Worthen%20%26%20Assessment&sort=best

EDITORS AND CONTRIBUTORS

Editors

Stephen P. Hundley is senior adviser to the chancellor for planning and institutional improvement at Indiana University–Purdue University Indianapolis (IUPUI), an urban-serving institution with 30,000 students. He also serves as professor of organizational leadership within the Department of Technology Leadership and Communication in IUPUI's School of Engineering and Technology. Hundley chairs the annual Assessment Institute in Indianapolis, launched at IUPUI in 1992 under the direction of his predecessor, Trudy W. Banta, and now the oldest and largest national event of its type. In 2017, he also assumed the role of executive editor of *Assessment Update*, an award-winning publication from Wiley/Jossey-Bass with a national readership. His prior administrative roles include program director, department chair, and associate dean for academic affairs and undergraduate programs in the School of Engineering and Technology; associate vice chancellor for strategic initiatives in the Office of the Executive Vice Chancellor and Chief Academic Officer; and interim associate vice chancellor for undergraduate education and dean of University College. Hundley earned his BS and MS degrees from Virginia Commonwealth University and PhD from American University in Washington DC.

Susan Kahn is director of planning and institutional improvement initiatives at Indiana University–Purdue University Indianapolis (IUPUI) and an adjunct faculty member in the Department of English in IUPUI's School of Liberal Arts and in University College. Previously, she was director of the Undergraduate Teaching Improvement Council (now Office of Professional and Instructional Development) for the University of Wisconsin System and senior academic planner and special assistant to the senior vice president for academic affairs, also at the UW System. After joining IUPUI, Kahn directed the Urban Universities Portfolio Project, a national initiative that produced the first generation of electronic institutional portfolios aimed at demonstrating institutional and educational effectiveness. She directed IUPUI's student ePortfolio effort from 2006 until 2018, guiding its development from a fledgling project to a campus-wide initiative designed to engage and empower students in their learning and development and to provide rich evidence for assessment. From 2011 until 2015, she served as chair of the board of directors of the Association for Authentic, Experiential, and Evidence-Based Learning, the professional association for ePortfolio researchers and practitioners. Kahn coedited *Electronic Portfolios: Emerging Trends in Student, Faculty, and Institutional Learning* (Stylus, 2001), among other publications; served as assessment editor for *About Campus* from 2006 to 2010; and is currently associate editor of *Assessment Update*. Kahn earned an AB in English from Smith College and an MA and a PhD, also in English, from the University of Wisconsin-Madison.

Contributors

Gianina R. Baker is assistant director of the National Institute for Learning Outcomes Assessment (NILOA), co-located at the University of Illinois Urbana-Champaign and Indiana University Bloomington. Her main research interests include student learning outcomes assessment at Minority-Serving Institutions, access and equity issues for underrepresented administrators and students, and higher education policy. Prior to her work with NILOA, she was the director of institutional effectiveness and planning at Richland Community College.

Trudy W. Banta is one of the pioneers in the scholarship of outcomes assessment in higher education. With federal funds, she founded the Center for Assessment Research and Development at the University of Tennessee, Knoxville. She is the founding editor of *Assessment Update*, a bimonthly periodical published by Jossey-Bass. At IUPUI, she founded the Division of Planning and Institutional Improvement. Recipient of 15 national awards for her work, Banta is the author or editor of 20 books and more than 400 chapters, articles, and reports. She has conducted 30 national conferences and 15 international conferences around the world, addressed meetings in a dozen countries, and consulted with faculty and administrators at more than 130 U.S. colleges and universities. Since her retirement in 2016, her title is vice chancellor and professor of higher education emerita.

Jeffery Barbee is an assessment and evaluation specialist at the Indiana University School of Medicine. His duties include leading assessment efforts with objective structured clinical examinations and working with faculty to develop tailored course assessments. He is also an adjunct instructor of music theory and applied low brass lessons at IUPUI. He earned his doctorate in musical arts and master's degree in higher education administration from the University of Missouri–Kansas City.

Stephen Biscotte helps support and manage the Pathways to General Education program as director of general education at Virginia Polytechnic Institute and State University. Biscotte's scholarship on general education, which focuses on the non–science, technology, engineering, and math (STEM) student experience in STEM general education courses, has appeared in *The Journal of General Education*. He has given presentations and workshops, both locally and nationally, on general education–related topics such as innovative structures, university reform efforts, and program evaluation. Biscotte also serves on the council of the Association for General and Liberal Studies. Prior to assuming his role at Virginia Tech, he was a high school science teacher for 11 years in Virginia and South Carolina.

Karen E. Black was the director of program review in the Division of Planning and Institutional Improvement at IUPUI and served as the director of the Assessment Institute in Indianapolis prior to her retirement. From 1992 to 2018, she managing editor of *Assessment Update*. She has published and presented on assessment of student learning outcomes and program review. As an adjunct faculty member, she taught courses in English and organizational leadership, and in IUPUI's first-year experience program.

Charles Blaich is the director of the Center of Inquiry at Wabash College and, since 2011, of the Higher Education Data Sharing Consortium, a 145-institution collaborative that shares data to improve educational effectiveness. He collaborated with researchers at the University of Iowa, University of Michigan, Miami University, and ACT to design and implement the Wabash National Study of Liberal Arts Education, a large-scale, longitudinal study investigating critical factors affecting the outcomes of a liberal arts education. Blaich's most recent publications include "Engaging With Diversity: How Positive and Negative Diversity Interactions Influence Students' Cognitive Outcomes" (coauthor; *The Journal of Higher Education,* 2017) and "Scope, Cost, or Speed: Choose Two–The Iron Triangle of Assessment" (*Change,* 2018).

Leslie A. Bozeman is the director of curriculum internationalization at IUPUI. In this role, she works to facilitate campus-level strategic initiatives pertaining to curriculum internationalization and global learning; increase faculty, staff, and administrator understanding of those concepts; and provide guidance on how to assess student learning outcomes in intercultural and global learning. Her experience over the past 25 years includes faculty development, undergraduate and graduate academic affairs, campus internationalization, campus and community global engagement, international development, cultural and intercultural education, study abroad, and teaching P–16.

A. Katherine Busby is the director of institutional research, effectiveness, and planning at the University of Mississippi. In this capacity, she provides strategic direction and leadership for the collection, analysis, interpretation, and dissemination of institutional data and oversees university-wide strategic planning and institutional effectiveness processes. Busby holds a BS and an MS in mathematics from the University of Mississippi and a PhD in assessment and measurement from James Madison University. Her research interests include measures of student development and leadership, instrument development, and validity issues. Active in professional associations, she is a former editor of *Research & Practice in Assessment*.

Anthony Chase is the evaluation and research specialist at the STEM Education Innovation and Research Institute at IUPUI. He received an MS in organic chemistry and a PhD in educational psychology from Purdue University. He primarily studies authentic educational environments and situated learning within STEM education.

Helen L. Chen is a research scientist at the Designing Education Lab in the Department of Mechanical Engineering at Stanford University. She serves on the board of directors of the Association for Authentic, Experiential and Evidence-Based Learning; is a coauthor of *Documenting Learning with ePortfolios: A Guide for College Instructors* (Jossey-Bass, 2011); and is coexecutive editor of the *International Journal of ePortfolio*. Her current research interests focus on engineering and entrepreneurship education, applications of design thinking for curricular change, the pedagogy of ePortfolios and reflective practice in higher education, and redesign of approaches to recording and recognizing learning in traditional transcripts and academic credentials.

Stephan C. Cooley is project analyst for research and initiatives at the Association for Institutional Research (AIR). He supports AIR's efforts to advance the practice and student success agenda of data professionals in the ever-evolving field of higher education. Cooley serves as the managing editor of *The AIR Professional File* and contributes to the conception and development of the association's educational opportunities. He previously coordinated AIR's online professional development opportunities for Integrated Postsecondary Education Data System (IPEDS) Keyholders. Prior to his work for AIR, Cooley served as the lead research assistant for three studies that examined effective school leadership, with funding from the Institute of Education Sciences. He holds an MS in foreign and second language education and a BA in French from Florida State University.

Darla K. Deardorff is a research scholar at Duke University and author or editor of 8 books, including *Demystifying Outcomes Assessment for International Educators: A Practical Approach* (Stylus, 2015), and more than 50 articles and book chapters. She is the founding CEO of ICC Global, an affiliated faculty member at numerous institutions around the world, and a frequently invited speaker and consultant. She also currently serves as executive director of the Association of International Education Administrators. Deardorff holds a doctorate from North Carolina State University.

Kyle Fassett is a doctoral student in higher education at Indiana University Bloomington and a project associate for the National Survey of Student Engagement and Faculty Survey of Student Engagement. His research interests include faculty teaching practices, collegiate experiences of LGBT students, and the roles of student affairs practitioners. He is the recipient of several awards from ACPA-College Student Educators International, including the Mid-Level Community of Practice's Outstanding Research, Contribution and/or Scholarship Award. He earned his master's degree in college student personnel from Bowling Green State University and his bachelor's degree in theater design from the State University of New York at New Paltz.

John G. Frederick, currently a higher education assessment consultant, has served as president of the Association for General and Liberal Studies and director of faculty learning and engagement at Central Piedmont Community College. Previously, he was the director of academic planning and assessment at the University of North Carolina at Charlotte (UNC-Charlotte), where he worked with academic units to plan, implement, and sustain their efforts in the assessment of student learning and strategic planning. Prior to joining UNC-Charlotte, he was a faculty member and director of student learning outcomes assessment at Miami Dade College. As a faculty member, he chaired the Learning Outcomes Assessment Team, working with the team to assess the college's general education student learning outcomes. As director, he supported the implementation and continuous improvement of assessment across the college.

Keston H. Fulcher is the executive director of the Center for Assessment and Research Studies and professor in graduate psychology at James Madison University (JMU). JMU has received an unprecedented 14 national recognitions related to student learning outcomes assessment. Fulcher's research focuses on structuring higher education for learning improvement. He serves on the advisory panel to the National Institute for Learning Outcomes Assessment and collaborates extensively with the Assessment Institute in Indianapolis.

Steven Graunke is the director of institutional research and assessment at IUPUI. He has participated in several research efforts related to HIPs, including assessment of a Themed Learning Community's ePortfolio project and use of predictive modeling to understand which students study abroad. Graunke helped faculty and staff attendees assess HIP experiences while serving as a facilitator for the IUPUI Research Academy. He has presented his work on the assessment of HIPS at several national conferences, including the Higher Learning Commission's Annual Conference and the Association for Institutional Research's annual AIR Forum.

Thomas W. Hahn is the director of research and program evaluation at the Center for Service and Learning and Institute for Engaged Learning at Indiana University–Purdue University Indianapolis (IUPUI). He is responsible for assessment, evaluation, and research in the areas of student civic learning, experiential learning, and success. Hahn has over 20 years of experience in assessment and program improvement in higher education. He oversees the annual IUPUI Research Academy on Community Engagement and Engaged Learning and chairs the campus subcommittee for the Experiential and Applied Learning Record. He received his undergraduate and graduate degrees from Old Dominion University in Norfolk, Virginia.

Michele J. Hansen serves as the assistant vice chancellor for institutional research and decision support (IRDS) at IUPUI. IRDS is a comprehensive institutional research office where members are engaged in institutional research, advanced statistical analyses, survey research, program evaluation, student learning assessment, program and administrative reviews, and data support for strategic enrollment management. Hansen's primary research interests are in the areas of learning outcomes assessment and program evaluation methods, effectiveness of interventions to enhance retention and academic success of undergraduate and graduate students (applying social psychology theories to higher education), survey research methods, and incremental and large-scale change management. Hansen received her bachelor's degree in psychology from Michigan State University and master's and doctoral degrees in social psychology from Loyola University Chicago.

Julie A. Hatcher is associate professor emerita of philanthropic studies in the Lilly Family School of Philanthropy at IUPUI and was executive director of IUPUI's Center for Service and Learning from 2012 to 2018. She is coeditor of the IUPUI Series on Service Learning Research (Stylus, 2011, 2013, 2016) and focuses her research on the role of higher education in democracy and civil society, civic learning outcomes in higher education, philanthropic studies, and civic-minded professionals. She serves on the national advisory board for the Carnegie Foundation's Community Engagement elective classification and consults with universities on strategies to enact the public purposes of higher education. Hatcher is the 2017 International Association for Research on Service-Learning and Community Engagement Distinguished Career Award recipient and the 2008 Dissertation Award recipient. She earned her PhD in philanthropic studies with a minor in higher education at Indiana University.

Krista Hoffmann-Longtin is assistant professor of communication studies in the School of Liberal Arts at IUPUI and an assistant dean for faculty affairs and professional development at the Indiana University School of Medicine. Her research focuses on communication education and faculty development in the sciences and health professions. An award-winning educator and researcher, she has published her work in *Communication Education*, *Academic Medicine*, and the *Journal of Faculty Development*. She teaches courses in communication theory and pedagogy and directs a graduate-level minor in science communication. Hoffmann-Longtin holds a BA from Ball State University, an MA from Purdue University, and a PhD from Indiana University.

Max Huffman is professor of law and codirector of program assessment and evaluation at the Indiana University Robert H. McKinney School of Law. He serves on the IUPUI Program Review and Assessment Committee and, for the past two years, has also served as codirector of the graduate studies track at the Assessment Institute in Indianapolis. Huffman has published work on teaching and assessment as well as in scholarly journals in the field of law.

Natasha A. Jankowski is director of the National Institute for Learning Outcomes Assessment (NILOA) and a research professor with the Department of Education Policy, Organization and Leadership at the University of

Illinois Urbana-Champaign. She is coauthor with her NILOA colleagues of the books *Using Evidence of Student Learning to Improve Higher Education* (Jossey-Bass, 2015) and *Degrees That Matter: Moving Higher Education to a Learning Systems Paradigm* (Stylus, 2017), and she has authored a variety of other book chapters, reports, and articles. She supports institutions and organizations nationally and internationally on meaningful assessment of student learning as well as effective communication of their assessment efforts.

Sherry Jimenez serves as the associate dean of assessment and interprofessional education at Lincoln Memorial University Debusk College of Osteopathic Medicine in Harrogate and Knoxville, Tennessee. She is responsible for administrative oversight and direction of assessment and clinical training activities in undergraduate, graduate, and continuing medical education in collaboration with medical, nursing, and allied health programs. A fellow of the National Academy of Osteopathic Medical Educators, Jimenez was recognized by the American Association of Colleges of Osteopathic Medicine's Society for Osteopathic Medical Educators with the Innovations in Medical Education Award in 2015. She is a 2013 corecipient of the Arnold P. Gold Foundation's Humanism in Medicine grant, which resulted in the cofounding of Marian University College of Osteopathic Medicine's Meaningful Medicine Mentoring Program.

Jillian Kinzie is associate director, Center for Postsecondary Research and the National Survey of Student Engagement, at Indiana University Bloomington and senior scholar with the National Institute for Learning Outcomes Assessment. She leads student engagement and educational effectiveness research efforts and consults with colleges and universities on using data on undergraduate quality and learning outcomes to enhance teaching and learning and improve the conditions for student success.

Gabrielle Kline is a senior at IUPUI double majoring in chemistry and biology with plans to pursue graduate study. She has participated in research and evaluation projects for IUPUI's STEM Education Innovation and Research Institute during the past two years. She is also deeply involved in her sorority and IUPUI's Chemistry Club.

Gil Latz is vice provost for global strategies and international affairs and professor of geography at The Ohio State University. He has published widely on internationalization, diversity, community engagement, and global learning for all—and how these areas intersect—as well as the internationalization of higher education in the United States and Asia. His research also focuses on regional development and resource management policy in both rural and urban areas in East Asia, North America, and Europe. Latz's national leadership includes service as senior associate for internationalization at the Center for Internationalization and Global Engagement in the American Council on Education and president of the Association of International Education Administrators (2015–2017). He earned his doctoral and master's degrees in geography from the University of Chicago.

Ahebé Sonia Ninon is the director of assessment and planning in the Division of Student Affairs at IUPUI. Ninon collaborates with other directors to further the division's efforts to make evidence-based decisions and represents the division on a variety of campus committees. She has a master's degree in social and applied economics and a master's degree in public administration from Wright State University.

Kristin Norris is the director of assessment for the Office of Community Engagement at IUPUI. She works with internal and external stakeholders to track, assess, and demonstrate the value of community-engaged activities to inform decision-making, support the institution's mission and strategic priorities, and transform higher education. She is passionate about student civic outcomes and the public purposes of higher education. Norris earned her BS from Purdue University, MS in hospitality and tourism management from Indiana University, and PhD in higher education administration from Indiana University. She is an editorial fellow for *Metropolitan Universities* and chair of IUPUI's Program Review and Assessment Committee.

Megan M. Palmer is an associate professor of higher education in the Indiana University (IU) School of Education-Indianapolis, associate dean of faculty affairs and professional development and diversity in the IU School of Medicine, and vice chair for education and faculty development and associate professor in the Department of Emergency Medicine at the IU School of Medicine. Her research focuses on college teaching, medical education, faculty development, and the experience of faculty. She holds a PhD from IU, an MS from Colorado State University, and a BA from the University of St. Thomas in Minnesota. Prior to her work at IU, Palmer served in a variety of student affairs administrative positions.

Jeremy D. Penn is the assessment coordinator in the College of Education at the University of Iowa. Prior to joining the University of Iowa, he served as a director of assessment for a large division of student affairs, a director of assessment and testing, and a high school math teacher. He was the president of the Association for the Assessment of Learning in Higher Education from 2018 to 2019.

Tracy Penny Light is president and board chair of the Association for Authentic, Experiential, and Evidence-Based Learning and associate professor of history at Thompson Rivers University in British Columbia, Canada. Her educational research explores the use of ePortfolios to foster deep learning. She has coauthored two books on ePortfolio implementation and practice, *Electronic Portfolios and Student Success* (with Helen L. Chen; Association of American Colleges & Universities, 2015) and *Documenting Learning with ePortfolios: A Guide for College Instructors* (with Helen L. Chen and John Ittelson; Jossey-Bass, 2011). Her historical research explores gender and sexuality in Canadian history, with a particular emphasis on medicine and popular culture. Publications include *Bodily Subjects: Essays on Gender and Health, 1800-2000* (with Wendy Mitchinson and Barbara Brookes; McGill-Queen's University Press, 2015) and *Feminist Pedagogy in Higher Education: Critical Theory and Practice* (with Jane Nicholas and Renee Bondy; Wilfrid Laurier University Press, 2015).

Amy A. Powell is the director of the learning communities program at IUPUI and teaches in IUPUI's first-year experience program. Powell is a cocoordinator of the high-impact practices track at the Assessment Institute in Indianapolis. She has served as resource faculty at the National Summer Institute on Learning Communities and represents IUPUI in the National Learning Communities Consortium. Prior to joining the learning communities program, Powell was an instructional technology consultant at IUPUI's Center for Teaching and Learning, leading faculty development in online course design, ePortfolio pedagogy, critical reflection, and the integration of pedagogy and technology. She holds a BA in music education from the University of Minnesota and an MS in education in instructional systems technology from Indiana University.

Caroline O. Prendergast is a doctoral student in the assessment and measurement program at James Madison University. She received her MEd in measurement, evaluation, statistics, and assessment from Boston College. Her research interests include the use of assessment to support learning improvement, approaches to building assessment capacity, and issues of equity in assessment.

Terrel L. Rhodes is vice president in the Office of Quality, Curriculum and Assessment and executive director of Valid Assessment of Learning in Undergraduate Education (VALUE)at the Association of American Colleges & Universities (AAC&U). A faculty member for 25 years, he focuses on the quality of undergraduate education, access, general education, ePortfolios, and assessment of student learning. His work on VALUE, a faculty-driven assessment project on student learning, and the VALUE Institute aims to use authentic student work to demonstrate meaningful learning across the outcomes essential to student success. For the past 10 years, he has led AAC&U's ePortfolio initiatives, including the AAC&U annual ePortfolio Forum, to enhance student learning.

Leah Ewing Ross is senior director for research and initiatives at the Association for Institutional Research (AIR). She leads AIR's national research, scholarship, and innovation agenda to effectively position institutional research and related fields within the changing landscape of higher education. Ross partners with stakeholders to create forward-looking models to advance evidence-based decision-making and to equip higher education professionals with the knowledge and tools they need as leaders within their organizations. Prior to joining AIR, she worked in consulting, scholarly publications, association management, and college admissions. Ross holds a PhD in educational leadership from Iowa State University, an MS in higher education administration from Florida State University, and an AB in English from Mount Holyoke College.

Jane Marie Souza serves as the associate provost for academic administration and chief assessment officer at the University of Rochester. She is a board member and president-elect of the Association for the Assessment of Learning in Higher Education and past editor-in-chief for the organization's publication, *Intersection*. Souza has served on accreditation teams for multiple agencies, including the New England Association of Schools and Colleges; the Middle States Commission on Higher Education; the Accreditation Council for Pharmacy Education; and the Council on Podiatric Medical Education, of which she is also a member. She has presented her work at conferences of the Association for Institutional Research; the Association for the Assessment of Learning in Higher Education; the Assessment Institute in Indianapolis; the Drexel Assessment Conference, where she served as keynote speaker; and the Association for Medical Education in Europe.

Monica Stitt-Bergh is an educational psychologist and associate specialist at the University of Hawai'i at Mānoa Assessment Office where she provides technical support and offers workshops on learning outcomes assessment. She has taught courses on writing and on social science research methods and has published and offered conference presentations on learning outcomes assessment, writing program evaluation, self-assessment, and writing across the curriculum.

Jennifer Thorington Springer is the interim associate dean of student affairs and associate professor of English in the School of Liberal Arts at IUPUI. She served as the founding director of the IUPUI RISE Program, which focuses on transformative pedagogy, including high-impact practices and various forms of experiential learning, from 2014 to 2018. Born and raised in Barbados, Springer's own border-crossing and personal background as a transnational subject directly influences her areas of study: Caribbean and African American literatures as well as Africana and women's studies. Springer's research primarily examines literary constructions of Black diasporic identities and ways in which race, class, gender, sexuality, and nationality further complicate those identities.

C. Edward Watson is associate vice president for quality, pedagogy, and LEAP initiatives and chief information officer with the AAC&U. He previously served as director of the Center for Teaching and Learning at the University of Georgia. He is the founding executive editor of the *International Journal of ePortfolio*; the executive editor of the *International Journal of Teaching and Learning in Higher Education*; and coauthor/editor of two recent books, *Teaching Naked Techniques: A Practical Guide to Designing Better Classes* (Jossey-Bass, 2017) and *Playing to Learn with Reacting to the Past: Research on High Impact, Active Learning Practices* (Palgrave MacMillan, 2017).

H. Anne Weiss is a PhD candidate at Indiana University and director of assessment for Indiana Campus Compact. Weiss has been researching the public mission of higher education for 15 years and, for more than 7 years, planning robust and rigorous inquiry projects that explore institutional, student, and community success metrics for civic and community engagement in higher education; institutional performance of the public mission of higher education; and students' political engagement and learning during college. They received their MA in applied communication from Indiana University.

Dawn M. Whitehead is vice president of the Office of Global Citizenship for Campus, Community, and Careers at the Association of American Colleges & Universities, where she works with member institutions to lead globally focused and community-based learning projects and programs that are integrated into curricular and cocurricular initiatives. Her areas of expertise are African studies, curricular change, curriculum internationalization, global service-learning, and global learning.

Kathleen Wise is the associate director of the Center of Inquiry and the Higher Education Data Sharing Consortium at Wabash College. Wise received her undergraduate degree from Yale University and her MBA from the University of Chicago. She joined the Center of Inquiry in 2004 and has worked with well over 100 colleges and universities to evaluate programs, offices and institutional assessment plans, and to improve student learning. Her most recent publications include "Engaging With Diversity: How Positive and Negative Diversity Interactions Influence Students' Cognitive Outcomes" (*The Journal of Higher Education,* 2017) and "The More Things Change, the More They Stay the Same: New Challenges to Using Evidence to Improve Student Learning" (*Research & Practice in Assessment,* 2018).

Sarah B. Zahl is the assistant dean for accreditation logistics and advancement at the Marian University College of Osteopathic Medicine, where she is responsible for the overall strategic direction and operational activities associated with accreditation. In addition to her administrative role, she holds faculty appointments as assistant professor of family medicine and assistant professor of education. Zahl has published her research in academic journals and regularly presents her work at national and international conferences. She has also earned grants and fellowships for her scholarship and practice. Her academic and research interests include accreditation management, outcomes assessment, and tracking student success factors during graduate study.

John Zilvinskis is an assistant professor of higher education at Binghamton University. He also serves as a research affiliate for the Institute for Justice and Well-Being and a doctoral faculty fellow for the College of Community and Public Affairs. Prior to joining Binghamton University, he was a research project associate with the Center for Postsecondary Research at Indiana University, where he worked primarily with data drawn from the National

Survey of Student Engagement. Zilvinskis's research has been published in *Research in Higher Education*, the *Review of Higher Education*, and the *Journal of Diversity in Higher Education*. In addition, he coedited a volume of *New Directions for Higher Education* on the topic of learning analytics, and he is a two-time winner of the Association for Institutional Research's Charles F. Elton Best Paper Award.

AAC&U. *See* Association of American Colleges & Universities

AAEEBL. *See* Association for Authentic, Experiential, and Evidence-Based Learning

AAHE. *See* American Association for Higher Education

AALHE. *See* Association for the Assessment of Learning in Higher Education

ABET. *See* Accreditation Board for Engineering and Technology

ABET, Inc., 95

Academic and Student Affairs Sides of the House: Can We Have an Open Concept Learning Design? (Roberts), 84

academic development. *See* faculty development

accountability, 29n2, 202–3, 206–7
  of graduate and professional programs, 115–16

accreditation, 107, 112, 119, 204

Accreditation Board for Engineering and Technology (ABET), 95, 114

ACPA. *See* American College Personnel Association

actionable, 198

active learning, 95–97

AGLS. *See* Association for General and Liberal Studies

Agrawal, M., 85

AIR. *See* Association for Institutional Research

Albertine, S., 207

American Association for Higher Education (AAHE), 4

American College Personnel Association (ACPA), 80–81

American Council on Education, 78

Aoun, J. E., 179

APLU. *See* Association of Public and Land-grant Universities

application, of knowledge, 96

Arasaratnam-Smith, L. A., 48

Articulating Learning Outcomes in Doctoral Education (Denecke), 116

ASK Standards: Assessment, Skills, and Knowledge Content Standards for Student Affairs Practitioners and Scholars (ACPA), 81

Assessing Civic Competency and Engagement in Higher Education (Torney-Purta), 67

assessment
  current state of, 5
  definitions of, 2, 19, 71, 180
  evaluation compared to, 180
  findings use of, 10
  origin and growth of, 2–5
  See also specific topics

assessment cycle, 158–59

Assessment Institute in Indianapolis (Institute), 1
  focuses of, 9–10
  mission of, 6
  partners of, 6–8, 194
  trends and, 11–14
  See also National Institute for Learning Outcomes Assessment

assessment levels, 9

assessment methods, 9

"assessment movement," 2–3

assignment charrette process, 21–22, 208–9
assignment design, 22–23
Association for Authentic, Experiential, and Evidence-Based Learning (AAEEBL), 7
in meta-trends, 196–98
Association for General and Liberal Studies (AGLS), 7, 198–99
Association for Institutional Research (AIR), 7, 188, 199–200
Association for the Assessment of Learning in Higher Education (AALHE), 6–7, 194–96
student affairs and, 81–82
See also meta-trends
Association of American Colleges & Universities (AAC&U), 7, 29n2, 92–93, 200–2
HIPs and, 33–34, 40
on signature assignments, 184
VALUE rubrics from, 117–18, 183, 209
Association of Public and Land-grant Universities (APLU), 29n2
Astin, A. W., 4–5
authentic embedded assessment
lifelong learners and, 183
signature assignments as, 183–84
See also ePortfolio assessment
authenticity
in ePortfolio assessment, 143, 183–84
in meta-trends, 208–9
NILOA on, 21–23
rubrics and, 183

Barr, R. B., 4
Barrette, C. M., 126
Becoming a Student-Ready College: High-Impact Practices and Intentionality by Design (McNair), 38–39
Bentley University, 52–53
Blaich, C. F., 207
Bland, C. J., 129

Boettcher, C., 47
Bok, D., 168
Bond, L., 110
Borrego, M., 93
Boyer, Ernest L., 4
Bresciani Ludvik, M., 208
business analogy, 158–59
Buyarski, C. A., 183–84
Bybee, R. W., 94

Cambridge, Darren, 145–46
Campus Compact, 66
Canetto, S. S., 99
CARS. See Center for Assessment & Research Studies
CBGL. See community-based global learning
Center for Assessment & Research Studies (CARS), 7
Center for Postsecondary Research (CPR), 7–8, 34–35, 202–4
challenges and debates, 23–25
charrette, 21–22, 208
Chism, N. V. N., 127–29
citizenship, 46–47, 50–51
holistic assessment and, 177–79
civic identity, 65
civic-minded graduate (CMG), 63–65
Cleven, A. J., 86
CMG. See civic-minded graduate
cocurricular assessment, 85, 198
cocurricular programs, 79, 83–84
cocurricular transcripts, 38
Coleman, C. M., 5
collaboration, 23, 187
community engagement and, 71
in faculty development, 129–30
in graduate and professional programs, 116
HPAC, 119
IPEC, 113, 118
in student affairs, 86–87
communication, 27–28, 70
for community engagement, 60, 71–72

among faculty and staff, 187
to stakeholders, 186
community, 62
impact on, 70
community-based global learning
(CBGL), 47
community-engaged learning
CMG in, 63–65
communications or assessment in, 70
community impact in, 70
current trends in, 63–69
definition of, 62
direct measures and, 66
documentation in, 68–69
Education for Democracy in, 66
faculty in, 69
future trends in, 69–71
history of, 62–63
indirect measures and, 67
main points on, 72
mutual benefits in, 67–68
outputs in, 69
partnerships in, 66–68
questions on, 72
reciprocity in, 61–62, 67–68
transdisciplinary in, 62–65, 71
community engagement, 12
collaboration and, 71
communication for, 60, 71–72
definition of, 61–62
HIPs in, 67
reciprocity in, 61–62, 67–68
Community Engagement Classification,
61
Competency Model for Community
Engagement Professionals, 71
compositional equity, 185
consensus, 27
content knowledge, 96
contexts, 9
Cooper, M. A., 207
cost allocation and quality, 201
Cox, M. F., 93
CPR. *See* Center for Postsecondary
Research

creative arts, 102
CRM. *See* customer relationship
management
Croxton, R. A., 38
culturally responsive assessment, 23,
85–86, 186–88
IDI, 54
IES, 49–50, 52
customer relationship management
(CRM), 78

data disaggregation, 185–86
data-informed decision cultures,
199–200
data leveraging, 176
data literacy, 179
deans, 77
Deardorff, D. K., 48
Deardorff's Process Model of
Intercultural Competence, 50
degree completion
in planning, 178–79, 189
Degree Qualifications Profile (DQP),
114–15, 117
Degrees That Matter (Jankowski and
Marshall), 27
democracy, 63, 66
Denecke, D., 115, 117
dentistry, 108–9, 113
digital literacy, 147–48
direct measures, 40
community-engaged learning and,
66
in learning improvement and
innovation track, 163
dispositional skills, 144, 208
diversity, 13–14
ethnicity, 37
as meta-trend, 207
planning for, 184–86
STEM and, 98–100
student affairs and, 82–83
doctoral research, 111
Dolan, E. L., 101
Doscher, S., 47, 54

Douglas, T. C., 93
DQP. *See* Degree Qualifications Profile

*Educating Lawyers: Preparation for the
    Practice of Law* (Sullivan, Welch,
    Bond, and Shulman), 110
educational development. *See* faculty
    development
educational quality, 1
Educational Testing Service (ETS),
    66–67
Education for Democracy, 66
EIA. *See* Excellence in Assessment
embedded assessment, 180, 183–84
emerging ideas, 10
employment
    meta-trends and, 203
    planning and, 179, 188
engineering. *See* STEM
Engineering Criteria 2000, 95
entrustable professional activities
    (EPAs), 112–13, 116
ePortfolio assessment, 48, 51–52, 209
    AAEEBL and, 196–97
    artifact-by-artifact in, 143–44
    authenticity in, 143, 183–84
    current trends on, 140–47
    definition of, 139
    description of, 138
    digital literacy and, 147–48
    dispositional learning and, 144
    faculty roles and, 148–49
    folio thinking and, 141–42
    future trends on, 147–49
    as HIP, 138, 140–43, 183
    holistic approach to, 145–46
    identity and, 143, 197
    "ineffable" related to, 144–45
    integration and, 144
    learning and, 147
    as learning experience, 139–40
    main points on, 150
    media in, 139, 142
    "meta" and, 142–43, 146–47
    pivotal experiences and, 146

print portfolios compared to, 138–39
    quality and, 141–42
    questions on, 150
    reflections and, 144–45
    scaffolding and, 141–42
    self-knowledge in, 138
    taxonomy for, 149
    technology and, 148
    traditional assessments and, 137
    as web presentations, 139
ePortfolios, 48, 51–52
equity, 23, 175–76, 185, 202
    HIPs and, 38–39, 40–41
ethical reasoning, 161–63, 166
ethnicity, 37
ETS. *See* Educational Testing Service
evaluation
    assessment compared to, 180
    See also specific topics
evaluation lack, in faculty development,
    124–25
evidence-based criteria, 128, 130
evidence-based decision-making, 206
evidence-based learning, 7, 196–97,
    198
evidence-based pedagogy and change,
    96–98
Ewell, Peter, 3, 204
Excellence in Assessment (EIA), 29n2
Ezell Sheets, J. K., 178

faculty development, 13, 41, 80–81,
    205, 210–11
    activities of, 125
    assessment engagement of, 126–27
    assignment charrette process and, 21
    availability of, 126
    challenges related to, 127
    collaboration in, 129–30
    current trends, 127–29
    evaluation lack in, 124–25
    evidence-based criteria and, 128, 130
    future trends, 129–31
    in health professions, 128
    history of, 125–27

impact of, 125–26
main points on, 132
motivation in, 127
publishing on, 131
questions on, 132
ROI and, 125–26, 128, 131
scaffolding in, 130–31
for STEM, 96–98
theory base for, 129
unit of analysis in, 130
Farro, S., 99
federal government, 3
    Morrill Acts, 60, 92
Finley, A., 185
Finney, Sara, 37
Florida International University (FIU),
    54
folio thinking, 141–42
formative assessment data, 182
Freeman, S., 95–96
Friedrichs, J., 47
Froyd, J. E., 95
Fuentes, D. G., 86
funding, for STEM, 91–92

Gambino, L. M., 208
Gansemer-Topf, A. M., 84
Gardner, D. P., 2–3
Gelmon, S. B., 63
gender, STEM and, 98, 99
general education, 198–99
George, M. D., 94
global citizenship, 46–47
    at FIU, 50–51
    literacies for, 179
global learning, 11–12
    CBGL and, 47
    challenges and, 53–54
    current trends in, 46–54
    customized tools for, 52–53
    Deardorff's Process Model of
        Intercultural Competence, 50
    definitions of, 45, 47–48
    ePortfolios in, 48, 51–52
    future trends in, 54

GPI and, 50–51
    history of, 45–46
    IES for, 49–50
    intercultural competence
        measurement in, 49–50
    main points on, 55–56
    pedagogies for, 50–51
    questions on, 56
    strategy in, 49
    systems thinking approach to, 54–55
    terminology in, 49
Global Perspective Inventory (GPI),
    50–51
global perspectives, 47
Good, M. R., 5
GPI. *See* Global Perspective Inventory
graduate and professional programs,
    12–13
    ABET and, 114
    accountability of, 115–16
    accreditation in, 107, 112
    collaboration in, 116
    current trends, 112–15
    dentistry, 108–9, 113
    doctoral research, 111
    DQP in, 114–15, 117
    EPAs in, 112–13, 116
    future trends, 115–16
    history of, 108–11
    HPAC for, 119
    interprofessional accreditation
        advisory group for, 119
    IPEC and, 113, 118
    IPE in, 113, 116, 119
    law, 110, 114
    licensing exams, 111
    literature review of, 108–11
    main points, 119–20
    medicine, 108, 113
    nursing, 109–10
    pharmacy, 109
    professional formation outcomes in,
        118–19
    proposed doctoral framework in,
        114–15

questions on, 120
student debt, 111
summative assessments in, 107
graduate education, 182

Han, S., 37
Hardrick, J., 47
Hartman, E., 47
HBCUs. *See* Historically Black Colleges
and Universities
health professions, 108–10, 113, 128
Health Professions Accreditors
Collaborative (HPAC), 119
HEDS. *See* Higher Education Data
Sharing Consortium
Henderson, C., 93
heuristic, 158–60, 170–71
higher education, 60
Higher Education Community Service
Honor Roll (The Honor Roll),
61
Higher Education Data Sharing
Consortium (HEDS), 8, 204–5
*High-Impact Educational Practices: What
They Are, Who Has Access to Them,
and Why They Matter* (Kuh), 34
high-impact practices (HIPs), 11, 208
AAC&U and, 33–34, 40
cocurricular transcripts and, 38
in community engagement, 67
current trends of, 35–40
definition of, 33
direct assessment of, 40
ePortfolio assessment as, 138,
140–43, 183
equity and access of, 38–39, 40–41
future trends of, 40–41
history of, 34–35
holistic assessment and, 178
impact of, 35
implementation fidelity and, 182
IUPUI and, 39, 41, 181–82
main points on, 42
NSSE and, 37
practice of, 34–35

quality and fidelity of, 36
questions on, 42
scaling of, 39–40
service-learning as, 62–63
student affairs and, 82
tracking and documentation of,
36–38
Hilton, M. L., 94
HIPs. *See* high-impact practices
Historically Black Colleges and
Universities (HBCUs), 20–21, 23
Historically Black Colleges and
Universities' Collaboration for
Excellence in Educational Quality
Assurance, 23
history, 12
of community-engaged learning,
62–63
of faculty development, 125–27
of global learning, 45–46
of graduate and professional
programs, 108–11
of HIPs, 34–35
of NILOA, 20–21
of STEM, 92–94
of student affairs, 77–79
holistic assessment
citizenship and, 177–79
HIPs and, 178
in planning, 176–78
of skills, 177
student development in, 177
HPAC. *See* Health Professions
Accreditors Collaborative
Hughes, J. A., 86
human literacy, 179
Hurtado, S., 185
Hurtig, J. K., 126
Hutchings, P., 4

identity, 65, 138
ePortfolio assessment and, 143, 197
IDI. *See* Intercultural Development
Inventory
IE. *See* institutional effectiveness

IEOs. *See* international education
    opportunities
IES. *See* Intercultural Effectiveness Scale
Ikenberry, S. O., 29n1
implementation fidelity
    HIPs and, 182
    of learning improvement and
        innovation track, 166–67
improvement, 23, 157, 187, 204–5
    See also learning improvement
        and innovation track; planning,
        decision-making, and
        improvement
improvement culture creation, 186–88
*Improving Learning in General Education:
    An AGLS Guide to Assessment and
    Program Review*, 199
inclusive assessment, 23
Indiana Campus Compact, 8
Indiana University–Purdue University
    Indianapolis (IUPUI), 6
    global learning at, 53
    HIPs and, 39, 41, 181–82
    Pledge Grants at, 39
indirect measures
    community-engaged learning and,
        67
    in planning, 180–81
ineffable outcomes, 26
information technology (IT), 86–87
Institute. *See* Assessment Institute in
    Indianapolis
Institute for Engaged Learning in
    its Division of Undergraduate
    Education, 41
institutional effectiveness (IE), 200–201
institutional missions, 189
institutional research (IR), 86, 188,
    200–201
institutional self-assessment process, 61
integration, 9
    ePortfolio assessment and, 144
    in liberal education, 201
    in STEM, 101, 102
intended program, 166–67

Intercultural Development Inventory
    (IDI), 54
Intercultural Effectiveness Context
    Model, 52
Intercultural Effectiveness Scale (IES),
    49–50, 52
internal alignment, 24
international education opportunities
    (IEOs), 52–53
interprofessional education (IPE), 113,
    116, 119
Interprofessional Education
    Collaborative (IPEC), 113, 118
Involvement in Learning (National
    Institute of Education), 3
IPE. *See* interprofessional education
IPEC. *See* Interprofessional Education
    Collaborative
IR. *See* institutional research
IT. *See* information technology
IUPUI. *See* Indiana University–Purdue
    University Indianapolis

Jacobs University (Bremen, Germany),
    50
James Madison University (JMU), 7,
    158, 168–69
Janke, E. M., 61
JMU. *See* James Madison University
Jones, G., 37

Kelley, T. R., 100
Kennedy, T. J., 95
Kiely, R., 47
Kilgo, C. A., 178
Kim, E., 126
Kinzie, J., 157–58, 177
Kirkpatrick, D., 128–29
Knowles, J. G., 100
Kolek, E. A., 37
Kuh, George, 29n1, 33–35, 37, 82,
    177, 208
    on ePortfolios and HIPs, 140–41
    on HIPs, 140–41, 178, 181
    on improvement, 157–58

Labov, J. B., 94, 96
Landorf, H., 47
language, 184–85
law, 110, 114
Learning Improvement and Innovation,
   187–88
learning improvement and innovation
   track
   business analogy on, 158–59
   coordination in, 168–69, 171
   critiques on, 163–64
   direct measures in, 163
   heuristic for, 158–60, 170–71
   implementation fidelity of, 166–67
   improvement model in, 160–61
   intended program in, 166–67
   measurement in, 161, 163, 167–68
   program theory in, 164
   purpose of, 158
   questions on, 171–72
   rationale in, 162–63, 164, 165
   resources on, 170–71
   RFP in, 168–69
   SLOs in, 162–67, 170–71
   social dynamics in, 168–70
   strategy 1 in, 161–64
   strategy 2 in, 164–68
   strategy 3 in, 168–70
   teaching patterns in, 159–60
   technical practices in, 164–68
   traditional assessment-focused report
      in, 161–64
   traditional assessment model
      compared to, 160–61
Learning Improvement Summits,
   158
learning management system (LMS),
   198
liberal education, 200–2
Liberal Education and America's
   Promise program, 34
licensing exams, 111
lifelong learners
   ABET and, 114
   accountability and, 115

authentic embedded assessment and,
   183
authenticity and, 183
planning for, 177, 179
STEM and, 94
Light, Penny, 141–42
LMS. *See* learning management system

MacPhee, D., 99
Major, T. Jr., 207
Marshall, D. W., 27
mathematics. *See* STEM
Matthews-DeNatale, Gail, 143
McDonald, N., 207
McNair, T. B., 38–39, 185, 207
Measuring Up, 4–5
media, 139, 142
medicine, 108, 113, 128
"meta," 142–43, 146–47
meta-high-impact practice, 142–43
meta-trends, 14, 194
   AAEEBL in, 196–98
   AALHE in, 194–96
   accountability with improvement in,
      203, 206–7
   actionable in, 198
   AGLS in, 198–99
   AIR in, 199–200
   assessment, teaching, learning
      integration as, 203–4
   authenticity in, 208–9
   cost allocation and quality as, 201
   CPR in, 202–4
   data-informed decision cultures as,
      200
   diversity in, 207
   employment and, 204
   evidence-based decision-making, 206
   general education in, 198–200
   HEDS in, 204–5
   inquiry in, 195
   integration and bundling as, 201
   leadership and stakeholders, 207
   liberal education as, 200–2
   LMS in, 198

NSSE in, 202–4
outcomes expansion in, 208–9
processes and outcomes in, 209
professional development in,
    209–10
public good and equity as, 202
quality and outcomes data in, 203–4
recognition in, 210
support in, 195
teams in, 194–96
TILT as, 209
as work in progress, 210–11
Miami University of Ohio, 49–50
Missouri State University, 85
Mitchell, P. H., 63
models diversification, 24–25
monitor learning, 205
Montenegro, E., 85–86, 184–85
Moore, A. C., 38
Morrill Acts (1862, 1890), 60, 92

NACE. *See* National Association of
    Colleges and Employers
NASPA. *See* National Association of
    Student Personnel Administrators
National Association of Colleges and
    Employers (NACE), 179
National Association of Student
    Personnel Administrators
    (NASPA), 80–81
National Institute for Learning
    Outcomes Assessment (NILOA),
    5, 8, 11, 29n1, 194
    on authenticity, 21–23
    on challenges and debates, 23–25
    on charrette, 21–22
    on conversations, 26
    description of, 20
    on future, 25–27
    HBCUs and, 20–21, 23
    history of, 20–21
    on improvement, 157
    on improvement and equity, 23
    Institute and, 19
    on internal alignment, 24

main points on, 28
main trends of, 28
on models diversification, 24–25
on partner expansion, 24, 26
questions from, 29
on stakeholders, 27–28
on story, 27
on technology, 26–27
track of, 20–21
on trends, 21–25
on value, 25
National Institute of Education, 3
National Science Foundation (NSF),
    91, 92
National Survey of Student
    Engagement (NSSE), 7–8,
    202–4
    HIPs and, 37
    as indirect assessment, 181
*A Nation at Risk: The Imperative for
    Educational Reform* (Gardner),
    2–3
neurocognitive skills, 208
Newkirk-Kotfila, Elise, 83
NILOA. *See* National Institute for
    Learning Outcomes Assessment
NILOA at Ten: A Retrospective (Kuh and
    Ikenberry), 29n1
NILOA track, 19–20
1980s pop culture (POPC), 160–63
NSF. *See* National Science Foundation
NSSE. *See* National Survey of Student
    Engagement
nursing, 109–10

Odell, M. R. L., 95
O'Donnell, K., 35, 37, 208
Ohio Northern University, 126
Ohio State, 53
Ouellett, M., 124
outcomes assessment, 2

Palomba, C. A., 2, 82, 210
partner expansion, 24, 26
partners, 6–8, 294

See also meta-trends
partnerships
   in community-engaged learning,
      66–68
   for student affairs, 83
Pascarella, E. T., 178
pharmacy, 109
PISA Test. *See* Program in International
      Student Assessment
pivotal experiences, 146
PKAL. *See* Project Kaleidoscope
planning, decision-making, and
      improvement (planning), 13–14,
      190
   data leveraging in, 176
   degree completion in, 178–79,
      189
   for diversity, 184–86
   employment and, 179, 188
   formative assessment data in, 182
   holistic assessment in, 176–78
   improvement culture creation in,
      186–88
   indirect measures in, 180–81
   for lifelong learners, 177, 179
   multiple data in, 180, 185
   practice of, 186–89
   social value of, 176
   student equity in, 175–76
   success demonstration from,
      188–89
   what to assess in, 176–79
Pledge Grants, 39
POPC. *See* 1980s pop culture
power structures, 64
predictive analytics, 26–27
print portfolios, 138–39
process assessment, 181
*Professional Competency Areas for Student
      Affairs Educators* (ACPA and
      NASPA), 81
professional development, 41, 210
   in student affairs assessment,
      80–81
   See also faculty development

Program in International Student
      Assessment (PISA Test), 46
Project Kaleidoscope (PKAL), 92–93
publishing, on faculty development,
      131

qualitative measures, 182
quantitative measures, 182

race, 99
   See also diversity
Ramsden, P., 129
reciprocity, 61–62, 67–68
representational equity, 185
representative sample, 68
request for proposals (RFP), 168–69
return on investment (ROI), 128–29
RFP. *See* request for proposals
Roberts, Darby M., 84
*Robot-Proof: Higher Education in the Age
      of Artificial Intelligence* (Aoun),
      179
ROI. *See* return on investment
Ross, J., 86
rubrics, 66–67, 117–18, 161, 183,
      209

SAAL. *See* Student Affairs Assessment
      Leaders
Satterfield, J., 85
scaffolding
   ePortfolio assessment and, 141–42
   in faculty development, 130–31
Schiller, J., 85
Schilling, K. L., 2
Schilling, K. M., 2
Schneider, C. G., 37
scholarly teaching, 101
Scholarship of Teaching and Learning
      (SoTL), 4
*Scholarship Reconsidered: Priorities of the
      Professoriate* (Boyer), 4
Schuh, J. H., 84
Schweingruber, H. A., 94
science. *See* STEM

self-knowledge, 138
service-learning, 62–63
Shelley, M. C., 99
Shelton, T., 61
Shulman, L. C., 110
Shulman, L. S., 4
signature assignments, 183–84
Singer, S. R., 94
Sloane, K., 183
SLOs. *See* student learning outcomes
Smith, K. A., 93, 95
Smith, K. L., 5
Snow, L., 85
social change, 64
social dynamics, 168–70
social issues, 64
social trustee, 65
SoTL. *See* Scholarship of Teaching and
     Learning
Space Race, 92
Spellings Commission on the Future of
     Higher Education, 25
*Spellings Report on the Future of Higher
     Education*, 5
stakeholders, 9, 207–8
  communication to, 186
  expectations of, 189
  NILOA on, 27–28
Stanny, C. J., 187
Statement of Aspirational Practice (AIR),
     177
states, 3
STEM, 12
  active learning in, 95–97
  challenges for, 92
  change in, 93–94
  constraints in, 97–98
  creative arts and, 101
  current trends of, 94–100
  diversity and, 98–100
  Engineering Criteria 2000, 95
  evidence-based pedagogy and change
     in, 96–98
  faculty development for, 96–98
  funding for, 91–92

future trends of, 100–102
gender and, 98, 99
goals enhancement for, 94–96, 102
history of, 92–94
initial interest in, 97
integration in, 100–101, 102
interdisciplinary in, 100–101
lifelong learners and, 94
main points on, 102–03
NSF and, 91, 92
PKAL in, 92–93
professionals and, 93
questions on, 103
race and, 99
recruitment and retention in,
     98–100
Space Race and, 92
term origin of, 91
Stewart, D-L, 83
Stitt-Bergh, M., 160
*Strada–Gallup 2017 College Student
     Survey*, 188
student affairs, 131
  ACPA and, 80–81
  assessment profession on, 84–85
  background on, 76–77
  cocurricular programs and, 79,
     83–84
  collaboration in, 86–87
  CRM in, 78
  cultural responsiveness in, 85–86
  deans and, 77
  description of, 76
  diversity and, 82–83
  future trends in, 84–87
  HIPs and, 82
  history of, 77–79
  holistic view for, 77, 82–83
  IR in, 86–87
  IT in, 86–87
  main points on, 87
  "mechanical record" in, 78
  partnerships for, 83
  professional development in, 80–81
  questions on, 88

role of, 78–79
student services in, 79
survey software for, 79
trends in, 79–84
Student Affairs Assessment Leaders
    (SAAL), 81
student debt, 111
student diversity. *See* diversity
student feedback, 203–4
student learning outcomes (SLOs),
    162–67, 170–71
Student Personnel Point of View
    (American Council on Education),
    78
student services, 79
Study Group on the Conditions of
    Excellence in American Higher
    Education, 3
Sullivan, W. M., 110
summative assessments, 107
surveys
    NSSE, 7–8, 37, 181, 202–4
    *Strada–Gallup 2017 College Student
        Survey*, 188
survey software, 79
Suskie, L., 180
Sweat, J., 37
systems thinking approach, 54–55

Tagg, J., 4
TCU. *See* Texas Christian University
technological literacy, 179
technology, 86–87
    ABET, 95, 114
    ePortfolio assessment and, 148
    NILOA on, 26–27
    See also STEM
Terenzini, P. T., 2
Test to Measure Intercultural
    Competence, short version
    (TMIC-S), 50
Texas Christian University (TCU), 51
TILT. *See* Transparency in Learning and
    Teaching
Timmer, J. D., 157–58

TMIC-S. *See* Test to Measure
    Intercultural Competence, short
    version
track areas, 10
traditional assessments, 160–64
    ePortfolio assessment and, 137
transdisciplinary, 62–65
Transparency Framework, 20
Transparency in Learning and Teaching
    (TILT), 209
Tuning USA, 5

underserved and underrepresented
    students, 38–40
U.S. Department of Education
    (USDE), 112

VALUE (Valid Assessment of Learning
    in Undergraduate Education)
    Institute, 20, 22, 114
    global learning and, 48
    HIPs and, 40
VALUE rubrics, 117–18, 183, 209
values, 25, 65, 176
VCU. *See* Virginia Commonwealth
    University
VCU Globe, 52–54
Virginia Commonwealth University
    (VCU), 52–53
Voluntary System of Accountability
    (VSA), 29n2
Wang, X., 98–99
Wankat, P. C., 95
Wayne State University, 126
web presentations, 139
Welch Wegner, J., 110
Wenk, Laura, 146
Whalen, D. F., 99
Wilson, M., 183
Winkelmes, M. A., 210
Winslow-Edmonson, C., 85
Wolfgram, S. M., 37
writing, 159–60

Yancey, Kathleen, 139–40, 147